THE
CASE FOR
PALESTINE
WHY IT MATTERS AND
WHY YOU SHOULD CARE

DAN KOVALIK

HOT BOOKS

Hot Books books may be purchased in bulk at special discounts for sales promotion, corporate gifts, fund-raising, or educational purposes. Special editions can also be created to specifications. For details, contact the Special Sales Department, Skyhorse Publishing, 307 West 36th Street, 11th Floor, New York, NY 10018 or info@skyhorsepublishing.com.

Hot Books® and Skyhorse Publishing® are registered trademarks of Skyhorse Publishing, Inc.®, a Delaware corporation.

Visit our website at www.skyhorsepublishing.com.
Please follow our publisher Tony Lyons on Instagram @tonylyonsisuncertain.

10 9 8 7 6 5 4 3 2 1

Library of Congress Cataloging-in-Publication Data is available on file.

Cover design by Brian Peterson

Print ISBN: 978-1-5107- 8059-0
Ebook ISBN: 978-1-5107- 8060-6

Printed in the United States of America

This book is dedicated to the memory of Heba Zegout, a talented painter and parent of four children, who was killed on October 11, 2024, when Israeli forces bombed her apartment building. Heba wrote to me shortly before she, along with two of her children, were killed in the bombing, simply stating, "We are sitting with the children. There is bombing. I feel afraid." I never heard from Heba again. Heba's two surviving children are now orphans, and their whereabouts are unknown.

ACKNOWLEDGMENTS

Many people helped me along my journey of learning and understanding about the Palestinians struggle. First and foremost, I am grateful to my students who initially inspired my curiosity about the truth of Palestine: Khalil Al-Wazir, Yara Zarir, Enas Alsaffadi, and Bisan Nimer. I am also grateful to my friends in Gaza whom I have stayed in touch with over the years, including during the current Israeli assault on Gaza: Maysaa Ghazi, another great artist and the sister of Heba Zegout; Ola Al Asi, a brave journalist from Gaza City; and Rola Abu Aziza, who has generously been helping her fellow brothers and sisters in Gaza survive during the Israeli assault.

I also wish to thank those who helped me in my travel through the West Bank, including Amal Wadan and her husband Mohammad, Fadia Barghouti, Khaldoun Barghouti, Uri Davis, Zakaria Odeh, and Saleh. I also want to acknowledge my dear friend Abir in Beirut, who has been an immense help to me in my travels in Lebanon. Finally, I would like to thank Kate Daher, a great teacher and friend and someone who has guided me in my understanding of Palestine.

CONTENTS

FOREWORD

The Case for Palestine is written by a friend of mine. But that's not why it's so important. The Palestinians are dying for more people to read this book. Because if enough people knew what Dan Kovalik knows, Joe Biden—who ended a half century in office rightly known as Genocide Joe—would have never been able to help kill all those children in your name.

This book sets the scene for what happened in the infanticide of 2023/24. In the femicide. In the genocide. For it was all those things and more. Many perished in the slaughter but so did much of what people believed. About Israel, about the so-called "west," about the "human rights" narrative we are so selectively fed. About the limits of the politics we knew—before. Because things will never be the same again.

A whole new western generation just watched their own Vietnam War, this time in 5G, live, HD, with slo-mo.

They saw the reality of colonial war; they saw the heroism of resistance; they saw the cowardice of their compatriots and how that was replaced by outrage as people came to know, and as people came to change.

In fifty years of involvement in the cause of Palestine, I have known many massacres. But I never knew such a transformation in attitudes—so much so fast.

In days, weeks, months, way less than a year, Palestine became the moral centre of the world. For the majority world, it had long been. For the western hegemon, it quickly became so. Governments began to fall over it. Oppositions began to fall, too. Great media institutions began to fail over it. New ways of seeing things arose like a great wave which swept so much detritus away. And this wave is still coming after them. Them?

The rulers who misruled us, the media which misled us, the academia which mistaught us, the books which lied to us.

New leaders like Dan Kovalik are now among us. New books like his are our weapons. Bear them proudly and find willing hands to carry them everywhere.

I have waited a long time to be able to approve this message.

—George Galloway MP
House of Commons
Westminster

PREFACE

What we are witnessing in Gaza is a mass killing of children in slow motion. There is no food left.

—Jason Lee, Save the Children

There is a whole segment of Israeli Society that is a copy of Nazim. They're transformed into paranoids from a master race, exactly like Hitler youth.

—Moshe Zimmerman, Israeli historian

As one can imagine, writing this book has been like aiming at a moving target. Every day brings new, and sadly more horrifying events, as the US/Israeli war on Gaza and the West Bank continues. The war is now into its 153rd day as I write these, the final words I will be able to write before *The Case for Palestine* goes to print. I fear that by the time this book is published, the more appropriate title may be, *The Eulogy for Palestine*. I pray this is not the case.

Many of us have been waiting with bated breath for the news of a cease-fire that has not come, and which now seems will not come for some time. While we have been teased with the possibility of such a cessation in the slaughter, including by President Joe Biden, who predicted the imminence of such while licking an ice cream cone, it is evident that the United States and Israel do not want an end to this anytime soon.

A revealing interview with US National Security Council spokesperson John Kirby in *The New Yorker* reveals this fact.[1] In this interview, while Kirby states that the Biden administration would like to see a short humanitarian pause in Gaza of around six weeks, it does not believe a "general cease-fire" is in the interest of Israel, and the United States therefore does not support one. The result is that the war will go on indefinitely, and most likely to the end—that is, to the end of Gaza.

While the figure generally given at this point of Palestinians killed in Gaza is around 30,000 (the vast majority being women and children)—a figure that has seemingly not budged for weeks—I agree with commentators such as Ralph Nader that this has to be a gross undercount. And it seems that it would have to be in light of the fact that the figure is based upon numbers being provided by the Palestinian Health Ministry. Given that there is nearly no functioning hospital left in Gaza due to their systematic destruction by the Israeli military, it seems virtually impossible for the Health Ministry to be able to keep a running tally of the dead and wounded, especially now that people are beginning to die quietly in their homes of starvation and disease. That is why Ralph Nader, for example, believes that the number of dead in Gaza is probably closer to 200,000, and I think he is right.

As Nader opined on March 5, 2024,

> In recent days, the situation has become more dire. In the March 2, 2024, *Washington Post*, reporter, Ishaan Tharoor writes: "The bulk of Gaza's more than 2 million people face the prospect of famine—a state of affairs that constitutes the fastest decline in a population's nutrition status ever recorded, according to aid workers. Children are starving at the fastest rate the world has ever known. Aid groups have been pointing to Israel restricting the flow of assistance into the territory as a major driver of the crisis. Some prominent Israeli officials openly champion stymying these transfers of aid."
>
> Tharoor quotes Jan Egeland, chief of the Norwegian Refugee Council: "We must be clear: civilians in Gaza are falling sick from hunger and thirst because of Israel's entry restrictions. . . . Life-saving supplies are being intentionally blocked, and women and children are paying the price."[2]

We are now daily seeing gruesome photos of dead, severely emaciated Palestinians—mostly children—who resemble Nazi concentration camp victims. And, in many ways, that is exactly what they are.

Famed Palestinian novelist, Susan Albulhawa—raised in an orphanage in Jerusalem but now a resident of Philadelphia—bravely traveled for two weeks to Gaza in late February to early March 2024. Albulhawa wrote about her time there, including in a must-read article, "History Will Record That Israel Committed a Holocaust." In this piece, Albulhawa writes:

> Journalists and politicians call it war. The informed and honest call it genocide.
>
> What I see is a holocaust—the incomprehensible culmination of 75 years of Israeli impunity for persistent war crimes.
>
> Rafah is the southernmost part of Gaza, where Israel crammed 1.4 million people into a space the size of London's Heathrow Airport.
>
> Water, food, electricity, fuel, and supplies are scarce. Children are without school—their classrooms having been turned into makeshift shelters for tens of thousands of families.
>
> Nearly every inch of previously empty space is now occupied by a flimsy tent sheltering a family.
>
> There are barely any trees left, as people have been forced to cut them down for firewood.[3]

Albulhawa explains that while she had read everything she could about the situation in Gaza, and watched every video, "no matter how gruesome . . . nothing can truly prepare you for this dystopia. What reaches the rest of the world is a fraction of what I've seen so far, which is only a fraction of this horror's totality." What impressed Albulhawa about what she saw was not just the death and devastation, but the absolute "degradation" of the people there—a degradation brought about by Israel's purposeful denial of all of the necessities of life, but especially water, to the people of Gaza. As Albulhawa explains, "The scarcity of running or clean water degrades the best of us. Everyone does their best with themselves and their children, but at some point, you stop caring. At some point, the indignity of filth is inescapable. At some point, you just wait for death, even as you also wait for a ceasefire." As she sums it up, "Gaza is hell. It is an inferno teeming with innocents gasping for air. But even the air here is scorched."

And despite the crocodile tears of US government officials about the civilian death toll in Gaza, and their claims that they so desperately want to alleviate the death and suffering, the Biden administration's every action belies such claims. Thus, as detailed below, the Biden administration cut off all funding to UNRWA—the lifeline for Palestinians, not just in Gaza, but indeed for six million Palestinians throughout the Middle East region—and appears to have no intention to reinstate it.

As discussed further below, the United States, Canada, and a number of other European nations completely cut off funding to UNRWA within hours after the International Court of Justice found that South Africa's claims of genocide against Israel were "plausible" and ordered preliminary measures to be taken to halt it. The cessation of benefits was based on Israel's claim that twelve UNRWA officials, out of 30,000 total, had some role in the militant attacks of October 7.

Evidence of this has always been lacking, and now UNRWA has come forward with allegations that UNRWA staff were kidnapped and tortured by Israeli forces who tried to coerce them into falsely confessing about participating in militant activities. Reuters cited an UNRWA report for claims that "said several UNRWA Palestinian staffers had been detained by the Israeli army and added that the ill-treatment and abuse they said they had experienced included severe physical beatings, waterboarding, and threats of harm to family members."[4]

This in turn follows a new UN report detailing the horrendous mistreatment of Palestinian women and girls by Israeli forces—mistreatment that has included murder, sexual assault, and rape. Thus, according to the February 19, 2024, UN report,

> Palestinian women and girls have reportedly been arbitrarily executed in Gaza, often together with family members, including their children, according to information received. "We are shocked by reports of the deliberate targeting and extrajudicial killing of Palestinian women and children in places where they sought refuge, or while fleeing. Some of them were reportedly holding white pieces of cloth when they were killed by the Israeli army or affiliated forces," the experts said.

The experts expressed serious concern about the arbitrary detention of hundreds of Palestinian women and girls, including human rights defenders, journalists and humanitarian workers, in Gaza and the West Bank since 7 October. Many have reportedly been subjected to inhuman and degrading treatment, denied menstruation pads, food and medicine, and severely beaten. On at least one occasion, Palestinian women detained in Gaza were allegedly kept in a cage in the rain and cold, without food.[5]

The UN report continued, "'We are particularly distressed by reports that Palestinian women and girls in detention have also been subjected to multiple forms of sexual assault, such as being stripped naked and searched by male Israeli army officers. At least two female Palestinian detainees were reportedly raped while others were reportedly threatened with rape and sexual violence,' the experts said. They also noted that photos of female detainees in degrading circumstances were also reportedly taken by the Israeli army and uploaded online."

This UN report came out as the Israeli claims of mass rapes on October 7, as promoted by the *New York Times*, continued to fall apart in the face of the great journalist work done by *The Grayzone*, *The Electronic Intifada*, and *The Intercept*. The *New York Times* ended up being forced to walk back its story—which portrayed these claims as fact—given the denial of family members of an alleged rape victim that she had been raped, the denial of Kibbutz Be'er residents that rapes had occurred in the kibbutz on October 7 as the *Times* had claimed, and the revelation that two of the individuals who contributed to the *Times* story had absolutely no journalistic experience but were in fact biased supporters of Israel, bore deep-seated hatred toward Palestinians, and were attempting to promote the rape claims to justify the brutal assault on Gaza.[6]

Back to the issue of the White House's feigned concern for the welfare of Palestinians in Gaza, the *Washington Post* reported that the Biden administration has secretly made over one hundred arms shipments to Israel during the first 150 days of the war on Gaza, making the slaughter of civilians there possible.[7]

What about the airdrops of food by the United States, and what about Biden's plan to build a new port on the Gaza shore for the delivery of humanitarian aid? In short, these are at best a Band-Aid to cover a gaping wound that the United States itself has helped to create, and it is being done for purely propaganda purposes and for the purpose of giving Biden political cover in the face of an electorate that is progressively rising up against his policies in Gaza. And indeed, Biden aides have anonymously told the press just that.

Thus, as explained by journalist Aaron Maté from *The Grayzone*, which has done amazing work covering October 7 and its aftermath, the airdrops "amount to a few trucks' worth of aid—compared to the thousands of trucks that Israel is blocking with US support. 'The food, water, and medical supplies so desperately needed by people in Gaza are sitting just across the border,' Doctors Without Border said Friday. 'Israel needs to facilitate rather than block the flow of supplies.'"[8] What's more, as Maté notes, Israel has been firing upon crowds that have gathered to try to receive the aid which the relatively few trucks allowed into Gaza have brought.

These incidents have now become known as the "flour massacres," referring to the most notorious event when, as the BBC would later confirm despite Israel denials, Israeli forces fired upon Palestinians in Gaza who tried to gather flour being handed out by aid trucks.[9] The result of this one incident, according to the BBC, was 112 dead and 760 wounded.

As Maté further explains, in terms of the promised port, Biden's

own aides acknowledge that this is a ruse. According to the *Washington Post*, administration officials quietly concede that "only by securing the opening of additional land crossings would there be enough aid to prevent famine." And given that the pier will take at minimum 30 days to complete, that "[raises] questions about how famine in Gaza will be staved off in the critical days ahead," the *New York Times* notes.

The White House has given the answer: rather than compel Israel to open those land crossings and prevent famine, it is instead adopting the Israeli position that the land crossings can be used as a tool of leverage against Hamas—and that Israel can control everything that gets in.

As Israel actively blocks hundreds of trucks waiting to bring aid to Gaza by land, and as the Biden administration dithers on plans for a water port, famine is setting in. Even by the end of February, the UN and international aid groups were sounding the alarm about the imminence of mass death due to hunger and thirst. As one media account related on February 28:

> "Here we are, at the end of February, with at least 576,000 people in Gaza—one-quarter of the population—one step away from famine," Ramesh Rajasingham, the deputy chief of the UN humanitarian agency (OCHA), told the UN Security Council (UNSC).
>
> One in six children under the age of two in northern Gaza suffers from acute malnutrition and wasting and practically all the 2.3 million people in the Palestinian enclave rely on "woefully inadequate" food aid to survive, he told the meeting on food security in Gaza.

"If nothing is done, we fear widespread famine in Gaza is almost inevitable and the conflict will have many more victims," he said.

Israel's assault upon Palestinians in the West Bank, described in detail below, is intensifying as the world's gaze is on Gaza. As France 24 explains, "Since October 7, according to the Palestinian Authority, more than 420 Palestinians have been killed in the West Bank by Israeli forces or settlers. Thousands of others have been arrested. Palestinian prisoner advocacy groups say the number of incarcerated Palestinians has jumped from 5,200 before October 7 to about 9,000."[10] About a third of these are being held in administrative detention, meaning that they are being held indefinitely and without charge.

Sadly, one Palestinian arrested and being held in administrative detention is my new friend Fadia Barghouti, who I met in the West Bank in December 2023, and who you will learn more about below. Fadia's husband and one of her sons were already in jail when she was arrested. As her brother Khaldoun told me, she is now being held in an Israeli prison near Haifa, far away from her home village and her family, and her family has been unable to have any contact with her.

Notwithstanding all of these horrors, the worst in Gaza may very well be yet to come in the form of Israel's planned ground invasion of Rafah, where around 1.5 million Palestinians are living in makeshift tents. Netanyahu has said that he will order this invasion whether a temporary cease-fire is agreed to or not, and while I doubt much of what is said by Netanyahu, I take him at his word about this. And the results of this, as the United States knows full well, would be disastrous. Thus, a leaked cable from United States Agency for International Development (USAID) concludes that

"A potential escalation of military operations . . . within Southern Gaza's Rafah Governorate could result in catastrophic humanitarian consequences, including mass civilian casualties, extensive population displacement, and the collapse of the existing humanitarian response, multiple relief actors have warned USAID's Levant Disaster Assistance Response Team," the cable says.

In its "Key Points," the cable says, "An offensive in Rafah would likely block the entry and transport of fuel and life-saving humanitarian assistance throughout the enclave, rendering critical infrastructure inoperable and leaving people in Gaza without food, medicine, shelter, and water."[11]

However, the same cable sadly notes that Rafah, already suffering a major bombing campaign by Israel, may have already reached a point of no return.

In short, the situation for the Palestinian people, especially in Gaza, is dire. Indeed, I agree with the memes being posted on social media that say, "If you ever wondered what you would do as a German during the Holocaust, you know now, because you're doing it." That is to say, the crimes against the Palestinians, only made possible by the massive assistance of the United States, are so grave that one's actions or inactions at this time to stop them will be the measure of that individual for all times. One's very soul is at stake in the face of this genocide, and this, in the end, is the strongest case for defending Palestine.

INTRODUCTION

We care a lot about the Palestinians. We are on the verge of achieving our freedom, it will not really be complete until our brothers the Palestinians, who fought with us and supported us, will achieve their freedom.

—Nelson Mandela (1992)

I am both astonished and outraged by the fact that those who represent the descendants of a people who were persecuted for centuries for religious or racial reasons. . . . That the descendants of this people who are today the decision-makers of the State of Israel, that they could not only colonize an entire people, partly drive them out of their land and seek to expel them for good. . . . But also, after the massacre of October 7, engaged in a real massive slaughter on the populations of Gaza and continue, incessantly, hitting civilians, women, and children. And to see the silence of the world, the silence of the United States, protectors of Israel, the silence of the Arab states, the silence of the European states who claim to be defenders of culture, humanity, human rights.[1]

—Edgar Morin (102 years old), Jewish World War II resistance fighter who fought as a lieutenant in Charles De Gaulle's Forces Françaises Combattantes

As I finish up this book, Israel has begun a major bombing campaign of Rafah where 1.4 million Gazans have fled to because they were told by Israel that this would be a "safe zone" for them. Israel waited until the first kickoff of the Super Bowl to begin this bombing, knowing that the gaze of the world, and especially of the United States, would be focused elsewhere. I have been seeing a number of people on social media refer to this as the "Super Bowl Massacre."

The US Senate, giving the green light to Israel to carry out this massacre, voted overwhelmingly on Super Bowl Sunday to move forward consideration of an appropriation bill that would provide Israel $14 billion in emergency military aid, and to give President Joe Biden carte blanche authority to provide stockpiled arms to Israel without notice to Congress. This same bill would prohibit funding to Gaza's lifeline—the United Nations Relief and Works Agency for Palestine Refugees in the Near East (UNRWA). Just two days later, the Senate approved this bill even after it witnessed the carnage in Rafah.

Despite the Biden Administration's claims that it was concerned about the civilian killings in Gaza, and in Rafah in particular, and that it made these concerns known to President Benjamin Netanyahu, *Politico* reported that the truth appeared to be otherwise. As *Politico* explained, "The Biden administration is not planning to punish Israel if it launches a military campaign in Rafah without ensuring civilian safety. Three US officials, granted anonymity to detail internal discussions, told *NatSec Daily* no reprimand plans are in the works, meaning Israeli forces could enter the city and harm civilians without facing American consequences."[2]

There was something poetic about the timing as the Super Bowl has become a monument to the US military and war, with the game being immediately preceded by the national anthem, a giant US flag spanning the gridiron, a US Marine color guard playing under an Air Force flyover costing around $4 million. As important as the game itself are the multimillion-dollar commercials that are designed to bring us all together and make us feel warm and fuzzy about ourselves as we watch this sickening display of our dying Empire. Some of the commercials even reference Jesus. All the while, I couldn't help but think of the line of one of Woody Allen's characters in *Crimes and Misdemeanors*, who lamented—after spending the day watching TV including professional wrestling and evangelical preachers asking for money—"if Jesus came back today, he wouldn't stop throwing up."

* * *

My commitment to Palestine and the Palestinian cause, and my willingness to speak out about it, came relatively late in life. Like many people in the United States, I was raised with an instinctual sympathy for Israel. Some of this was religious, having been raised Roman Catholic and being taught that Israel was the Holy Land and the rightful homeland of the Jews. Some of this arose from my sympathy for the Jewish people as the victims of the Holocaust and the belief that Israel was rightfully granted to them as a safe haven from oppression afterwards.

For most of my life, I had not even encountered Palestinians. The first time I did was in the mid-1980s at my Catholic high school, Moeller, in Cincinnati, Ohio when two young Palestinians were invited to make a presentation about the necessity for a two-state solution to the Israeli-Palestinian conflict. Ironically, our high school sports teams were known as the Holy Crusaders, and our mascot was a knight on horseback with a sword and shield, presumably in the process of invading and plundering the Arab world, including historic Palestine.

While I found these Palestinians very likeable, and their arguments compelling, my response, which I openly verbalized to them, was that Israel was an important ally of the United States—if not the most important ally—and that we therefore simply could not afford to support a second state there. And that was that. I would not encounter Palestinians again, at least as far as I knew, until decades later.

In 2012, I began teaching International Human Rights at the University of Pittsburgh School of Law (Pitt). I taught this course until June 2023. During my time teaching at Pitt, I frequently had Palestinian students in my class who came to study on an Open Society Institute fellowship. One of my first such students was Khalil al-Wazir, a young Palestinian from Gaza. Khalil was named after his uncle, Khalil al-Wazir, the number two leader of the PLO under Yasir Arafat. Khalil's namesake was a Communist, a heroic fighter, and was eventually assassinated in 1986 by Israeli commandos. My student Khalil was proud to show me a photo of himself as a child sitting on Yasir Arafat's lap.

While Khalil's uncle was a guerilla fighter, Khalil does not come close to resembling a fighter. Instead, Khalil is an intellectual who can only be described as a nerd. He is short, with a small frame, and wears black horned-rim glasses that seem much too big on his baby face. Khalil would sit right in front of me in class, smiling and gleeful at my left-wing, anti-imperialist rantings. However, Khalil himself rarely participated in class. He privately told me that he believed the other students would probably see him as biased given his Palestinian background. In any case, he thought I was doing just fine in expressing views that he sympathized with.

As of the time of this writing, Khalil is living with his wife and two children in the middle of Gaza, having been forced to move out of Gaza City due to Israeli bombing. As he explained to me in an email, he and his family are living like nomads, cooking with fire and spending the day looking for water. Incredibly, his emails are nonetheless optimistic, and he has recently mentioned his desire to get a PhD in the United States.

I only spent one class day of the semester talking about Palestine—a topic I was just starting to learn about in any detail, but which I thought was important to address. I focused on the controversial report of Justice Richard Goldstone on Israel's 2008–2009 military offensive against Gaza known as Operation Cast Lead, which resulted in the deaths of 1,400 Palestinians and thirteen Israelis—a pretty typical ratio (around 100 to 1) of dead Palestinians to dead Israelis in any conflict between them. Richard Goldstone, a former justice of the Constitutional Court of South Africa and chief prosecutor of the United Nations International Criminal Tribunals for the former Yugoslavia and Rwanda, was appointed by the United Nations to investigate and report on the human rights issues arising from Operation Cast Lead.

The report of Goldstone, who himself is Jewish, was controversial not because of the facts found by Goldstone, but because of his ultimate conclusion that Israel had committed war crimes and possible crimes against humanity during Operation Cast Lead. In my view, this conclusion should not have been controversial given the terrible facts detailed by the report—facts which themselves are largely undisputed. But, any criticisms of Israel are by definition matters of controversy, no matter who is making them. Indeed, as the *Guardian* would later explain, "If the appointment of a Jewish Zionist judge with impeccable international credentials was meant to appease Israel, it failed. The Israeli government and its supporters in the Israeli media went for Goldstone with a vengeance."[3]

The following are some of Goldstone's findings which, in my view as an international law expert, support the conclusion that Israel committed war crimes and crimes against humanity during Operation Cast Lead:

- the intentional attack on a refugee shelter run by the UN Refugee and Workers Agency for Palestinian Refugees (UNRWA) in the Near East;
- the intentional attack upon the Al-Quds Hospital;
- the intentional attack upon the al-Wafa Hospital;
- the intentional destruction of the el-Bader flour mill that adversely impacted the food supply of the residents of Gaza;
- the intentional destruction of the Sawafeary chicken farm, again negatively impacting the food supply of Gaza;
- the intentional destruction of the water and sewage installations;
- the intentional destruction of civilian housing, killing scores of civilians;
- the intentional destruction of other various civilian infrastructure;
- the "shooting of civilians who were trying to leave their homes to walk to a safer place, waving white flags and, in some of the cases, following an injunction from the Israeli armed forces to do so."
- the intentional destruction of a mosque killing fifteen civilians;
- the intentional obstruction of emergency medical help to the wounded;
- the shelling of a "crowd" gathered in a tent to conduct a funeral for the dead.[4]

For its part, UNWRA corroborated Goldstone's findings, detailing the massive destruction of civilian infrastructure necessary to sustain human life:

During Israel's Operation "Cast Lead" in the Gaza Strip in December 2008 to January 2009, 6,268 homes were destroyed or severely damaged; 186 greenhouses were destroyed; 931 impact craters in roads and fields were counted; universities faced US$25 million in damages; 35,750 cattle, sheep and goats, and more than one million chickens and other birds were killed; and 17 percent of the cultivated area was destroyed. "Cast Lead" caused a total of US$181 million in direct and US$88 million in longer-term costs for Gaza's agriculture; generated about 600,000 tonnes of rubble and US$44 million in environmental costs; and water and sanitation infrastructure suffered almost US$6 million in damages.[5]

The destruction of greenhouses in Gaza by Israel in the 2008–2009 Cast Lead operation is an important event upon which to focus because a number of defenders of Israel, including Hillary Clinton, have recently been blaming Palestinians for the demise of the greenhouses, many originally built by Israeli settlers, and for why Gaza has not been economically viable since Israel and the settlers withdrew from Gaza in 2005. A recent article by *Mondoweiss* debunks this victim-blaming. This article first explains that,

> According to the *New York Times,* two months prior to the withdrawal, in July of 2005, Israeli settlers demolished about half of the greenhouses, "creating significant doubts that the greenhouses could be handed over to the Palestinians as a living business." There are other reports that rather than leave their greenhouses behind for the Palestinians some settlers decided to burn them to the ground.[6]

Still, as *Mondoweiss* explains, Palestinians, with significant international aid, took control of many of the remaining greenhouses and quickly got them up and running. However, many of these greenhouses ended up failing, not because of anything the Palestinians had done, but because Israel, which had completely fenced in Gaza before withdrawing and controlled all ingress and egress, would not allow the Palestinians to bring their produce to market through the Karni crossing (despite Israel's written agreement to keep it open 24/7). Tons of produce were therefore just left to rot and many of the greenhouses thereby went under. And, during Operation Cast Lead which followed, Israel took out another 186 greenhouses. The truth about these greenhouses is emblematic of Israel's cruel treatment of Gaza and its effective victim blaming to deflect criticism for its own misdeeds.

Despite the strong factual support for Goldstone's legal conclusions of international law violations, he was eventually bullied into distancing himself from his own report. As the *Guardian* explained, "Goldstone was vilified by pro-Israel groups as a 'self-hating Jew' and his report was likened to a blood libel, a false charge against Jews with roots in medieval antisemitism." This episode shows how perilous it is for anyone, and I mean anyone, to dare criticize Israel, and I am painfully aware of this.

Khalil and I became friends during his yearlong studies at Pitt. In the course of our discussions, Khalil told me things about Gaza that, much to my embarrassment, I had no idea about. For example, when Khalil told me about his plans to go home to Gaza after his studies at Pitt to be with his fiancée and hopefully work for a Palestinian human rights organization, he detailed how he planned to get there. He said that he would fly to Cairo, Egypt where he would be inevitably arrested at the airport, detained for several days, and deported to Gaza by land through the Rafah border crossing.

This, Khalil explained, was the only viable way for any Palestinian to get back to Gaza because Israel had destroyed Gaza's airport long ago, and Gaza was otherwise completely fenced in by Israel, with no other way to enter or leave. And even getting permission to go through the Rafah crossing was not guaranteed. I was told the very same by other students from Gaza, including Enas Alsafaddi, who I also became friends with. This was completely shocking to me. How could this be possible, and how is it that I didn't know?

As a number of commentators, such as Noam Chomsky, have explained, Gaza is the "largest open-air prison in the world," and has been so for years. Some have gone so far as to describe it as a concentration camp, noting that it is not fair to refer to it as a prison given that the 2.3 million people living there—around half of them being children—have not been convicted of any crimes.

As Amnesty International explained in a 2017 annual report on Palestine,

Gaza remained under an Israeli air, sea and land blockade, in force since June 2007. The continuing restrictions on imports of construction materials under the blockade, and funding shortages, contributed to severe delays in reconstruction of homes and other infrastructure damaged or destroyed in recent armed conflicts. Continuing restrictions on exports crippled the economy and exacerbated widespread impoverishment among Gaza's 1.9 million inhabitants. The Egyptian authorities' almost total closure of the Rafah border crossing with Gaza completed its isolation and compounded the impact of the Israeli blockade.[7]

The grisly result of this total isolation and blockade of Gaza is human suffering that is almost impossible to describe.

The UN predicted back in 2012 that Gaza would indeed be "unlivable" by 2020, and it is fair to say that this prediction came true. A 2020 *Washington Post* article indeed concluded as much. As this article explained, the sea bordering Gaza is "full of sewage, pumped in because there's not enough electricity and infrastructure to run Gaza's war-ravaged sewage system. Hospitals, schools, and homes are similarly running on empty, worn down by the lack of clean water, electricity, infrastructure and jobs or money. Barely anyone has enough clean water to drink. The only local source of drinking water, the coastal aquifer, is full of dirty and salty water. By 2020—basically, now—that damage will be irreversible, water experts have warned."[8]

The horrors confronting children in Gaza from this situation have been particularly terrible. In a 2017 interview in the Israeli paper *Haaretz*, "Gaza Kids Live in Hell: A Psychologist Tells of Rampant Sexual Abuse, Drugs and Despair," trauma treatment expert Mohammed Mansour explained:

> I encountered a large number of cases of sexual abuse among the children. That's a phenomenon that has always existed, but in this visit, and also in the previous visit, in August, it suddenly reached far larger dimensions. It's become positively huge. More than one-third of the children I saw in the Jabalya [refugee] camp reported being sexually abused. Children from ages 5 to 13.[9]

Dr. Manour made it abundantly clear that it is the Israeli blockade and the resulting "de-development" of Gaza that is leading to this dire situation:

> Most people don't work, and those who do, earn pennies—the average salary is 1,000 shekels a month [$285]. Mentally and physically, parents are simply not capable of supporting their children. They are immersed in their own depression, their own trauma. . . .
>
> I've seen the starvation. I visit meager, empty homes. The refrigerator is off even during the hours when they have electric power, because there's nothing in it. The children tell me that they eat once a day; some eat once every two days.

As Dr. Manour concluded, "The trauma does not end and will not end. Adults and children live in terrible pain, they're only looking for how to escape it. We also see growing numbers of addicts."

After learning of this immense suffering of the Palestinian people, I began to write publicly about it, feeling that I could no longer be silent, especially given my own government's support for Israel and its policies. I also felt I would not be a good friend to the Palestinians I had become friends with, if I did not speak out. As I opined, the destruction of the very social fabric of Gaza is according to plan. Israel is intent on the destruction of the Palestinian people, and it is engaged in what I have said for years is "a slow, patient, but systematic genocide."

I also wrote a piece in the peer-reviewed legal journal *The Jurist* about an incredible incident involving a Palestinian doctor named Izzeldin Abuelaish and the tragedy he suffered following a speech he gave at the Jewish Community Center (JCC) in the Squirrel Hill neighborhood of Pittsburgh. My then wife and I had lived in Squirrel Hill when we first moved to Pittsburgh, and we had been members of the JCC where we worked out at their gym. Our two sons attended the JCC summer camp and played on a soccer team there named after the city of Haifa in Israel/Palestine.

Squirrel Hill was the site of the terrible tragedy where the Tree of Life Synagogue was attacked by a lone gunman who killed eleven parishioners. My wife and I attended a moving candlelight vigil in honor of the Tree of Life victims in Squirrel Hill shortly after it happened. A number of Palestinians I know also attended this vigil as they too felt devastated by the tragedy.

Famously, right-wing Israeli Education Minister Naftali Bennett came to Pittsburgh to ostensibly console the survivors of the shooting, but his main goal was to use the tragedy to promote the State of Israel and its struggle against the Palestinians. He even likened the lone gunman, who was motivated by a combination of anti-Semitism and anti-immigrant sentiment—the Tree of Life was, after all, a progressive synagogue that did a lot of good work with the immigrant community—to a Hamas fighter back in Israel/Palestine. Many Jews in Pittsburgh and beyond were offended by Bennett's attempt to hijack the tragedy for his right-wing political ends, with members of the Pittsburgh Jewish community in the If Not Now When coalition—a Jewish group seeking a peaceful and just end to the Israeli-Palestinian conflict—protesting his visit and his policies back home, including his attempt to expel African asylum-seekers from Israel.[10] Ironically, Bennett's (anti-Black) racism is something he has in common with the Tree of Life shooter.

The story of Harvard-trained Dr. Abuelaish is a terrible one. As I explain in the *Jurist* article,[11] during Operation Cast Lead, Dr. Abuelaish regularly reported from Gaza in fluent Hebrew about the conflict. He was invited to address an audience at the JCC about his views on the conflict in 2009. Dr. Abuelaish has been an outspoken voice for peace and coexistence between Israel and the Palestinian people, and that was his very welcome message to the JCC audience. He also talked about his three daughters and their dreams for a peaceful future.

Within hours of his address to the JCC, Israeli armed forces shelled Dr. Abuelaish's home in Gaza, killing his three daughters and his niece. In my *Jurist* piece, I quote an AP article which explained that "when his home was hit, an Israel TV station delivered a real-time report from a sobbing Abuelaish to Israelis. 'My daughters have been killed,' he cried as a journalist listened at the other end of the line as the audio aired live."

The occasion for writing my article about Dr. Abuelaish in 2021 was his traveling then from Canada, where he had immigrated after the death of his daughters and niece, to Israel to appeal to the Israeli Supreme Court for a simple apology for the killing of his family members. The Supreme Court ultimately rejected his appeal, with Dr. Abuelaish stating that "With this decision, they killed, and they are insisting to kill, to torture, to stab them again and again and again."

Still, Dr. Abuelaish to this very day continues to advocate for peace and coexistence between Israel and Palestine, even as his own losses of loved ones continue to mount. Indeed, I just learned that "twenty members of Abuelaish's extended family were killed after an airstrike on the Jabalya refugee camp in late October," 2023.[12]

As I explained in my *Jurist* article, a total of three hundred children died in the Operation Cast Lead operation that claimed Dr. Abuelaish's daughters and niece. As I opined in this legal journal piece: "It is Palestinian children who always bear the brunt of such assaults, and the killing of Palestinian children occurs with such frequency that, at a minimum, they demonstrate such a lack of concern for the lives of civilians as to amount to a violation of international humanitarian law which requires an affirmative attempt by armed actors to protect civilians. In other words, to put a finer point on it, these killings amount to war crimes."

Just as Richard Goldstone found out, verbalizing such conclusions will bring about swift backlash, and this was true in my case as well. Thus, in response to this article, I was accused of anti-Semitism in a publication known as *The Jewish News Syndicate* (*JNS*).[13] In "The Absurdity of a Human-Rights Professor's Anti-Semitism," the author mined my *Jurist* article and other pieces I had written, including the one in which I accused Israel of engaging in a "slow-moving genocide," to make its case that I am somehow a bigot. Given that there now appears to be a fast-moving genocide being carried out by Israel in Gaza for everyone to see, I feel a bit vindicated in my observations back then.

The claims of anti-Semitism against me were very painful. I have always viewed myself as an anti-racist and someone who has great respect for Judaism and the Jewish people. And, in my view, there is nothing cited in that *JNS* article that contradicts this, but the mere allegation is enough to convict one in the minds of many readers. And, while I was never given a reason, when my teaching contract was up the next year, I was told it was not being renewed. I wonder if the *JNS* article had something to do with this, but I will probably never know.

In 2021, I twice visited both Lebanon and Syria. These trips were eye-opening for me and upended a lot of assumptions I had about the Middle East and the forces at work there.

For example, I was surprised to learn upon two visits in 2021 to Syria—Palestine having once been part of Greater Syria along with Jordan, Lebanon and part of Turkey—that Israel, in close collaboration with the United States, backed militant forces there which targeted Christian churches and communities, as well as other historic sites and antiquities, for destruction.

In May and August of 2021, I visited the picturesque town of Maaloula, Syria—an ancient city literally built into the mountains bordering Lebanon. Visiting Maaloula is like traveling back to Biblical times, in a number of ways. In addition to its centuries-old architecture, Maaloula is one of the few cities in the world that stills speaks Aramaic—the nearly dead language spoken by Jesus Christ. This makes Maaloula, a quite placid town, an ideal stop for Christian pilgrims. On my second visit there, I was fortunate enough to hear songs sung in Aramaic echoing in the valley.

However, the normal peace of Maaloula (which means "entrance" in Aramaic) was violently shattered in September 2013 when forces of the Free Syrian Army (FSA)—a coalition of militant groups backed by the US[14] and Israel[15] along with other countries and who were referred to by US officials as "moderate rebels"—invaded the town.

As witnesses I talked with in Maaloula, including nuns at the Convent of St. Thecla, explained, these forces attempted to destroy the convent as well as the nearby Church of Saints Sergius and Bacchus Monastery—at over 2,000 years old, one of the oldest Christian churches in the world. Thankfully, the stone construction of these edifices made it difficult for the FSA to bring them down by fire as they attempted to do, but they did manage to burn down the nearby forest, steal and destroy ancient Christian relics, smash the tomb of St. Thecla, and even kidnap some of the nuns of the convent.

The goal of the FSA was to destroy this Christian town, which it saw as anathema to the radical (if not heretical) form of Islam the FSA espoused and an impediment to its ultimate plan of setting up an Islamic Caliphate in Syria.

In August, I also visited Homs and the Saint Mary Church of the Holy Belt (circa. 59 AD) where the same thing played out in 2011–2012. At that time, as a priest of the church explained, the FSA tried to burn down this church, which is reputed to house a portion of the belt of the Virgin Mary. As they approached the town, some of the priests, escorted by the Syrian Armed Forces, secreted the belt out of town and hid it. However, again, the FSA managed to destroy a number of ancient relics and paintings and to burn the wooden portions of the church.

What may surprise many people who depend upon the mainstream Western press for their news, it was the Syrian Armed Forces of Bashir Al-Asad, with help from Hezbollah, who fought off the FSA and saved both Homs and Maaloula, as well as the ancient churches therein, from total destruction.

Lest one doubt this account of events, an interview conducted by the *National Catholic Reporter* (*NCR*) is illuminating. Thus, *NCR* interviewed Issam Bishara, the Catholic Near East Welfare Association's (CNEWA) regional director for Lebanon, Syria, and Egypt about the welfare of the 2.5 million Christians living in Syria amid the clashes in the Christian communities. In a rather leading question, the *NCR* reporter, Tom Gallagher, asked Bishara, "Have Christians been specifically targeted by Assad and his government forces?" However, Gallagher received an answer that he was apparently not expecting. Thus, in response, Bishara stated unequivocally,

> No. On the contrary, the regime is still providing protection to the Christian communities in almost all places where the regime is still controlling the ground. But the problem occurred especially in Homs after the protestors and the Islamic groups had controlled a part of the city (Bab Amro Quarter) where around 200 Christians were killed. The other concern is related to terrorism, which can target anyone and any place and especially Christian military officers and their communities.[16]

Ultimately, as *NCR* noted, most of the Christians in Homs had to find shelter and security elsewhere (many in the capital of Damascus) due to the invasion of the FSA, with the Christian population of the city reduced from 160,000 to 1,000 between 2011 and 2012. And, when some of them tried to return to Homs, many found their homes in ruins.

As we shall see below, this assault against Christians and Christian churches has been playing out in the West Bank and Gaza as well, and in these instances by Israel directly.

On these trips to Syria and Lebanon, I met some incredibly kind and generous Palestinians who treated me to incredible hospitality, including great meals, and who took me on tours of Palestinian refugee camps. The unique kindness and sweetness of the Palestinians I have met over the years has made a huge impression on me. In truth, I did not really know what true hospitality was until I met Palestinians. Other Westerners have told me the very same.

I met Amal, a Palestinian from the West Bank, in Syria. She immediately treated me as a friend and introduced me to a number of Palestinians in Beirut when we returned there after our Syria trip. The only way for most people to travel to Syria is to fly to Beirut and then travel by land a few hours to Damascus. The same trip is made in reverse in order to return home. This circuitous route is made necessary by the fact that the airport in Damascus, Syria, is largely out of commission because of the periodic bombing of the airport by Israel and less frequently by the United States. In addition, because of brutal Western sanctions against Syria, no Western commercial airlines would fly into the airport even if it were fully functional.

While in Beirut, Amal introduced me to a lovely Palestinian woman named Abir. Abir is one of the sweetest people I have ever met. She was always happy to pick me up at my hotel—the Mayflower where I stayed because that was the famous haunt of legendary journalist Robert Fisk when he stayed in Beirut—and take me around town. Abir would often sing joyously along with the radio as she drove me in her SUV.

One place Abir took me was the place of her birth—the infamous Shabra and Shatila Palestinian refugee camps in Beirut. These camps house Palestinians whose families were forced to flee from what was then

Palestine during the 1948 Nakba in which over 750,000 Palestinians were forcibly and violently displaced by Israeli forces in the course of creating the Israeli state. As refugees, these individuals, including Abir, are people without a country. While they have a legal right of return to their former homes in what was once known as Palestine, this right has sadly been honored in the breach and has been treated as wholly theoretical. In the meantime, the refugees do not have full citizenship in Lebanon.

The first thing that struck me when I visited the refugee camps in Beirut was that these were not "camps" in the sense that I had imagined. The notion of a "camp" conjured the vision of people living in rows of tents on a dirt surface, and this might have been an apt description of the camps when they were first created. Today, however, these refugee camps are in fact little cities, with concrete housing, markets, barber shops, and other commercial establishments. With that said, the infrastructure is austere. The camps are electrified with conspicuous rows of wires set up haphazardly between all the buildings. Many of these are not insulated, and people are sometimes electrocuted when it rains. In addition, there is not a proper sewage system, and the smell of raw sewage is palpable as one enters.

In 1982, when Abir was six years old and living here, she was a witness to one of the more brutal events in the history of the Israeli-Palestinian conflict.

Israel invaded Lebanon in June 1982 with the stated goal of attacking the forces of the Palestinian Liberation Organization (PLO) which at the time was based in Beirut and was carrying out attacks of Israel from there. However, as is invariably the case in such operations, Israel had its sights set on much more than the PLO.

Thus, as Al Jazeera relates,

- The PLO withdrew from Lebanon by September 1, 1982. Assurances were provided by the United States and a multinational force that the remaining Palestinian refugees and civilians would be protected.
- Two weeks later, the Israeli military besieged Sabra and Shatila and provided cover for their allies, a right-wing Lebanese militia called the Phalange, to carry out the mass killings.

- The killing continued for 43 hours, from 6 p.m. on Thursday, 16 September, until 1 p.m. on Saturday, 18 September.
- While accurate figures on the number of people killed are difficult to ascertain, estimates have put the death toll at between 2,000– 3,500 civilians.
- Testimonies from the mass killing describe horrific acts of slaughter, mutilation, rape, and mass graves. Images from the aftermath were aired on television worldwide and caused global outrage.[17]

It should be noted that this massacre was a replay of a very similar, but less known, massacre in another Lebanese refugee camp known as Tal al-Za'tar—"the largest, poorest and most isolated of the Palestinian refugee camps in the Beirut area, with a population of about twenty thousand Palestinians and perhaps ten thousand impoverished Lebanese, mainly from the south."[18]

The six-year-old Abir witnessed the terrible carnage at Sabra and Shatila, in which her aunt was killed, before her very eyes. Abir, taking my hand, gave me a tour of the camps, showing me the important sites and memorials of the massacre and the dead. While there, she bought me a ring and a beautiful little keepsake chest with an engraving of the Dome of the Rock mosque on the Temple Mount in Jerusalem to remember my visit.

I was and continue to be impressed how people like Abir, and the other Palestinians I have met, can endure such horrors and still find happiness and joy in their lives and show some of the greatest generosity I have ever received. This is a humbling experience, and it is impossible to avert one's eyes again from the plight of the Palestinian people thereafter or to remain silent about it.

CHAPTER 1

A SHORT HISTORY OF ZIONISM AND THE FOUNDING OF ISRAEL IN HISTORIC PALESTINE

I know a lady in Venice who would have walked barefoot to Palestine for a touch of his nether lip.
—William Shakespeare, *Othello* (1603)

Let us not ignore the truth among ourselves . . . politically we are the aggressors and they (Palestinians) defend themselves . . . the country is theirs, because they inhabit it, whereas we want to come here and settle down, and in their view, we want to take away from them their country.
—David Ben-Gurion, Founding Father and First Prime Minister of Israel

Once upon a time, there was a land called Palestine. Defenders of Israel would like you to forget that land, that it ever existed or that a people indeed lived on this land before the founding of Israel in 1948. Rather, they would have us believe that those who founded Israel as a safe haven for Jews—"a people without a land"—did so in "a land without a people."

To the extent they do acknowledge the existence of people on this land, Zionists would have us believe that these people left the land as part of a "voluntary transfer"; that is, of their own accord.[1]

1

However, all of this is far from the truth. One goal of this book is to keep the memory of this land, its people, and their displacement and oppression alive—even as this very memory is being violently obliterated as I write these words.

This historic memory is critical in understanding the current events taking place in Israel/Palestine, and how the claims about these events rarely jibe with the reality. For example, it is important to know and understand the utter falsity of a "voluntary transfer" of Palestinians in 1948 as Israeli Prime Minister Benjamin Netanyahu is now openly talking about his plan for another "voluntary migration" of Palestinians from Gaza,[2] somehow pretending that the current bombing of Gaza to smithereens could result in the "voluntary" anything of the Palestinians living there.

Writing not long ago in his 2006 book, *The Ethnic Cleansing of Palestine*, Ilan Pappe—an Israeli Jew born to German-Jewish parents who fled the Holocaust and himself a veteran of the Israeli Defense Forces (IDF)—explained the collective amnesia around these events even into the twenty-first century.[3]

Discussing specifically the major, violent ethnic cleansing of Palestinians in 1948 to make way for the creation of Israel—an event Palestinians refer to as the Nakba (catastrophe)—Pappe writes:

It is the deep chasm between reality and representation that is most bewildering the case of Palestine. It is indeed hard to understand, and for that matter to explain, why a crime that was perpetrated in modern times and at a juncture in history that called for foreign reporters and UN observers to be present, should have been totally ignored. And yet, there is no denying that the ethnic cleansing of 1948 has been eradicated almost totally from the collective global memory and erased from the world's conscience. Imagine that not so long ago, in any given country you are familiar with, half of the entire population had been forcibly expelled within a year, half of its villages and towns wiped out, leaving behind only rubble and stones. Imagine now the possibility that somehow this act will never make it into the history books and that all diplomatic efforts to solve the conflict that erupted in that country will totally sideline, if not ignore, this catastrophic event. I, for one, have searched in vain through the history of the world as we know it in the aftermath of the Second World War for a case of this nature and a fate of this kind.

As Pappe further explains, the Nakba, in which "close to 800,000 people had been uprooted, 531 villages had been destroyed, and eleven neighborhoods emptied of their inhabitants . . . has ever since been systematically denied, and is still today not recognized as an historical fact, let alone acknowledged as a crime that needs to be confronted politically as well as morally."

And so, dear reader, you would be forgiven if you did not know of these events or even the word Nakba, and if you in fact believe, as our leaders and press would have you think, that the history of Israeli-Palestinian relations somehow began on October 7, 2023, and that Israel bears no responsibility in precipitating the terrible events of that day.

The reason that the public is desperately kept in the dark about such history is simple—because if the public had awareness of it, they would not consent to the support of Israel in again ethnically cleansing Palestinians from their land, destroying their towns and villages, again "leaving behind only rubble and stones." Indeed, to the extent that there are currently unprecedented protests against Israel's current war on Gaza, it is because at least part of the public has been gradually, and quite recently, educated about this history by people like Ilan Pappe.

As we know from historians like Pappe, the Nakba was carried out with the type of brutality that other settlers have carried out against indigenous populations, including "the poisoning of the water supply . . . with typhoid, numerous cases of rapes and . . . dozens of massacres." And indeed, as Pappe explains, "The fact that the expellers were newcomers to the country, and part of a colonization project, relates the case of Palestine to the colonist history of ethnic cleansing in North and South America." However, while the ethnic cleansing in the Americas is largely (though certainly not entirely) a matter of past history, the ethnic cleansing of Palestinians continues to this day, in real time, and can be viewed on our smartphones, computers, and TVs. And more importantly, it is an ethnic cleansing that can be halted before it is too late.

History did not begin with the Nakba either. Rather, the dispossession of the Palestinians from their historic land had been decided for them for many years prior, with Britain and the United States willing partners in the plan. The concrete plan for this dispossession came in the form of the infamous Balfour Declaration of 1917. As the BBC explains, the Balfour Declaration "can be seen as a starting point for the Arab-Israeli conflict. The declaration by the then foreign secretary was included in a letter to Lord Walter Rothschild, a leading proponent of Zionism, a movement advocating self-determination for the Jewish people in their historical homeland—from the Mediterranean to the eastern flank of the River Jordan, an area which came to be known as Palestine."[4] Note here, what is now a familiar phrase, and one which some claim is anti-Semitic when said by pro-Palestinian activists—"from the River to the Sea."

At the time of the Balfour Declaration, however, it must be pointed out that the vast majority of people who were living in the area from the river to the sea were in fact Palestinians who, by the way, are themselves Semitic peoples—a fact which is also forgotten in the discussions of the Israeli-Palestinian conflict. One rarely hears the accusation, for example, that someone is anti-Semitic because they harbor anti-Palestinian sentiments. And indeed, I would contend, that form of anti-Semitism is fully endorsed by the governments and mainstream media of the United States, Israel and many other Western countries. Indeed, it is this pervasive form of anti-Semitism that allows the current atrocities against the Palestinians to take place.

According to the Jewish Virtual Library, at the time of the Balfour Declaration, there was a total population in Palestine of 660,000 people, only 60,000 (or 8.1 percent) of whom were Jewish.[5] And yet, through the Balfour Declaration, it was decided that this land of mostly Palestinians—the land at that time in the Ottoman Empire and under Turkish rule—would be given away to Jewish settlers who would come mostly from Europe. The full Declaration reads as follows:

Foreign Office
November 2nd, 1917

Dear Lord Rothschild,
I have much pleasure in conveying to you. on behalf of His Majesty's
Government, the following declaration of sympathy with Jewish Zionist
aspirations which has been submitted to, and approved by, the Cabinet.

His Majesty's Government view with favour the establishment in
Palestine of a national home for the Jewish people, and will use their
best endeavors to facilitate the achievement of this object, it being clearly
understood that nothing shall be done which may prejudice the civil and
religious rights of existing non-Jewish communities in Palestine or the
rights and political status enjoyed by Jews in any other country.

I should be grateful if you would bring this declaration to the knowledge of the Zionist Federation.

Yours,
Arthur James Balfour

There are many notable things about this controversial letter. First, note
that the letter clearly refers to the land of "Palestine." In addition, while
the letter makes a vague reference to support for a "national home for the
Jewish people"—a concept that seems unobjectionable, especially given
the very real oppression suffered by Jews in Europe—all parties to the
letter understood what this really meant: "the use of the phrase 'national
home' was . . . intended to disguise what the British knew and the Arabs
feared: the Zionists intended to create a state for Jews in a province that
was more than 90 per cent Arab."[6]

Note also that the letter provides "that nothing shall be done which
may prejudice the civil and religious rights of existing non-Jewish communities in Palestine or the rights and political status enjoyed by Jews
in any other country." However, this promise, if it can be construed as
such, to uphold the rights of the unnamed "non-Jewish communities"
was forgotten before the ink on the letter was even dry. As Ilan Pappe
puts it, "Balfour promised to protect the aspirations of the non-Jewish

population—a strange reference to the vast native majority—but the declaration clashed precipitously with both the aspirations and natural rights of Palestinians for nationhood and independence."[7]

While certainly, the letter was the product of some concern about the maltreatment of Jews in Europe—a legitimate concern I certainly acknowledge and welcome—this was really the least of the concerns. Rather, this World War I–era letter, which was also supported by then (quite racist) US President Woodrow Wilson, was mainly the product of the old-fashioned Western imperial desires to colonize a strategic part of the Middle East. And they saw the creation of a Jewish homeland as a vehicle to do so.

Moreover, it should also be noted that while supporting a Jewish homeland in the Middle East to deal with European anti-Jewish persecution may seem like a laudable goal in some ways, many also see it as a manifestation of anti-Semitic sentiment—that is, the Europeans would deal with their "Jewish problem" by simply getting rid of the Jews. And they would do so by taking away the land of other peoples who had nothing to do with the persecution of the Jews in Europe. The Europeans, and especially the Germans, would do this in a big way after World War II, "atoning" for the Nazi German Holocaust which the West did little to stop by offshoring their guilt to Palestine and the Palestinians who had nothing to do with the Holocaust and making the Palestinians pay for the West's crimes.

This is reminiscent of the fate of the most famous Palestinian in history—Jesus Christ—who is said to have suffered and died for the sins of all of humankind. But in his case, Jesus chose this fate voluntarily, if not without some hand-wringing beforehand in the Garden of Olives.

This strange form of "atonement," if you could call it that, persists to this day. And, in order to justify it, Palestinians, in addition to being made to bear the punishment for Europe's mistreatment of the Jewish people, must also be made to bear its guilt. And thus, there is a bizarre projection of the Europeans' responsibility for the Holocaust upon the Palestinians, with the latter even being called "Nazis" by many defenders of Israel to this day—and thus, the November 12, 2023, stunt of Israeli president Isaac Herzog claiming that a copy of *Mein Kampf* was found in the bedroom of a Palestinian child. This would be comical if the results were not so serious.

Germany, not surprisingly, is one of the worst offenders when it comes to this displacement and projection of guilt and punishment, attempting as it does to make up for its own genocide against Jews by vigorously supporting another genocide—this one against the residents of Gaza. Consequently, Germany has increased its military support to Israel tenfold during Israel's current Gaza onslaught.[8]

Betraying their imperial/colonial ambitions, Britain and France made a deal at around the same time as the Balfour Declaration to carve up the Middle East. As an article on Al Jazeera explains, "The British also promised the French, in a separate treaty known as 1916 Sykes-Picot agreement that the majority of Palestine would be under international administration, while the rest of the region would be split between the two colonial powers after the war. The [Balfour] declaration, however, meant that Palestine would come under British occupation and that the Palestinian Arabs who lived there would not gain independence."[9]

The year 1916 was significant in British history for another reason—the Easter Rising in Ireland, all of which was then occupied by Great Britain. On Easter in that year, over 1,700 Irish Republicans who sought independence from Britain mounted an armed insurrection against British rule. British forces brutally put down the uprising and executed its leaders, including James Connolly, who would become a symbol of the Irish independence struggle, a struggle which continues to this day in what is known as Northern Ireland—a part of Ireland still under British rule. It is not surprising then, that the Irish demonstrate so much sympathy for the Palestinian struggle against Israeli occupation as they see it akin to their own. And indeed, it is akin to their own.

As Al Jazeera explains, while there is much debate about the whys and wherefores of the Balfour Declaration, there seems to be consensus upon the following reasons for it:

- Control over Palestine was a strategic imperial interest to keep Egypt and the Suez Canal within Britain's sphere of influence.
- Britain had to side with the Zionists to rally support among Jews in the United States and Russia hoping they could encourage their governments to stay in the war [World War I] until victory.

- Intense Zionist lobbying and strong connections between the Zionist community in Britain and the British government; some of the officials in the government were Zionists themselves.
- Jews were being persecuted in Europe and the British government was sympathetic to their suffering.[10]

But again, as to the last bullet point—the British concern for the well-being of the Jews—not all officials in the British government believed that the Balfour Declaration reflected such a bona fide concern, but that it in fact reflected quite the opposite. As an article in the London *Guardian* explains, "The only Jewish member of the British cabinet, Edwin Samuel Montagu, the secretary of state for India, argued against issuing the Declaration. Montagu called Zionism 'a mischievous political creed' and wrote that, in favoring it, 'the policy of His Majesty's Government is antisemitic.' David Alexander, president of the Board of British Jews, Claude Montefiore, president of the Anglo-Jewish Association, and most Orthodox rabbis also opposed the Zionist enterprise. They insisted that they had as much right as any Christian to live and prosper in Britain, and they did not want Weizmann, however Anglophile his tastes, telling them to settle in the Judean desert or to till the orange groves of Jaffa."[11]

The other motivation behind the Declaration, and one which endures to this day, is the desire among certain sects of Western Christians—today, they are called Evangelicals—who wanted to "pry [Palestine] from the Ottoman Empire" and pave the way for "the return of the Jews to Palestine as a chapter in the divine scheme, precipitating the second coming of Christ and the creation of a pietist state there."[12]

As we shall see later, this goal has been a disaster for the actual Palestinian Christians who live in Palestine and have lived there since the very beginning of Christianity. But this version of Christianity—one at great variance with the Christianity I know from the Bible—is unconcerned with the well-being of real, living human beings and instead focuses on some imagined apocalyptic future in which the "righteous" are taken to Heaven while the "unrighteous" are damned and die in an eternal fire. It is also a religion based on hubris as it rests on a belief that we as humans could somehow usher in these divine events.

It should also go without saying that Jews, who do not accept Jesus as their savior, do not fare well in the imagined future of these Christian zealots and are not the intended beneficiaries of the self-described Christian Zionists' efforts. Indeed, it can be said that many Christian Zionists are truly anti-Semitic.

This marriage between Christian Fundamentalism and Zionism was and continues to be an uneasy and unholy alliance, but it is a powerful alliance nonetheless, and one that drives US policy toward Israel in a big way.

MSNBC did a story on this on October 22, 2023, just two weeks after the beginning of the current crisis. This article is appropriately titled, "The dispiriting truth about why many evangelical Christians support Israel. For Christian Zionists, what happens to the Jews and Palestinians is, to put it very mildly, collateral damage."[13] As this article explains,

> Evangelicals' support isn't simply driven by a theology that compels them to love the Holy Land, detached from its convulsive domestic and global political implications. For many "Christians Zionists," and particularly for popular evangelists with significant clout within the Republican Party, their support for Israel is rooted in its role in the supposed end times: Jesus' return to Earth, a bloody final battle at Armageddon, and Jesus ruling the world from the Temple Mount in Jerusalem. In this scenario, war is not something to be avoided, but something inevitable, desired by God, and celebratory.
>
> At the heart of Christian Zionism is not a love for Israel but rather Christian nationalism. What happens to the Jews and Palestinians is, to put it very mildly, collateral damage. Christian Zionists are anticipating, and hoping for a war to end all wars, and a resulting Christian world that they claim will vanquish evil and bring peace. Only those who accept Jesus as their savior will benefit from these events that Christian Zionists claim the Bible predicts will happen. Nonbelievers—including Jews and Muslims—will not survive them.

In other words, the Christian Zionists, who have great political clout in the United States—indeed, Trump's chief of the CIA and then secretary of state Mike Pompeo is a zealous Christian Zionist as was Trump's vice president, Mike Pence[14]—are pushing for war and conflagration and seem to be getting their wish. Mike Pence recently displayed his fanatical support for Israel and its military aims when he was photographed signing an Israeli mortar shell that would inevitably be used to kill people. Even the Israeli newspaper *Haaretz* criticized him for this act, stating, "when former US Vice President Mike Pence—a representative of a country that has the power to use military and financial support to Israel to change the course of the war—signed a mortar while on a visit to the Lebanese border last week, he was sending a message of gleeful killing and uncritical thinking."[15] Sadly, there are all too many US officials who are "gleeful" about killing and who are ruled by "uncritical thinking," especially when it comes to Israel.

One other fact mentioned in the MSNBC piece must also be emphasized—that, in the scenario of Armageddon that Christian Zionists believe in, Jesus in his Second Coming will rule from the Temple Mount in the Old City of East Jerusalem—an area recognized by international law as Palestinian territory. Recall that President Trump, urged on by Christian Zionists such as Mike Pompeo and Mike Pence, flouted international law and the will of the Palestinians by recognizing all of Jerusalem, including East Jerusalem, as the capital city of Israel and then moving the US Embassy from Tel Aviv to Jerusalem. President Joe Biden has not reversed this illegal and incendiary policy.

For many centuries, since the early 700s, the Temple Mount has been the site of the iconic Al-Aqsa Mosque—the third most holy site in the world for Muslims. This site has become a major focus of conflict between Israelis and Palestinians, with Israeli politicians, soldiers and settlers often engaging in provocative acts there, including invading the holy site, and harassing, beating, and arresting Muslim worshippers en masse. These types of ugly and hateful activities are cheered on by the Christian Zionists who wish to wrest control over this site from the Muslims in furtherance of their apocalyptic fantasies in the same way that the Christian Zionists back in 1917 wanted to wrest control of all of Palestine from the Turkish Empire.

Indeed, a major conflict began at Al-Aqsa on October 1, 2023—just days before the attacks by Hamas and other armed militants on October

7—when thousands of Israeli settlers began "carrying out provocative tours of the mosque complex following calls by ultranationalist Jewish groups."[16] These provocations were aided and abetted by Israeli police who prevented young Palestinians from entering the area and forced Palestinian businesses in the Old City to close during these incursions.

The settlers' provocative acts were not limited to the Muslim site or to Muslims but were also carried out against Christians in the Old City of Jerusalem where the mosque is located. These acts included spitting upon Christians. Such open anti-Christian hatred is not an isolated event. Indeed, "Since Israel's most conservative government in history came to power late last year, concerns have mounted among religious leaders—including the influential Vatican-appointed Latin Patriarch—over the increasing harassment of the region's 2,000-year-old Christian community."[17] We will discuss in more detail the assault upon the real live Christians of Palestine and elsewhere.

Even greater provocations took place earlier in April 2023, during the holy day of Ramadan. At this time, Israeli police invaded the Al-Aqsa compound, "beat worshippers with batons and used tear gas and sound bombs to force them out of the prayer halls."[18] The police ended up arresting four hundred worshippers at the mosque.

As Al Jazeera explained, this event also was not an isolated one:

In recent years, the Al-Aqsa Mosque compound has been an annual flashpoint during Ramadan.

Last year [2022], more than 300 Palestinians were arrested and at least 170 wounded as Israeli forces launched incursions at the compound during the holy month. This followed deadly violence in the occupied West Bank in late March, in which 36 people were killed.

In May 2021, Israeli forces stormed the compound using tear gas, rubber-coated steel bullets and stun grenades against worshippers during Ramadan. Hundreds of Palestinians were injured, drawing international condemnation.[19]

As Al Jazeera explains, the violence at the Al-Aqsa compound in May 2021, and the response of Palestinian militants to this violence, resulted in the eleven-day Israeli assault on Gaza that resulted in the deaths of 256 Palestinians, including sixty-six children. Recall that the *New York Times*, in a sea change from its usual pro-Israeli coverage, would print the photos of the Palestinian children killed in this offensive on a full page of the newspaper.

As one can see from the above, it is not a coincidence that the military uprising by Hamas and other militants beginning on October 7, 2023—an uprising we are led to believe came out of nowhere has been dubbed "Operation Al-Aqsa Flood."

In the end, what cannot be denied is that the plan for the creation of a Jewish state back in 1917 has been disastrous for the Palestinian people who were not privy to or consulted on this plan of the imperial powers. These imperial powers, it must be emphasized, were engaged in the mass slaughter of their own peoples by the many millions in the course of World War I at the very time they were hatching this plan for Palestine. What could go wrong from a plan concocted by such leaders?!

The Palestinians' once peaceful land quickly became a troubled one and has remained so ever since. As Al Jazeera writes in a sad passage:

> Khalil Sakakini, a Jerusalemite writer and teacher, described Palestine in the immediate aftermath of the war [World War I] as follows: "A nation which has long been in the depths of sleep only awakes if it is rudely shaken by events, and only arises little by little. . . . This was the situation of Palestine, which for many centuries has been in the deepest sleep, until it was shaken by the great war, shocked by the Zionist movement, and violated by the illegal policy [of the British], and it awoke, little by little."
>
> Increased Jewish immigration under the mandate created tensions and violence between the Palestinian Arabs and the European Jews. One of the first popular responses to British actions was the Nebi Musa revolt in 1920 that led to the killing of four Palestinian Arabs and five immigrant Jews.[20]

For his part, Ilan Pappe writes, "The moment British Foreign Secretary Lord Balfour gave the Zionist movement his promise in 1917 to establish a national home for Jews in Palestine, he opened the door to the endless conflict that would soon engulf the country and its people. . . . By the end of the 1920s, it was clear that this proposal had a potentially violent core, as it had already claimed the lives of hundreds of Palestinians and Jews."[21] In response, the British reluctantly stepped in to try to create some stability in Palestine, though solidly on the side of the Zionist settlers, and thus began what would be known as the British Mandate, which would last until the founding of the new State of Israel.

From the very beginning, the Zionist idea of a Jewish state went hand in hand with the expulsion of the indigenous Palestinians. As Pappe explains: "From the founder of the Zionist movement, Theodor Herzl, to the main leaders of the Zionist enterprise in Palestine, cleansing the land was a valid option. As one of the movement's most liberal thinkers, Leo Motzin, put it in 1917: 'Our thought is that the colonization of Palestine has to go in two directions: Jewish settlement in Eretz Israel and the resettlement of Arabs of Eretz Israel in areas outside the country. The transfer of so many Arabs may seem at first unacceptable economically, but is nonetheless practical. It does not require too much money to resettle a Palestinian village on another land.'"[22] Note that Motzin focuses on the economic costs of the desired ethnic cleansing and says nothing of its morality.

It must be emphasized that these two pillars of the Zionist project as described by Motzin—Jewish settlement and Arab removal—continue to be the essential pillars of the Israeli project to this very day. Indeed, as discussed in more detail below, we are seeing the manifestation of these goals today in a much bigger way than even manifested during the Nakba of 1948.

As we learn from Pappe's detailed analysis of the situation, the Palestinians were used to the change of nations that ruled over their land, whether they be Roman invaders or Muslim empires or the British, and they were always willing to accommodate to this rule. Still, there was some resistance, and even some mob violence carried out by Palestinians during the years of the British Mandate, but it was very different than what was taking place in Europe against Jews, and it had very different motivations.

Thus, an article in the *London Review of Books*, reviewing works by Israeli historians Tom Segev and Naomi Shepherd, who counter the narratives long promoted by Israeli apologists, discusses a violent mob attack by Palestinians against Jewish settlers in 1929 in the city of Hebron. As this article explains, the Zionist leader and founder of Israel David Ben-Gurion "called it a pogrom, but according to Segev this is a misuse of the term. Pogroms, as in Russia and the Ukraine, were officially sponsored. The motivation was anti-semitism; the Arabs, on the other hand, were reacting to fear of Zionist domination. 'Most of Hebron's Jews were saved because Arabs hid them in their houses,' Segev writes, adding that Zionist archives list 435 Jews who escaped death in this way, a higher number than in European pogroms."[23]

And the Zionist settlers in Palestine, moreover, were not the heroic Davids fighting the Goliath of British imperialism as we have been led to believe for so long. Rather, "For Israel's new historians, among them Segev and Naomi Shepherd, the Zionist project is part of the saga of white settlement, as in north America and Rhodesia. The settlers declared independence only when they no longer required the mother country's soldiers to subdue the natives."[24]

This is critical for assessing the Israeli-Palestinian conflict even to this day. Thus, if the Israeli settlers are seen, and I believe rightly, as colonizers, and the Palestinians seen as the indigenous peoples being violently and unjustly colonized and displaced, the violence of the one cannot be judged the same as the violence of the other. The violence of the slaveholder, after all, is not judged the same as the violence of the enslaved person when rebelling against the slaveholder. In any case, as one might expect, the Israelis as the colonizers have inflicted much more violence against the Palestinians than the Palestinians have inflicted against them.

As Ilan Pappe explains, even when that "declaration of independence" by the Zionists came in late 1947, the Palestinians, though engaging in some sporadic acts of resistance that were quickly quelled, were largely willing to take a wait-and-see attitude as to what would happen. For the Palestinians, their main concern was maintaining a certain sense of "normality" in their lives, agriculture and business, which led them to confront the new regime with a certain level of stoicism and passivity. And indeed, the militant leaders of the new Israeli state grew frustrated with the Palestinians' passivity, the Zionist leaders desperately wanting a pretext to justify the violent ethnic cleansing they had planned for the Palestinians.

But though such a pretext never really came, the Zionists went ahead with the violent ethnic cleansing anyway. And they did so because the ethnic cleansing of the Arab population was an inherent part of their plan all along. That is, as my Palestinian friend in the West Bank eloquently told me, "*it is not our resistance that they oppose, but our existence.*"

As Pappe explains, the Zionist plan was a unique one, and one more terrible than any of the other invaders, even the Romans who came in the form of the Crusaders, had in store for the indigenous population. As Pappe writes, as the British Mandate was ending, and the Zionists became ascendant, Palestinian "villagers and city dwellers waited patiently to see what it would mean to be part of a Jewish state or any other new regime that might replace British rule. Most of them had no idea what was in store for them, that was about to happen would constitute an unprecedented chapter in Palestine's history; not a mere transition from one ruler to another, but the actual dispossession of the people living on the land."[25]

By 1948, the Jewish settlers constituted only one-third of the population of Palestine (and the vast majority of these were European settlers who were newcomers immigrating after 1917) and owned less than 6 percent of the land.[26] And yet, the United Nations, in General Assembly Resolution 181—the result of the intense lobbying by the Zionists as well as the guilt the Europeans rightly felt from the Holocaust—allocated 56 percent of the land, and the very best land, for the creation of the new Jewish state. The injustice of this, and the inevitability of the violence that would take place as a result of implementing this plan, is seen when one considers that "within the borders of the UN-proposed state, they [the Jewish settlers] owned only eleven percent of the land, and were the minority in every district."[27]

And, unbeknownst to the UN, the founders of Israel planned to take much more land than that allotted by the UN Resolution.

Violence would come swiftly as the Zionist leaders, led by David Ben-Gurion, had been planning and preparing for it for some time. And this plan indeed had a name—Plan Dalet (or Plan D). While defenders of

Israel attempt to vilify the Palestinians as terrorists, Plan Dalet explicitly called for the infliction of terror upon the Palestinian population, which put up little resistance, and this terror continues to be inflicted against the Palestinians to this day.

As the Institute for Middle East Understanding explains, "Almost immediately after the partition plan was passed, the expulsion of Palestinians by Zionist militias began, months before the armies of neighboring Arab states became involved. By the time these militias and the new Israeli army finished, the new state of Israel covered 78 percent of Palestine. The remaining 22 percent, comprising the West Bank, East Jerusalem, and Gaza, fell under the control of Jordan and Egypt, respectively."[28]

One of the most iconic and disturbing acts of violence and terror occurred in the Palestinian village of Deir Yassin. The assault on this village was carried out by two Israeli militias—the Stern Gang and the Irgun led by Menachem Begin. Begin would go on to be the founder of the right-wing party that would combine with other parties to become the Likud—the party of current prime minister Benjamin Netanyahu. Begin would also become prime minister of Israel from 1977 to 1983. Begin was an unapologetic terrorist, having been involved in such terrorist plots as the 1946 bombing of the King David Hotel that killed ninety-one people, including twenty-five Brits, forty-one Arabs, and seventeen Jews.[29] The assault upon Deir Yassin would be another of Begin's terrorist attacks.

While Israelis long denied the atrocities of Deir Yassin—wanting instead to portray the massacre there as part of a "war of independence" rather than the war for domination and dispossession it was—the terrible truths about this massacre had to be acknowledged given the release of accounts by Israelis who themselves carried out the atrocities. In 2017, the Israeli newspaper *Haaretz* ran a story on these accounts, which it described as making "for difficult reading."[30] *Haaretz* describes one "harsh account" by

Prof. Mordechai Gichon, a lieutenant colonel in the Israel Defense Forces reserves, who was a Haganah intelligence officer sent to Deir Yassin when the battle ended. "To me it looked a bit like a pogrom," said Gichon, who died about a year ago. "If you're occupying an army position—it's not a pogrom, even if a hundred people are killed. But if you are coming into a civilian locale and dead people are scattered around in it—then it looks like a pogrom. When the Cossacks burst into Jewish neighborhoods, then that should have looked something like this."

According to Gichon, "There was a feeling of considerable slaughter and it was hard for me to explain it to myself as having been done in self-defense. My impression was more of a massacre than anything else. If it is a matter of killing innocent civilians, then it can be called a massacre."

As will be discussed further below, the Israelis continue to carry out pogroms against the Palestinians to this very day.

A piece on Al Jazeera describes the Deir Yassin massacre and its significance as follows:

On April 9, 1948, just weeks before the creation of the State of Israel, members of the Irgun and Stern Gang Zionist militias attacked the village of Deir Yassin, killing at least 107 Palestinians.

According to testimonies from the perpetrators and surviving victims, many of the people slaughtered—from those who were tied to trees and burned to death to those lined up against a wall and shot by submachine guns—were women, children and the elderly.

As news of the atrocities spread, thousands fled their villages in fear. Eventually, some 700,000 Palestinians would flee or be forcibly displaced at the outset of Israel's creation, making the massacre a decisive moment in Palestinian history.[31]

As Al Jazeera notes, these villagers were "murdered in cold blood and buried in mass graves" despite the fact that "Palestinians and some Israeli historians say the villagers had signed a non-aggression agreement with the Haganah, the pre-Israeli-state Zionist army." The article goes on to describe the terrible events at Deir Yassin:

According to a 1948 report filed by the British delegation to the United Nations, the killing of "some 250 Arabs, men, women and children, took place in circumstances of great savagery."

"Women and children were stripped, lined up, photographed, and then slaughtered by automatic firing and survivors have told of even more incredible bestialities," the report said. "Those who were taken prisoners were treated with degrading brutality."

Israeli historian Benny Morris said the militias "ransacked unscrupulously, stole money and jewels from the survivors and burned the bodies. Even dismemberment and rape occurred."

On December 4, 1948, a number of prominent Jewish intellectuals, including Albert Einstein, Hannah Arendt, and Sydney Hook, so disturbed by the events at Deir Yassin, and by the US reception for one of the masterminds of the massacre, Menachem Begin, penned a letter to the *New York Times* vigorously protesting. Einstein et al. focused their ire on Begin's fledgling political party that would ultimately become the Likud Party, which has now governed Israel for the past twenty-plus years and counting.

In this letter, the authors mince no words, even referring to Begin's party as "fascist" and akin to Nazism. This letter reads in full as follows:

TO THE EDITORS OF NEW YORK TIMES:
Among the most disturbing political phenomena of our times is the emergence in the newly created state of Israel of the "Freedom Party" (Tnuat Haherut), a political party closely akin in its organization, methods, political philosophy and social appeal to the Nazi and Fascist parties. It was formed out of the membership and following of the former Irgun Zvai Leumi, a terrorist, right-wing, chauvinist organization in Palestine.

The current visit of Menachem Begin, leader of this party, to the United States is obviously calculated to give the impression of American support for his party in the coming Israeli elections, and to cement political ties with conservative Zionist elements in the United States. Several Americans of national repute have lent their names to welcome his visit. It is inconceivable that those who oppose fascism throughout the world, if correctly informed as to Mr. Begin's political record and perspectives, could add their names and support to the movement he represents.

Before irreparable damage is done by way of financial contributions, public manifestations in Begin's behalf, and the creation in Palestine of the impression that a large segment of America supports Fascist elements in Israel, the American public must be informed as to the record and objectives of Mr. Begin and his movement.

The public avowals of Begin's party are no guide whatever to its actual character. Today they speak of freedom, democracy and anti-imperialism, whereas until recently they openly preached the doctrine of the Fascist state. It is in its actions that the terrorist party betrays its real character; from its past actions we can judge what it may be expected to do in the future.

Attack on Arab Village

A shocking example was their behavior in the Arab village of Deir Yassin. This village, off the main roads and surrounded by Jewish lands, had taken no part in the war, and had even fought off Arab bands who wanted to use the village as their base. On April 9, terrorist bands attacked this peaceful village, which was not a military objective in the fighting, killed most of its inhabitants (240 men, women, and children) and kept a few of them alive to parade as captives through the streets of Jerusalem. Most of the Jewish community was horrified at the deed, and the Jewish Agency sent a telegram of apology to King Abdullah of Trans-Jordan. But the terrorists, far from being ashamed of their act, were proud of this massacre, publicized it widely, and invited all the foreign correspondents present in the country to view the heaped corpses and the general havoc at Deir Yassin.

The Deir Yassin incident exemplifies the character and actions of the Freedom Party. Within the Jewish community they have preached an admixture of ultranationalism, religious mysticism, and racial superiority. Like other Fascist parties they have been used to break strikes, and have themselves pressed for the destruction of free trade unions. In their stead they have proposed corporate unions on the Italian Fascist model.

During the last years of sporadic anti-British violence, the IZL and Stern groups inaugurated a reign of terror in the Palestine Jewish community. Teachers were beaten up for speaking against them, adults were shot for not letting their children join them. By gangster methods, beatings, window-smashing, and wide-spread robberies, the terrorists intimidated the population and exacted a heavy tribute. The people of the Freedom

Party have had no part in the constructive achievements in Palestine. They have reclaimed no land, built no settlements, and only detracted from the Jewish defense activity. Their much-publicized immigration endeavors were minute, and devoted mainly to bringing in Fascist compatriots.

Discrepancies Seen

The discrepancies between the bold claims now being made by Begin and his party, and their record of past performance in Palestine bear the imprint of no ordinary political party. This is the unmistakable stamp of a Fascist party for whom terrorism (against Jews, Arabs, and British alike), and misrepresentation are means, and a "Leader State" is the goal.

In the light of the foregoing considerations, it is imperative that the truth about Mr. Begin and his movement be made known in this country. It is all the more tragic that the top leadership of American Zionism has refused to campaign against Begin's efforts, or even to expose to its own constituents the dangers to Israel from support to Begin.

The undersigned therefore take this means of publicly presenting a few salient facts concerning Begin and his party; and of urging all concerned not to support this latest manifestation of fascism.[32]

This letter, written contemporaneously with the terrible events in Deir Yassin, is inconvenient for those who to this very day attempt to deny that a massacre there ever took place. It is equally inconvenient to those who try to claim Einstein as an adherent to the violent Zionist project in Palestine.

Einstein and his colleagues, judging the Zionist leaders by their actions and not their rhetoric, saw reality for what it was, and that the emerging State of Israel was not in fact manifesting the values of freedom and democracy it purported to value. Sadly, this letter and its message have largely been lost to history, and Begin's party, which has now been in power in Israel for the better part of almost half a century, is currently outdoing him in terms of violence, terror and ethnic cleansing.

Before we move away from our discussion of Menachem Begin, there are some interactions he had with two different US political figures that are revealing about the ability of the United States to change Israeli war policy and about whether we can take seriously President Biden's current claims that he is trying in vain to change Israel's brutal policies in Gaza.

The first incident involved President Ronald Reagan, who was in office at the same time Begin was Israeli prime minister. As the *New York Times* reported at the time, Reagan halted Israel's bombing of civilians in Lebanon with one phone call to Begin. As the *Times* explained, "Israeli dive-bombers and artillery last week gave west Beirut its worst pounding of the 10-week siege, threatening for a time to add American peacemaking efforts to the burgeoning casualty lists. A shocked President Reagan telephoned Prime Minister Menachem Begin to "express his outrage" at the killing of civilians and warned he was considering calling home his mediator, Philip C. Habib. The cease-fire was reinstated and Mr. Reagan later saw 'great reason for hope.'"[33]

Around the same time, Begin had a very different conversation with another US politician. That politician shocked Begin by the eagerness he showed for the latter's killing of civilians in Lebanon. Specifically, the politician stated, "It was great! It had to be done! If attacks were launched from Canada into the United States, everyone here would have said, 'Attack all the cities of Canada, and we don't care if all the civilians get killed.'"[34] Even Begin found this statement to be "offensive." That US politician was then Senator Joseph Biden.

These two incidents are strong evidence for the proposition that (1) the US president has the power to stop the Israeli targeting of civilians if he/she wishes to; and (2) that President Joseph Biden simply does not wish to.

Returning to the Nakba, there were many more atrocities committed against other villages and cities in Palestine. For example, the village of Tantura was another site of a terrible massacre by Israeli forces. Again, while Israeli officials have denied this massacre for decades, the recent discovery of mass graves, along with a recent documentary, have supported the Palestinian claims about the atrocities. As the *Guardian* explained recently, in 2023, the discovery of three different mass graves in Tantura support the longtime Palestinian claims "that men living in Tantura, a fishing village of approximately 1,500 people near Haifa, were executed after surrendering to the Alexandroni Brigade and their bodies dumped in a mass grave. . . . Estimates have ranged from 40 to 200 people."[35]

The *Guardian* piece quotes "Adnan Al Yahya, now 92, [who] was seventeen when Tantura fell to Israeli forces. He has testified in several academic and journalistic publications over the years that he and a friend were forced by soldiers to dig a grave at the site and throw dozens of bodies in. 'I will never forget that day, it's still very clear to me. I lost my belief in God that day," Haj Yahya said on the phone from his home in Germany. "'The world should know what happened to us in Tantura.'"

The documentary, *Tantura* includes interviews with Israelis involved in the massacre there. In this film, available on YouTube, these Israelis laugh as they discuss rape and other atrocities carried out by Israeli forces.

According to the Israeli historian Benny Morris, one of the first Israeli historians to reveal the truth about the Nakba, there are a dozen known incidents of rape during the Nakba, but that there were probably many more that went unreported. As he explains in a very recent interview,

In Acre four soldiers raped a girl and murdered her and her father. In Jaffa, soldiers of the Kiryati Brigade raped one girl and tried to rape several more. At Hunin, which is in the Galilee, two girls were raped and then murdered. There were one or two cases of rape at Tantura, south of Haifa. There was one case of rape at Qula, in the center of the country. At the village of Abu Shusha, near Kibbutz Gezer [in the Ramle area] there were four female prisoners, one of whom was raped a number of times. And there were other cases. Usually more than one soldier was involved. Usually there were one or two Palestinian girls. In a large proportion of the cases the event ended with murder. Because neither the victims nor the rapists liked to report these events, we have to assume that the dozen cases of rape that were reported, which I found, are not the whole story. They are just the tip of the iceberg.[36]

When asked about the number of massacres carried out during the *Nakba*, Morris answers that there were twenty-four and that the carrying out of massacres indeed appears to have been integral to the ethnic cleansing carried out.

And by the way, lest one believe that Benny Morris is a bleeding heart whose account of events should be discounted as a consequence, this could not be further from the truth. Indeed, as Morris points out in the same interview, he is a lifelong Zionist who actually believes that the Nakba did not go far enough because it did not expel all of the Palestinians from the land.

Morris asserts (half-heartedly) that rapes and massacres are unjustified in all circumstances, but that the ethnic cleansing as such was the right thing to do. The ethnic cleansing, which Morris laments was only partial, depended upon rapes and massacres to be as successful as it was, but that does not seem to give Morris any pause. Morris stated coldly: "You can't make an omelet without breaking eggs. You have to dirty your hands."

Morris, as all other Zionists who are wedded to the idea of the necessity of ethnic cleansing (which is pretty much all of them), base their justification on the premise that the Palestinians harbor such animosity to the Israelis that they represent a ticking time bomb. Morris counts the Arabs living within Israel proper as Israeli citizens among these ticking time bombs and believes that they might have to be cleansed at some point. Indeed, Morris goes farther, believing that Arabs are indeed a ticking time bomb in the entire West, stating, "The phenomenon of the mass Muslim penetration into the West and their settlement there is creating a dangerous internal threat. A similar process took place in Rome. They let the barbarians in and they toppled the empire from within." Incredibly, Morris counts himself as a "leftist" and does not associate himself with the ultra-right-wing that currently governs Israel. But still, he is a racist, likening all Arabs to "barbarians."

There are two problems with the line of argument that Morris puts forth. First, if ethnic cleansing, and possibly genocide, are in fact necessary for the existence of Israel (at least as a Jewish-only state) to exist, then perhaps it does not have a moral or legal right to exist. But second, this argument is based on a false premise—that the Palestinians as a people harbor intransigent hatred for the Israelis and for Jews as a people. Judging from my conversations with many Palestinians over the years, I do not believe this is in fact true.

And indeed, there was a poll taken by the well-respected Zogby International, which found that the racial/ethnic hatred largely runs one way; that is, it is the Israelis who hate the Palestinians, and not the other way around. Thus, as the founder of Zogby International, John Zogby, an American of Lebanese Catholic heritage, recently tweeted, "On the 'the river to the sea' controversy: 7 yrs ago we polled Israelis & Palestinians. A strong plurality in both favored 1 state. When asked how that would look: Israelis said it meant expelling all Palestinians; Palestinians said it meant equal rights in 1 state. Just sayin'."[37] And again, my own anectdotal evidence from my interactions with Palestinians jibes with this finding.

The other argument that Morris makes—a typical one and therefore one worth analyzing—is that, as between Arabs and Jews, Jews are the more oppressed peoples, especially as seen from their treatment during the Holocaust. Morris and other Zionist defenders argue that this gives Jews the right for their own state. But again, it was not the Arabs who carried out the Holocaust; it was indeed a Western country (Germany) that did. This fact must be reiterated over and over. There was no more barbaric act in history than the Holocaust. So, who truly are the barbarians?! In no case should the sins of Germany be transferred upon the Palestinians, but that is the sleight of hand the West has successfully executed since World War II and to the present time.

It must be emphasized that the massacres carried out during the Nakba were not just limited to Muslim communities such as the ones above. Rather, Christian communities were targeted as well. An article in *Middle East Monitor* discusses these "inconvenient historical facts [which] are whitewashed completely to cement alliances with Christians in the West":

When the state of Israel was created in 1948, it is estimated that there were 350,000 Christians in Palestine; almost 20 per cent of the population at the time. Of the 750,000 Palestinians who were forced from their homes in the Nakba (the ethnic cleansing of Palestinians that is ongoing), some 50,000 were Christians; that's 7 per cent of the total number of refugees and 35 per cent of the total number of Christians living in Palestine at the time. Today it is believed that the number of Christians in Israel and occupied Palestine has fallen to 175,000, just over 2 per cent of the entire population, and the numbers continue to dwindle rapidly. . . .

> The goal of Plan Dalet . . . was to rid Palestine of its Palestinian charac-
> teristics and turn it into a Jewish country. According to Anders Strindberg,
> the Haganah Jewish terrorist group attacked numerous convents, hospices,
> seminaries and churches, which were either destroyed or cleared of their
> Christian owners and custodians.[38]

As discussed in greater detail below, this assault on Palestinian Christians
and historic Christian sites in Israel/Palestine continues to this very day.

In the aftermath of the Nakba and the violent displacement of the
Palestinian population, the United Nations General Assembly passed
Resolution 194, which provides that "refugees wishing to return to their
homes and live at peace with their neighbours should be permitted to do
so at the earliest practicable date, and that compensation should be paid
for the property of those choosing not to return and for loss of or damage
to property which, under principles of international law or equity, should
be made good by the Governments or authorities responsible."[39] The UN
has reaffirmed this resolution every year since 1948.

However, this Resolution has sadly been honored in the breach, with no
attempts ever made to enforce it. And indeed, as discussed below, the displacement of Palestinians has continued unabated over the years, and the
number of Palestinian refugees has swelled. As the Oxford Human Rights
Hub explained on the seventieth anniversary of the Nakba, "Palestinian
refugees and their descendants still constitute one of the largest and lon-
gest-standing unresolved refugee crises in the world. Nearly 5.3 million
refugees are registered with the United Nations Relief and Works Agency
for Palestine Refugees (UNRWA) and 1.5 million subsist in fifty-eight
refugee camps across Lebanon, Jordan, Syria, and the occupied Palestinian
territory (Gaza, West Bank, and East Jerusalem). Palestinian refugees,
who were forcibly displaced . . . are stripped of their UN-mandated Right
of Return and face substantial challenges to the full enjoyment of their
rights."[40]

Israel has desperately attempted, with some large degree of success,
to suppress the memory of the Nakba—an event that undermines the
mythology of Israel as a morally righteous nation literally carrying out the
will of God. There is more than one myth packed into this claim, with Ilan

Pappe famously saying that "most Zionists do not believe that God exists, but they believe that he promised them Palestine."

Over the years, a number of Israeli officials have even gone so far as to deny the very existence of the Palestinians, with Israeli Prime Minister Golda Meier, for example, quoted in 1969 as saying, "It was not as though there was a Palestinian people in Palestine considering itself as a Palestinian people and we came and threw them out and took their country away from them. They did not exist."[41] Recently, Israeli Finance Minister Bezalel Smotrich made a similar claim, stating that "There is no such thing as a Palestinian nation. There is no Palestinian history. There is no Palestinian language."[42]

To suppress the memory of the Nakba, Israel has gone so far as to ban even the mention of it in the grade school textbooks of Arabs in Israel/Palestine.[43] It is worth noting that the very fact that Israel controls what Arabs read in school is an example of how much control Israel has and exercises over the daily lives of Palestinians. As Zakariah Odeh, a Palestinian human rights advocate and resident of Jerusalem, explained to me, Israeli police enter the schools of Palestinian children in Jerusalem every morning to search and harass the students and to make sure that the school does not have any books that mention inconvenient truths.

In 2011, the Israeli legislature (the Knesset) went so far as to pass what is known as the Nakba law, which prevents any organizations receiving government funding from claiming that Israel is not democratic or arguing that Israel should not be a Jewish state.[44] The same law absolutely forbids people from commemorating "Nakba Remembrance Day." On the same day, by the way, the Knesset also passed a law permitting "Israeli housing developments in the Negev and Galilee to discriminate against potential new residents on the basis of ethnicity and economic status."[45]

In short, while one of the worst things you could say about someone is that they are a Holocaust or genocide denier, Israel has made it state policy to deny the reality of the Nakba. This denial and suppression of the truth, and downright propagandizing, have been necessary to defend Israel's indefensible behavior over the years and to justify the US's annual bankrolling of Israel to the tune of three to four billion dollars a year.

This imposed forgetfulness, however, is not in keeping with Jewish tradition, as we were reminded by Peter Beinart in a very poignant piece in *The Guardian*, "The Jewish Case for Palestinian refugee return." As Beinart wrote at the time:

> In Jewish discourse, this refusal to forget the past—or accept its verdict—evokes deep pride. The philosopher Isaiah Berlin once boasted that Jews "have longer memories" than other peoples.
>
> Why is dreaming of return laudable for Jews but pathological for Palestinians? . . .
>
> Many prominent Palestinians . . . have alluded to the bitter irony of Jews telling another people to give up on their homeland and assimilate in foreign lands. We, of all people, should understand how insulting that demand is. Jewish leaders keep insisting that, to achieve peace, Palestinians must forget the Nakba. But it is more accurate to say that peace will come when Jews remember.[46]

It is important always to emphasize that there are many Jews—for example Ilan Pappe, Norman Finkelstein, Noam Chomsky, Max Blumenthal, Gabor and Aaron Maté and many more—who have done as much as anyone to keep the historical memory of the Palestinian people and their dispossession alive. And indeed, in doing so, they are honoring the best of Jewish tradition. Those who would deny this memory betray this tradition, and there is nothing wrong in saying so.

CHAPTER 2

THE UNITED STATES ASSUMES THE SPONSORSHIP OF ISRAEL

Every time anyone says that Israel is our only friend in the Middle East, I can't help but think that before Israel, we had no enemies in the Middle East.

—Father John Sheehan, S.J.

I saw in Auschwitz that if a dominant group wants to dehumanize others, as the Nazis dehumanize me, the dominant group must first dehumanize themselves, the same holds nowadays in Israel. I am appalled how hateful, how dehumanized, that they do not see any human aspect in any Palestinian anymore. The Zionists have no right whatsoever to use the Holocaust for any purpose, they have given up everything which has to do with humanity and with empathy.

—Hajo Meyer, Holocaust survivor

For some time, the United States has been the major and uncritical backer of Israel, and Israel has depended upon this support for its very existence and for its ability to continue its suppression of the Palestinian people. However, this has not always been the case. Thus, while the United States did in fact support the Balfour Declaration of 1917 as well as the UN plan for the creation of Israel and the partition of Palestine, it is fair to say that this support was reluctant and not unconditional as it is today. Indeed, in

1957, the United States would push back against Israel in a big way, and in a manner that it would never do again.

Thus, in 1956, Israel conspired with Britain and France—then its biggest backers—to invade Egypt and take control of the Suez Canal. Recall that control of this canal was one of the key motivations behind the Balfour Declaration of 1917. The United States and its president, former General Dwight D. Eisenhower, were not privy to this plan.

Eisenhower was an interesting president. While a career military man, he was a reluctant warrior and critical of the misuse and overuse of military power, as many people who have actually seen the horrors of war usually are. In his farewell speech as President, Eisenhower would famously warn of the growing "military-industrial complex"—a term he coined—and its threat to the democratic functioning of the country.

An article in the *Irish News*, "'Genocide Joe' Biden has got the Gaza crisis wrong in every way"—an article critical of Biden's unconditional support for Israel's violent assault on Gaza—points to Eisenhower and the Suez Canal crisis of 1956–1957 as an example of how a US leader should respond to Israel's aggressions. Eisenhower was a hero of World War II and the Allied defeat of the Nazis and therefore had immense credibility with Israel. As the article explains,

> In April 1945 US troops reached the Buchenwald concentration camp complex. What they found horrified them. A week later General Eisenhower, along with Generals George S Patton and Omar Bradley, visited Ohrdruf, a sub-camp of Buchenwald. The camp was strewn with the bodies of inmates SS guards had killed before they fled. Eisenhower ordered the film of his visit and the scenes at Ohrdruf to be circulated as widely as possible to publicize the horrors of Nazism. However, Eisenhower's personal experience of those horrors did not blind him to the ambitious expansionist schemes of the newly invented Israel.[1]

This last sentence is an important one, noting that the fact that Eisenhower witnessed the "horrors" of the Holocaust did not mean that he was an unconditional supporter of Israel and its "ambitious expansionist schemes." This should be an obvious point, but because it is not so obvious to many,

I'll emphasize that witnessing the Holocaust's horrors, far from leading one to give unconditional support to Israel, could actually lead one to oppose many of Israel's actions, especially those involving ethnic cleansing and genocide.

And indeed, that can be said of a number of Jews who are either Holocaust survivors themselves or who are descendants of survivors of the Holocaust (an event Jews refer to as "the catastrophe," or *Shoah* in Hebrew). Such individuals would include Gabor Maté, Norman Finkelstein, and Ilan Pappe—all descendants of Holocaust survivors and all staunch opponents of Israel's policies toward the Palestinians. Indeed, in 2014, no less than 327 Jewish Holocaust survivors and descendants took out an ad in the *New York Times* condemning Israel's "ongoing massacre of the Palestinian people."[2]

None of this should be surprising, for the very fact that such individuals have a close connection to the genocide committed by the Nazis makes them especially sensitive to the issue of genocide in general and therefore particularly opposed to Israel's genocidal policies. It should go without saying that, as these individuals realize, the fact that Jews were the victims of the Holocaust does not privilege the Jewish state of Israel to then carry out a genocide against the Palestinians. And, the contrary argument, often made by Israeli apologists as a means to intentionally manipulate public opinion—with former Israeli Foreign Minister Abba Eban joking darkly that "There's no business like Shoah business"—should be rejected.

Russian Foreign Minister Sergei Lavrov recently made this point, reminding people that the Soviet Union lost 27 million people (the vast majority Russian) to Nazi Germany. Many Russians indeed died in Nazi concentration and death camps. And in truth, the Soviet Union did more and sacrificed more to defeat the Nazis than any other nation. Lavrov said that this does not give Russia carte blanche to do anything it wants in the world, and no one would ever suggest that. Lavrov stated that, similarly, Israel now is not justified in its brutal mass killing in Gaza because of the treatment the Jews endured also at the hands of the Nazis.

In 1957, Eisenhower, who was not willing to use US military power to support the designs of Israel, Britain, and France upon a canal in a far-flung land, took on then Israeli prime minister David Ben-Gurion, as well as his own Congress, to force Ben-Gurion to leave Egypt. As the *Irish Times* explains, Eisenhower would join seventy-five other nations at the UN to pass a resolution condemning Israel's actions and combined this with private threats to Ben-Gurion that the United States would sanction Israel if it did not relent. In response, Ben-Gurion withdrew, the lesson again being that a US president can change Israel's conduct if only he/she is willing to do so.

In the course of the conflict with Egypt, Israel, as per usual, took the opportunity to punish the Palestinians. Thus, on the way into Egypt, Israel massacred Palestinians living in the border refugee camps of Rafah and Khan Yunis—areas that are in the news now as Israel once again pummels the Palestinians there despite the fact that Israel has told the Palestinians in Gaza to flee to those very areas as "safe zones." As Palestinian historian Rashid Khalidi points out, Israel executed 452 young men in Rafah and Khan Yunis.[3] However, also as per usual, "News of the massacres was suppressed in Israel and veiled by a complacent American media."[4] The plight of the Palestinians would not even become a footnote to the 1956 Israeli-Egyptian conflict.

Eisenhower's actions in forcing Israel to withdraw from the Sinai would constitute one of the last times that a US president was willing to significantly take on Israel. Thus, while Eisenhower's successor, John F. Kennedy, also had such a willingness, he would be assassinated in 1963, less than three years after taking office. Some argue that Kennedy's death in fact marked the death of the hopes and aspirations of the Palestinian people for return and for statehood.

Indeed, journalist Rick Sterling recently penned an article about this very issue, arguing that Kennedy, who had visited Palestine as a young man in 1939, was very different from any other US president in regard to Israel/Palestine in four different respects: (1) his willingness to deal equally with both Israel and the Arab states, including with the nationalist leader of Egypt, Gamal Abdul Nasser; (2) his willingness to take on the Israeli lobby by simply enforcing US lobbying laws against Israel as it does against other nations that attempt to exert influence over US politicians; (3) his support of Palestinian rights, including the right of return, with Kennedy going so far as to criticize the Balfour Declaration, saying that "Palestine was hardly Britain's to give away"; and (4) his willingness, and indeed his efforts, to prevent Israel's acquisition of nuclear weapons.[5]

As Sterling concludes,

> We do not know for sure what might have happened had JFK not been assassinated. It is possible that Israel would have been stopped from acquiring the bomb. Without that, they may not have had the audacity to launch the 1967 attacks on their neighbors, seizing the Golan, West Bank, and Gaza Strip. If the Zionist lobby had been required to register as foreign agents, their influence would have been moderated. Perhaps Israel could have found a reasonable accommodation with Palestinians in one or two states.
>
> Instead, Israel hardened into an apartheid regime committing increasingly outrageous massacres. As Kennedy warned in 1960, Israel has become a "garrison state" surrounded by "hate and fear." The assassination of John F. Kennedy insured Zionist control of Israel, suffering for Palestinians and permanent instability.

Under Kennedy's successors, the United States would soon take over from the other Western powers, namely Britain and France, in becoming Israel's biggest and most loyal sponsor. As Sterling alludes, this sea change would take place in 1967.

As Palestinian historian Rashid Khalidi writes in his *The Hundred Years' War on Palestine* the Six-Day War that took place in 1967 and its aftermath marked the change in US-Israeli relations that would remain constant for the next fifty-plus years.[6] This is a relationship defined by constant aggression of the Israeli military—a military the United States took over support for from Britain and France—combined with, and facilitated by, unwavering diplomatic cover by the United States. In the case of the 1967 war, the United States performed diplomatic feats allowing Israel to succeed in the war and to gain significant Palestinian territory.

First of all, in the run-up to the war that the world saw coming because of Egypt's aggressive military maneuvers in the Sinai Peninsula, and Israel's counterthreats, US ambassador to the UN Arthur Goldberg would assure the Arab states that the United States was working to mediate

Egyptian-Israeli tensions and that it would restrain Israel from attacking in the meantime. All the while, Goldberg was secretly giving Israel the green light to engage in a first strike against the air forces of Egypt, Syria, and Jordan. When this first strike came, the neighboring Arab states were taken by surprise and the air forces of these three nations were quickly destroyed, allowing Israel, with its great air superiority, to then dispatch these nations' armies very quickly as well.

In addition, once the war was in full swing and Israel's forces were moving fast toward Damascus, Syria, Goldberg found a way to delay the vote at the Security Council for a cease-fire, allowing Israel to make greater inroads in the conflict, particularly in Syria.

And finally, and most importantly, the United States was instrumental in the passage of UN Security Council Resolution 242, a Resolution placing significant conditions upon the requirement that Israel withdraw from the territory it seized during the Six-Day War. These conditions, as Rashid Khalidi explains, have allowed Israel to maintain this territory to this day, again to the great detriment of the Palestinian people.[7] In the case of East Jerusalem and the Golan Heights, Israel has effectively annexed these areas, as Khalidi explains, while becoming the occupying power over Gaza and the West Bank, replacing Egypt and Jordan, respectively.[8]

But even more importantly, as Khaldi explains, Resolution 242, though not even mentioning the Palestinians, effectively recognized the boundaries between Israel and Palestine resulting from Israel's takeover of Palestine in 1948—a takeover that, you will recall, was much greater than that set forth by the 1947 UN Resolution creating Israel and partitioning the land of Palestine—and effectively destroyed the right of return of Palestinians to their land and homes that UN Resolution 194 still provides for, at least on paper.

As Khalidi laments, "Once again, the Palestinians were being dealt with by the great powers in a cavalier fashion, their rights ignored, deemed not worthy of mention by name in the key international decision meant to resolve the conflict and determine their fate. This slight further motivated the Palestinians' reviving national movement to put its case and cause before the international community."[9]

During the course of the Six-Day War in 1967, an incident took place that demonstrates the unreliability of Israel as an ally, and the lengths to which the United States is willing to go in order to protect Israel from criticism. Thus, while this war was taking place, Israel attacked the unarmed US naval ship named the USS Liberty, killing thirty-four Americans and wounding 171. As *The Intercept* wrote on the fiftieth anniversary of this event, this was "among the worst attacks in history against a noncombatant US naval vessel."[10]

Still, the details of the attack remain a mystery, at least to the public, as a consequence of the willingness of the United States to suppress the truth of this event in the interest of protecting Israel. As *The Intercept* explained in its piece, documents revealed by Edward Snowden, the whistleblower of the US National Security Agency (NSA), showed how much, even decades later, "the NSA was determined to keep even seemingly minor details about the attack classified," and secret, even from the survivors of the assault. Indeed, "The Liberty Veterans Association, an organization comprised of survivors of the 1967 attack, has called for a robust and transparent investigation into the incident for decades, to no avail."

While some believe that Israel attacked the ship full-well knowing it was firing upon a US vessel—an assertion supported by the fact that the USS *Liberty* was fired upon multiple time in "broad daylight" and was flying a huge US flag—those who say so, including the survivors themselves, have been vilified for giving such an opinion, even being accused of being anti-Semitic or slanderous of Israel."[11] One theory for Israel's actions is that it was trying to prevent the crew of the USS *Liberty* from being a witness to Israel's war crime of executing Egyptian POWs, but again, it is verboten to express such an opinion.[12]

The fact that survivors of the USS *Liberty*, many of whom suffer from PTSD, would be accused of anti-Semitism because they raise questions about Israel's attack on the ship shows to what large extent the defenders of Israel misuse and abuse the term "anti-Semitism." Obviously, these survivors have very good reasons to raise questions about their ship being fired upon and their friends dying and being crippled as a result; reasons that have absolutely nothing to do with the fact that the perpetrators were

Jewish or that the survivors have anti-Jewish prejudices. The same can be said of claims, often made, that Jews who criticize Israel are somehow self-hating Jews. The best retort to this type of accusation came from Woody Allen who once quipped, "yes, I hate myself, but it's not because I'm Jewish. I have many other reasons to hate myself."

But such claims of "anti-Semitism" have been successfully weaponized to destroy people who dare raise questions about Israel's actions or who express support for the Palestinian cause. Examples of this are former Labor MP Jeremy Corbyn, whose chances at becoming UK prime minister were destroyed because of his support for the Palestinians; Norman Finkelstein, who lost family in the Holocaust, being stripped of his academic career as a result of his public condemnation of Israel's treatment of the Palestinians; and with the president of Harvard, Claudine Gay, being forced to resign at least in part because she would not concede enthusiastically enough that Jewish students at Harvard were being intimidated by pro-Palestinian activism there. Congresswoman Rashida Harbi Tlaib was even censured by her congressional colleagues for pro-Palestinian statements she made, never mind the fact that she herself is Palestinian, and in fact, the only Palestinian in Congress. In essence, she was censured for being too proudly Palestinian, an offense many Palestinians are accused and found guilty of. As these examples demonstrate, while the question of Israel and its treatment of the Palestinians are matters of great public concern that deserve full-throated debate, only one side of this debate is permitted.

Moreover, whatever the truth is about the USS *Liberty* episode, it demonstrates how captive the US government is to Israel, with the government often elevating the interests of Israel over those of its own citizens as well as the cause of human rights and international humanitarian law.

The Biden administration's current response to Israel's brutal assault on Gaza is another case in point. Thus, even while Israel is in the dock in the International Court of Justice for alleged genocide, and even as the majority of Americans polled have expressed the desire for a cease-fire in Gaza, the Biden administration continues to double down on its military and diplomatic support for Israel and to oppose a cease-fire. And, as per usual, the United States has run diplomatic cover for Israel at the UN General

Assembly and Security Council, preventing any meaningful UN action that could end the conflict or even protect civilians in Gaza. The White House even continues to back Israel in the conflict despite the fact that it appears to be morphing into a regional war involving other countries like Yemen, Lebanon, Syria, Iran, and possibly Egypt.

This type of unconditional support for Israel makes many wonder, reasonably, whether it is the United States or its client state that is calling the shots; whether it is in fact the tail that is wagging the dog.

Press coverage of Israel and Palestine has also been greatly distorted by pro-Israeli bias that sometimes reaches absurd and almost comical extremes. One example of this is how the press goes out of its way to avoid talking about children being killed in Gaza while highlighting the (much less frequent) deaths of Israeli children at the hands of Palestinians. An example of this recently was the mainstream press referring to a three-year-old girl (she could properly be called a "baby") who was killed in Gaza as a "young lady" while referring to Israeli female soldiers (over the age of eighteen) as "girls."[13]

The satirical paper *The Onion* has caught on to such mental gymnastics, thus running a headline that read, "'New York Times' Invents Entirely New Numerical System to Avoid Reporting Gazan Death Toll.[14]

And indeed, *The Onion* headline is not too far off from reality. Thus, as a report from *The Intercept* showed, the three US papers of record have demonstrated an incredible anti-Palestinian bias in their coverage of the events of October 7 and thereafter. As *The Intercept* found, "In the *New York Times*, *Washington Post*, and *Los Angeles Times*, the words 'Israeli' or 'Israel' appear more than 'Palestinian' or variations thereof, even as Palestinian deaths far outpaced Israeli deaths. For every two Palestinian deaths, Palestinians are mentioned once. For every Israeli death, Israelis are mentioned eight times—or a rate sixteen times more per death than that of Palestinians."[15]

In addition to this lopsided coverage of Israeli versus Palestinian deaths, *The Intercept* found that the three newspapers "used emotive language to describe the killings of Israelis, but not Palestinians; and offered lopsided coverage of anti-Semitic acts in the United States, while largely ignoring anti-Muslim racism in the wake of October 7. Pro-Palestinian activists have accused major publications of pro-Israel bias, with the *New York Times* at its headquarters in Manhattan for its coverage of Gaza—an accusation supported by our analysis." *The Intercept* related that this type of bias was also reflected in the cable news coverage as well.

CNN is another outlet that has been outed for its bias for Israel and against Palestinians, and this outing came directly from CNN staff themselves. As the *Guardian* reported on February 4, 2024, "Journalists in CNN newsrooms in the United States and overseas say broadcasts have been skewed by management edicts and a story-approval process that has resulted in highly partial coverage of the Hamas massacre on 7 October and Israel's retaliatory attack on Gaza. 'The majority of news since the war began, regardless of how accurate the initial reporting, has been skewed by a systemic and institutional bias within the network toward Israel,' said one CNN staffer. 'Ultimately, CNN's coverage of the Israel-Gaza war amounts to journalistic malpractice.'" The *Guardian* reported that the skewing of the coverage includes "tight restrictions on quoting Hamas and reporting other Palestinian perspectives while Israel government statements are taken at face value. In addition, every story on the conflict must be cleared by the Jerusalem bureau before broadcast or publication."[16]

As all this demonstrates, the unconditional and indeed fanatical support the United States gives to Israel is having a corrosive effect on our democratic system, public discourse, and our society. At the same time, it has had a similarly corrosive effect on Israel, for this unconditional and uncritical support has encouraged the worst aspects of Israeli society, leading Israelis to believe that they have an automatic "get out of jail free" card for any offenses they commit.

The result is that Israel has become what people like Albert Einstein warned would happen in 1948—a hard-right, if not fascist, country that is now in the dock in The Hague for genocide. And the United States is right beside Israel in The Hague as an aider and abettor of this genocide.

Long gone now in Israel are the (barely) moderating influences of "labor Zionism" and "socialist Zionism," which a number of my former colleagues at the United Steelworkers Union (USW) adhered to and believed gave Zionism some legitimacy. When my friend and colleague Rich Brean used to argue about Israel in my latter years at the union, Rich would try to wave off the worst criticism of Israel by simply saying, "that's just Netanyahu, not all of Israel." The problem with this argument, however, is that there's virtually nothing left but Netanyahuism or worse in Israel. Yes, there are a few left-wing figures remaining in the Knesset, but they are few and far between and have little to no influence. Israel is now fully in the grips of the right wing, and it's because the Israelis want it that way; because they have voted for these forces over and over again. And in truth, it is so because this is the natural tendency of Zionism to begin with and because there was no one to moderate this tendency by saying "no" once in a while.

The US government could have and should have played this role, but, with few exceptions, its leaders decided it was not expedient to do so. And one of the reasons they have found it expedient not to do so is because of the huge amounts of money that pro-Israel lobbying firms and campaign PACs put into our political system. For example, in 2024, AIPAC, The American Israel Public Affairs Committee, plans to spend $100 million just on trying to unseat the seven congresspeople known collectively as "the Squad," including Summer Lee, a congressional representative in Pittsburgh.[17] That kind of money is more than enough to swing an election.

By the late 1970s, the hard right, then represented by Prime Minister Menachim Begin—remember Begin who Einstein called a "fascist"—became ensconced in the Israeli government and society, and, as usual, to the great detriment of the Palestinian people.

Ironically, this process would be solidified through the Camp David peace negotiations, hosted by President Jimmy Carter, between Israel and Egypt to settle the differences still unresolved by the Six-Day War of 1967 and the 1973 Yom Kippur War in which Egypt and Syria attempted, unsuccessfully, to gain back the land they lost in 1967—the Sinai Peninsula and the Golan Heights, respectively.

As Rashid Khalidi succinctly puts it,

Although under Carter the United States had come close to endorsing the Palestinians' national rights and their involvement in negotiations, the two sides found themselves farther apart than ever. Camp David and the Israeli-Egyptian peace treaty signaled US alignment with the most extreme expression of Israel's negation of the Palestinian rights, an alignment that was consolidated by Ronald Reagan's administration. Begin and his successors in the Likud, Yitzhak Shamir, Ariel Sharon, and then Benjamin Netanyahu, were implacably opposed to Palestinian statehood, sovereignty, or control of the occupied West Bank and East Jerusalem. . . . They believed that the entirety of Palestine belonged solely to the Jewish people, and that a Palestinian people with national rights did not exist. . . . Their explicit aim was to transform the entirety of Palestine into the Land of Israel.[18]

Begin's vision of a Jewish state "from the river to the sea" became the guiding principle of Israel, and of the United States as well, from that time forward. And, as a consequence, "conditions became even worse for the Palestinians."[19]

To add insult to injury, Begin, and his Egyptian counterpart Anwar Sadat, would be honored with a Nobel Peace Prize for their treachery. For his part, Jimmy Carter, the greatest ex-president of the United States, went on after leaving office to be a critic of Israel, even writing a book criticizing Israel as an apartheid state and arguing that Israeli apartheid is even worse than South Africa's apartheid system.[20] However, out of office, Carter sadly had no influence to shape international events.

The worst conditions created for the Palestinian people have been in Gaza. This is well detailed in a December 19, 2023, article by Sara Roy in the *New York Review of Books*, "The Long War on Gaza," in which she details how, "over 56 years," that is, since 1967, "Israel has transformed Gaza from a functional one to a dysfunctional one, from a productive economy to an impoverished one."[21]

Roy herself has been visiting Gaza for years, and she describes how, when the Palestinians living there discovered she is Jewish, they were surprised at first, but then became friendly and helpful. As she relates, she first started traveling there back in 1985, and, in her words, "Once I explained I was there to learn about their society and economy and how the occupation affected their lives, it didn't take long to gain their trust. In fact, being Jewish became an asset: people who barely knew me invited me into their homes and businesses. Many of them would later help me collect data when I lived in Gaza during the first intifada, or uprising, which began in 1987."

Roy explains that the vast majority of people in Gaza are refugees from the Nakba (indeed, about 70 percent), but that they have preserved the memory of their former homes and land. Indeed, she poignantly relates how some of her earliest memories of Gaza are "of young refugee children describing in great detail the homes and villages that their grandparents had lived in but that they had never seen. They were strikingly intimate with their ancestral homes. I remember the delight they took in their descriptive power and the self-esteem it gave them."

She then recounts the history of how Israel has slowly but surely, and intentionally, de-developed the economy and society of Gaza. As she explains, "Israel has never known what to do with this tiny strip of land. From the beginning of the occupation, the country's leaders recognized that Gaza would have to be pacified to preclude the creation of a Palestinian state—their primary objective—and minimize Palestinian resistance were they to annex the West Bank. During the first two decades of the occupation, from the Six-Day War of 1967 to the start of the first intifada, their preferred tactic was controlling Gaza's economy." And, they did this by importing 100,000 Palestinian workers into Israel to help develop Israel's economy. The result of this, she relates, was that the individual workers prospered while Gaza suffered "communal stagnation" and a lack of development.

Then, using the first Gulf War as a pretext, Israel in 1991 began regulating, and indeed greatly curtailing, the movement of Palestinians between Gaza and the West Bank and in and out of Gaza in general. Citing the Israeli human rights group, B'Tselem, Roy relates that "'Isolating Gaza from the rest of the world, including separating it from the West Bank, is part of a longstanding Israeli policy.'"

This process only accelerated after the Oslo Accords were agreed to in 1993, Roy explains, with Israel erecting a huge fence around all of Gaza in 1994—a fence that stands to this day. Then, in 2005, Israel officially "disengaged" from Gaza, removing all settlements and military personnel. However, while Israel has claimed that this meant that it ended the occupation of Gaza, Israel nonetheless is still the legal occupier under international law, Roy explains, as it "maintains 'effective control' over Gaza's borders (except for Rafah, which Egypt controls), sea access, airspace, and population registry."

Then, after Hamas came to power in 2007 through elections, Israel "recast its relationship with Gaza from occupation to warfare, as evidenced by the numerous deadly assaults it launched on the territory over the past seventeen years—among them Operation Summer Rains (2006), Operation Hot Winter (2008), Operation Cast Lead (2008–09), Operation Pillar of Defense (2012), Operation Protective Edge (2014), Operation Guardian of the Walls (2021), Operation Breaking Dawn (2022), and Operation Shield and Arrow (2023). Its international allies quickly accepted this shift: Gaza came to be identified solely with Hamas and treated as a hostile foreign entity."

As Roy explains, the goal of Israel during this long phase, was to destroy Gaza's market economy, and "more specifically, they aimed to keep it 'functioning at the lowest level possible consistent with avoiding a humanitarian crisis.' The goal, that is, was not to elevate people above a specific humanitarian standard but to ensure they stayed at or even below that standard."

An article in *The Nation* describes what it has meant for the people of Gaza to be kept "at or even below" the "specific humanitarian standard" set for them by Israel:

> For at least 15 years, between 2008 and 2023, Israeli policies were geared to put all Gazans—children and adults alike—on a diet. But the nutritional conditions of all Palestinians living under occupation had already been deadly. Twenty years ago, in 2003, the UN reported that because they were living under military occupation restrictions, 22 percent of Palestinian children under five were suffering from grave malnutrition, and 9.3 percent of children under the age of five were suffering from acute malnutrition, which meant that they had brain damage or were damaged for life from chronic malnutrition.
>
> Water supplies were compromised too. In 2016 the World Health Organization reported that Gaza under siege experiences life-threatening water problems.[22]

In addition, as Sara Roy explains, Gaza has been left with near 50 percent unemployment, 65 percent of the population "food insecure," and with 80 percent of the population depending upon international assistance to be able to eat. In other words, as Roy concludes, the "result of this policy was the transformation of the Palestinians in Gaza from a community with national, political, and economic rights into a humanitarian problem."

And, according to plan, Israel has been able to control the population of Gaza by threatening it as deemed necessary with the withholding of humanitarian aid necessary for their very survival, making the analogies of Gaza to a concentration camp quite apt. Recall that in 2018, President Donald Trump inflicted great punishment and suffering upon the Palestinians of Gaza by cutting $200 million of aid to them.[23]

Turning Gaza into a charity case inevitably affects the psyche of the people living there, destroying their self-esteem and stripping them of their dignity. And again, that is the point. This is about undermining the Palestinians as a people and a nation.

The two Palestinian areas of historic Palestine—Gaza and the West Bank—were completely cut off from each other, making the idea of a Palestinian state an impossibility. And indeed, that was the goal for Israel, having never intended to abide by the Oslo Accords, which called for Palestinian statehood.

This brings us to the events of October 7, 2023, when armed militants breached the fence of the Gaza concentration camp and went on the offensive.

CHAPTER 3

THE REALITY OF THE OCTOBER 7 ATTACKS

Those who make peaceful revolution impossible will make violent revolution inevitable.
— John F. Kennedy

Take the worst thing you can say about the Hamas, multiply it by 1,000 times and it still will not meet the Israeli repression and killing and dispossession of Palestinians.
— Dr. Gabor Maté, physician, writer, and descendant of victims of the Holocaust

On October 7, 2023, Hamas and allied militant groups broke through the border fence surrounding Gaza and also used homemade flight craft— essentially parachutes with a simple engine to propel them—to glide over the fence and attack targets within Israel. Apparently, a number of other Gazans not associated with these operations went through the openings the militants created in the border fence and also carried out attacks on their own.

As with all things involving Israel and Palestine, there has been much propagandizing about this event, and it is therefore necessary to analyze what really happened, at least to the extent it is possible to fully know the facts.

As an initial matter, it must be pointed out that, as occupied peoples, the Palestinians have the legal right to take up arms to resist their occupation. And, despite Israel's incessant protests to the contrary, Israel as the occupying power does not have a right to self-defense against the Palestinians. This is analogous to the respective rights of homeowners subject to a home invasion. The homeowners have the right to deter and defend themselves from the invasion; the invaders do not have a legal right to defend themselves from the homeowners. For most people, this makes patent sense.

With this said, there are always limits on what those who have a right of self-defense may do to defend themselves. In the case of the Palestinians, they must abide by the laws of war, meaning, in essence, that they may not intentionally target civilians for killing, maiming, or atrocities. At the same time, if one looks at the history of rebellion of the oppressed against their oppressors—for example, the Nat Turner slave rebellion or the attacks carried out by the abolitionist John Brown and his compatriots against slave owners (and their families as well)—these types of rebellions are always messy affairs, to say the least.

Others have compared Gaza to the Warsaw Ghetto—an area in which the Nazis imprisoned up to 460,000 Jews during World War II and kept them on subsistent rations just as Israel has kept the residents of Gaza since 2007. The Jews in the Warsaw Ghetto would mount a famous, and much celebrated, uprising against the Nazis as the latter entered the ghetto to remove the residents to the death camps. While this is a controversial comparison, the Jewish journalist, Masha Gessen, upon recently receiving the Hannah Arendt Prize—recall that Hannah Arendt herself had signed on with Albert Einstein in a letter condemning the Nakba back in 1948—recently made this comparison. In so doing, Gessen stated that "The biggest difference between Gaza and the Jewish ghettos in Nazi-occupied Europe is that many Gazans, most Gazans are still alive, and the world still has an opportunity to do something about it."[1]

I would contend that the facts show that while there were atrocities on October 7 committed by Palestinians (both militants and also non-militants who used the opportunity to enter Israel on their own)—atrocities that should surely be condemned—the main goal of the militant operations was military and aimed at military targets. Indeed, I would argue forcefully that the attacks on October 7 were more targeted against military forces than Israel's assault on Gaza after October 7 or indeed at any time that Israel has militarily attacked the Palestinians over the decades.

First of all, let's look at what Hamas has said about its operations on October 7. In late January 2024, Hamas put out a seventeen-page document about these operations that is well worth looking at.

As an initial matter, Hamas makes it clear who they are fighting against, and who they are not fighting against, and this is at great variance with claims that Israel and the West make about Hamas. Thus, in a section of this document titled, "Who is Hamas?" the group states:

1. The Islamic Resistance Movement "Hamas" is a Palestinian Islamic national liberation & resistance movement. Its goal is to liberate Palestine and confront the Zionist project. Its frame of reference is Islam, which determines its principles, objectives and means. Hamas rejects the persecution of any human being or the undermining of his or her rights on nationalist, religious or sectarian grounds.

2. *Hamas affirms that its conflict is with the Zionist project not with the Jews because of their religion. Hamas does not wage a struggle against the Jews because they are Jewish but wages a struggle against the Zionists who occupy Palestine.* Yet, it is the Zionists who constantly identify Judaism and the Jews with their own colonial project and illegal entity.

3. The Palestinian people have always stood against oppression, injustice, and the committing of massacres against civilians regardless of who commit them. *And based on our religious and moral values, we clearly stated our rejection to what the Jews were exposed to by the Nazi Germany.* Here, we remind that the Jewish problem in essence was a European problem, while the Arab and Islamic environment was—across history—a safe haven to the Jewish people and to other peoples of other beliefs and ethnicities. The Arab and Islamic environment was an example to co-existence, cultural interaction and religious freedoms. The current conflict is caused by the Zionist aggressive behavior and its alliance with the western colonial powers; therefore, we reject the exploitation of the Jewish suffering in Europe to justify the oppression against our people in Palestine[2] (emphasis added).

This is an important statement, as Hamas makes it clear that it is not against the Jews or Judaism, but against the Zionist project oppressing the Palestinians. Hamas also acknowledges the Holocaust and the suffering that Jews endured in the Holocaust, and they denounce this terrible crime. These words of Hamas matter and are worth considering as much as the stated beliefs and intentions of Israeli officials. As discussed further below, Israeli officials have made it very clear that their main issue is with the Palestinian people who they view as subhuman, and not just with Hamas.

Hamas also explains why it engaged in the October 7 operations it calls "the Al-Aqsa Flood." In addition to the Nakba, the further displacement and occupation that took place in 1967 and after, Hamas details the following as a reason for its military attack:

> The people in Gaza in 2018 . . . initiated the Great March of Return demonstrations to peacefully protest the Israeli blockade, their misery, humanitarian conditions, and to demand their right-to-return. However, the Israeli occupation forces responded to these protests with brutal force by which 360 Palestinians were killed and 19,000 others were injured including over 5,000 children in a matter of few months.
>
> . . . According to official figures, in the period between (January 2000 and September 2023), the Israeli occupation killed 11,299 Palestinians and injured 156,768 others, the great majority of them were civilians. Unfortunately, the US administration and its allies did not pay attention to the suffering of the Palestinian people over the past years but provided cover to the Israeli aggression. They only lamented the Israeli soldiers who were killed on Oct. 7 even without seeking the truth of what happened, and wrongfully walked behind the Israeli narrative in condemning an alleged targeting of Israeli civilians. The US administration provided the financial and military support to the Israeli occupation massacres against the Palestinian civilians and the brutal aggression on the Gaza Strip, and still the US officials continue to ignore what the Israeli occupation forces commit in Gaza of mass killing.[3]

This passage is important. One will often hear critics of the Palestinian resistance movement ask why the Palestinians don't try nonviolent tactics to oppose their occupation, oppression, and murder by Israel. The truth is, they have. But as even Gandhi recognized, such tactics only work against an opponent guided by enough of a conscience and sense of empathy to be swayed by such tactics. Gandhi acknowledged, for example, that such tactics would not work against the Nazis, who utterly lacked conscience and empathy, and that military action would be necessary to defeat them. It appears that Israel and the United States are in the category of opponents that are simply impervious to the suffering of the Palestinian people and therefore cannot be moved by their peaceful attempts to resist. Recall, for example, then-Senator Biden's statement to Israeli Prime Minister Begin in which he expressed his sympathy for Israel's mass killing of civilians in Lebanon at the time, and that he would have done the same to Canadians if presented with an analogous situation.

In addition, Hamas makes it clear that the international legal system has utterly failed the Palestinian people and has failed because the United States has managed to immunize Israel from all legal accountability, again another factor necessitating military resistance. As Hamas states,

> The US admin & its western allies have been treating Israel as a state above the law; provide it with cover to maintain prolonging the occupation and oppressing the Palestinians, allowing "Israel" to exploit to take further Palestinian lands and to Judaize their sanctities & holy sites. Despite the UN issuing 900+ resolutions over 75 years in favor of the Palestinian people, "Israel" reject abiding by any of these resolutions, the US VETO was always present at the UN Security Council to prevent any condemnation of "Israel's" policies and violations. That's why we see the US & western countries complicit & partners to the Israeli occupation in its crimes & suffering of the Palestinians.[4]

What Hamas says in this regard is irrefutable.

As Hamas asks rhetorically, throwing up its hands, "What was expected from the Palestinian people after all of that? To keep waiting and to keep counting on the helpless UN! Or to take the initiative in defending the Palestinian people, lands, rights, and sanctities; knowing that the defense act is a right enshrined in international laws, norms, and conventions."[5]

The fact that, even now, as Gaza and the people therein are being obliterated before our very eyes without any meaningful response by the UN demonstrates that the Palestinians could have waited until the end of time before seeing any relief from the UN for their suffering.

Hamas goes on to make it clear that its objectives on October 7 were purely military; that its targets were military bases and personnel, and *not* civilians. Hamas also categorically denies the rape allegations levelled by Israel, rape being against the moral values of Hamas as devout Muslims. Hamas has called for a full, independent investigation into the events of October 7.

As the smoke has cleared a bit, it appears that a significant percentage of the Israelis killed on October 7 were official police or military personnel. I say "official" because armed Israeli settlers who are carrying guns to protect the land they have stolen from Palestinians are NOT counted in this number but may arguably be legitimate military targets. In Hamas's statement about their October 7 operations, they mention these settlers, stating, "It is also a matter of fact that a number of Israeli settlers in settlements around Gaza were armed, and clashed with Palestinian fighters on Oct. 7. Those settlers were registered as civilians while the fact is they were armed men fighting alongside the Israeli army."[6]

In the end, according to France 24 news, analyzing Israel's own social security data, "The final death toll from the [October 7] attack is now thought to be 695 Israeli civilians, including thirty-six children, as well as 373 security forces and seventy-one foreigners, giving a total of 1,139."[7] That is, nearly a third of those killed by the militants were official members of the Israeli security forces, again not counting armed Israeli settlers.

Comparing this to the ratio of militants to civilians killed by Israel since October 7, it is not even close: the attack of the militants was much more targeted against military targets than Israel's operations. Thus, as of the time of this writing, "30,676 Palestinians have been killed during the Israeli attacks . . . , including 28,201 civilians. The death toll includes 12,040 children, 6,103 women, 241 health workers, and 105 journalists."[8] This means that nearly 92 percent of the Palestinians killed by Israel are civilian while a just over 8 percent are militants. And, of all those Palestinians killed, around 58 percent are women and children. As the Geneva-based Euro-Med Monitor concluded, "about 4 percent of the total population of the Gaza Strip—more than 90,000 people—are now dead, wounded, or missing."[9]

In short, the Israeli operations have been greatly more devastating on the civilian population of Gaza—in terms of the percentage of the civilians killed and absolute numbers—than the militant operations of October 7.

And, these numbers do not even fully tell the tale, because the other fact that has come out in the course of time is that Israeli forces killed an unknown number of their own civilians on October 7, but this number could be in the hundreds, with some Israelis even saying that they were being used as "human shields" by their own military.[10] The whys and wherefores of these "friendly fire" killings is discussed further below but suffice it to say that they lower the percentage of civilians to security forces killed by Palestinian militants even further. If we also deduct the number of civilians killed by nonmilitants who on their own breached the Gaza fence and carried out violence in Israel, this number drops even further.

In addition, it must be said at the outset that it is clear that both Israel and the United States have opportunistically used the events of October 7 to justify the mass slaughter and displacement of people from Gaza in order to carry out the ends that both have desired all along—the final solution of the "Palestinian problem," which amounts to ridding the land of all Palestinians.

And indeed, as has been pointed out by numerous mainstream sources by now, and as has become a matter of great controversy in Israel, it is also certain that the Israeli intelligence and security forces had warning of these attacks well in advance, raising the reasonable question of whether Israeli leaders permitted the attacks to take place in order to have a pretext they could use to justify their final solution. As the Associated Press (AP) reported on December 3, 2023:

> Israel's military was aware of Hamas' plan to launch an attack on Israeli soil over a year before the devastating Oct. 7 operation that killed hundreds of people, The New York Times reported Friday.
>
> It was the latest in a series of signs that top Israeli commanders either ignored or played down warnings that Hamas was plotting the attack,

which triggered a war against the Islamic militant group that has devastated the Gaza Strip.

The [New York] Times said Israeli officials were in possession of a 40-page battle plan, code-named "Jericho Wall," that detailed a hypothetical Hamas attack on southern Israeli communities.[11]

As the AP further related, "The document was seen by many Israeli military and intelligence officials," and "The Oct. 7 attack—in which 1,200 people were killed and 240 people were abducted and taken to Gaza—would uncannily mirror the one outlined in the battle plan." Indeed, as the AP emphasized, "The attack was planned in plain sight. A month before the assault, Hamas posted a video to social media showing fighters using explosives to blast through a replica of the border gate, sweep in on pickup trucks and then move building by building through a full-scale reconstruction of an Israeli town, firing automatic weapons at human-silhouetted paper targets." In addition, the AP wrote: "Adding to public outrage over the military's apparent negligence, the Israeli media has reported that military officials dismissed warnings from female border spotters who warned that they were witnessing Hamas's preparations for the attack."

We may never know for sure whether the Israeli government willfully ignored this intelligence in order to get the pretext for its destruction of Gaza, whether it was just incompetent in responding to the threats or whether there was some combination of the two, but all of this is worth considering, and there is no doubt that once the smoke has cleared, the Israeli public will call for a full accounting of the truth.

In any case, once the October 7 attacks did take place, Israel and the Western governments and press moved swiftly to promulgate and spread gross untruths about the nature of the attacks to justify Israel's much more brutal assault upon Gaza. As time has gone on, this propaganda campaign has been exposed, but sadly too late to prevent the terrible crimes we are now seeing against the Palestinian population.

One of the main goals of the operations on October 7 was to take hostages that could be exchanged for Palestinian prisoners being held by Israel—many of these "prisoners" being properly called hostages. The fact that Israel has taken such hostages is greatly downplayed by the Western press because it certainly puts the hostage-taking of the Palestinians into perspective.

Of the three hundred prisoners that the Palestinian militants listed as wanting returned for the hostages they were holding in the initial exchanges, thirty-three were women, and the majority of the remainder were children from ages from sixteen to eighteen, though one is fourteen years old.[12]

The reader may be surprised to learn that, according to UNICEF, Israel takes hundreds of children prisoner (or "hostage" as you will) each year. As UNICEF related in 2013, "Each year approximately 700 Palestinian children aged twelve to seventeen, the great majority of them boys, are arrested, interrogated and detained by Israeli army, police and security agents. In the past ten years, an estimated 7,000 children have been detained, interrogated, prosecuted and/or imprisoned within the Israeli military justice system—an average of two children each day."[13] That is, Israel takes three times more children prisoners per year for many years than all of the hostages taken by the Palestinian militants on October 7, the militants having taken 236, mostly adult, hostages.

Israel's system for handling these child prisoners is unique, and indeed, uniquely bad. As UNICEF explains, "In September 2009, in response to documentation of the prosecution of children as young as twelve in adult military courts, Israel established a juvenile military court. It is understood that this is the first and only juvenile military court in operation in the world. In fact, it uses the same facilities and court staff as the adult military court." As such, this system violates the Convention on the Rights of the Child, which Israel ratified in 1991, as "The Committee on the Rights of the Child has stated that States Parties to the Convention on the Rights of the Child should establish separate facilities for children deprived of their liberty, including distinct, child-centered staff, personnel, policies and practices."[14]

And, as UNICEF relates, the Israelis regularly treat these child prisoners in inhumane ways. As UNICEF concluded in its report:

Ill-treatment of Palestinian children in the Israeli military detention system appears to be widespread, systematic and institutionalized. This conclusion is based on the repeated allegations about such treatment over the past 10 years and the volume, consistency and persistence of these allegations. The review of cases documented through the monitoring and reporting mechanism on grave child rights violations, as well as interviews conducted by UNICEF with Israeli and Palestinian lawyers and Palestinian children, also support this conclusion.

The pattern of ill-treatment includes the arrests of children at their homes between midnight and 5:00 a.m. by heavily armed soldiers; the practice of blindfolding children and tying their hands with plastic ties; physical and verbal abuse during transfer to an interrogation site, including the use of painful restraints; lack of access to water, food, toilet facilities and medical care; interrogation using physical violence and threats; coerced confessions; and lack of access to lawyers or family members during interrogation.

Treatment inconsistent with child rights continues during court appearances, including shackling of children; denial of bail and imposition of custodial sentences; and transfer of children outside occupied Palestinian territory to serve their sentences inside Israel. The incarceration isolates them from their families and interrupts their studies.

These practices are in violation of international law that protects all children against ill-treatment when in contact with law enforcement, military, and judicial institutions.[15]

In addition, over the years there have been credible reports of Palestinian children being sexually abused at the hands of police and prison guards. For example, the Palestinian Prisoners Club (PCC), focusing only on detentions in the West Bank, reported in 2014 that an incredible 40 percent of children detained by Israeli forces were sexually abused.[16] In one year alone, they estimated that 240 Palestinian children in the West Bank had been so abused.

Recently, in July 2023—just months before the October 7 attacks—Save the Children reported on the terrible abuse of Palestinian children in Israeli custody. Indeed, "the group said some of the former child detainees it spoke to reported violence of a sexual nature, while many others were beaten, handcuffed, and blindfolded in small cages in detention centers and upon being moved between centers."[17] As Al Jazeera, reporting on the Save the Children report, explains,

There is a marked increase in the number of former child detainees who suffer nightmares and insomnia and have difficulty returning to their normal life, with many reporting a decrease in hope for their futures.

The study said 86 percent of the 228 former child detainees surveyed were beaten in detention, and 69 percent were strip-searched, adding that 42 percent were injured at the point of arrest, including gunshot wounds and broken bones.

They were also interrogated at unknown locations without the presence of a guardian or caregiver and are often deprived of food, water and sleep, the report says.

In addition, they were often refused access to legal counsel, according to the research.[18]

This point about being abused while being moved between centers was brought home to me when I visited the West Bank in December 2023. At that time, Fadia Barghouti, whose husband and son are currently being held as prisoners by Israel, told me that any time prisoners are moved, they risk being abused. The problem is so serious that prisoners, including her husband and son, are afraid to even meet with their own lawyers for fear that they will be assaulted on the way to the meeting. It is not uncommon that such assaults of prisoners in such circumstances can frequently be sexual in nature. And the relatives of the prisoners may also be subject to such assault while visiting them.

Indeed, while Israel, with the willing assistance of the Western press, has done a great job at concealing its use of sexual humiliation, assault, and rape (of mostly women, but also of men) as a means of ruling over the Palestinians it occupies, there is no doubt that this is indeed a well-documented phenomenon. As an article in the journal *Conflict and Society* explains, in addition to the regular occurrence of sexual assault and harassment at Israeli checkpoints and home raids by Israeli forces,

Palestinian women experience sexual violence while visiting their relatives in Israeli jails and when attending court hearings of their relatives. . . . There, the perpetrators can be prison guards or military court officers, female or male. Another situation in which Palestinian women report sexual violence is during interrogations. These include threats of rape and unwanted and forced touch, by both female and male interrogators, as well as rape. Aisha Awdat, for instance, claims to have been raped by an Israeli investigator on March 10, 1969. . . . Rasmea Odeh also reports she was raped in 1969 during interrogation. . . . In 2015, a Palestinian female detainee was raped by two female soldiers, one of whom is a doctor, who conducted a vaginal and anal search on her, apparently following an order of a Shin Bet [internal Israeli intelligence] agent. . . . These cases show that the exposure of Palestinian women to sexual violence is not limited to encounters with male combat soldiers or Israeli male soldiers in general. Spatially, as much as Palestinian women are subject to sexual harassment and assaults at checkpoints and during house raids, their vulnerability exceeds these spaces and includes interrogation rooms, courts, and prisons.[19]

Tragically, the abuse of Palestinian prisoners, adults and children, has only intensified since October 7.

As of October 7, Israel was holding around 5,200 Palestinians prisoner, and many of these (around 2,200) were being held in "administrative detention"—that is, without charge and without a definite sentence of confinement.[20] After October 7, clearly in retaliation for the militants' capture of the 240 Israeli hostages, this number skyrocketed, with Israel taking over 3,000 more Palestinians prisoner by November 24, bringing the total to over 8,000.[21] Thus, while Israel returned 150 prisoners (including women and children) to Hamas in the prisoner/hostage exchange in November,[22] it has more than made up for that by taking thousands more prisoner.

Human rights groups have reported that the treatment of the Palestinian captives is horrendous, and it has been so for years. In fact, as far back as the year 2000, Israeli authorities have admitted to the systematic torture of Palestinian detainees. As the *Guardian* reported then,

The Israeli internal security service, Shin Bet, used systematic torture against Palestinians and regularly lied about it, according to an Israeli government report which has been released five years after it was written.

The report covers the period 1988–1992, when Palestinian youths were mounting a sustained street revolt known as the Intifada. . . .

The Israeli human rights organisation, B'Tselem, estimates that thousands of Palestinian detainees—some 85 percent—were subjected to torture. B'Tselem said that since the beginning of the Intifada, 10 Palestinians have died and hundreds have been maimed as a result of Shin Bet torture.[23]

And, as the *Guardian* explained, "'The irregularities were not, for the most part, the result of not knowing the line between the permissible and the forbidden, but rather were committed knowingly,' the report says."

The mistreatment of prisoners has only intensified since October 7. First of all, the use of administrative detention has risen greatly since that time, rising from around 1,300 in early October to 4,000 in early December. As explained by Amnesty International this spike in administrative detention followed what was already "a 20-year high before the latest escalation in hostilities on 7 October."[24] Amnesty further explained, "Administrative detention is one of the key tools through which Israel has enforced its system of apartheid against Palestinians. Testimonies and video evidence also point to numerous incidents of torture and other illtreatment by Israeli forces including severe beatings and deliberate humiliation of Palestinians who are detained in dire conditions."[25]

The publication *New Arab* explained that, while reports of abuse against Palestinian prisoners are certainly nothing new, there has been a rise of such reports since October 7. The *New Arab* included the following account from former detainee Israa Ja'abis: "I left little girls in my prison cell crying. Why? Because unspeakable things are happening to them there. . . . Unimaginable things at the hands of the [Israeli] soldiers."[26] According to the piece, "Some of the recently released Palestinian detainees said that guards carried out abuse and collective punishment in the weeks that followed the war on Gaza. They described being hit with sticks, having muzzled dogs set on them, and their clothes, food and blankets taken away. The Palestinian Prisoners Society said some guards allegedly urinated on handcuffed prisoners."[27]

On January 3, 2024, the editorial board of the Israeli newspaper *Haaretz* ran an editorial condemning the abuse, some of it apparently lethal. In this piece, "Israel Must Stop Abusing and Humiliating

Palestinian Prisoners," the editorial board explained, "Since the start of the war, five Palestinian prisoners have died in Israeli prisons. Investigations have been opened into two of these deaths, since there were signs of violence on their bodies. In addition, two Gazan workers died under unclear circumstances."[28]

Haaretz cited testimony of abuse from a number of Palestinian prisoners, including "by both West Bank Palestinians and Arab citizens of Israel [i.e., Israeli citizens] held in Megiddo Prison's security wings." According to *Haaretz*,

> These prisoners say the guards handcuffed new inmates and beat them until they bled. One prisoner told his lawyer that they were repeatedly forced to lie on the floor and say "Am Yisrael Chai" (the people of Israel live). If they didn't, they would be beaten.
>
> "When we arrived, they divided us into two groups and made us wait," one detainee said. "Forty guards entered and beat us hard," said another. "In the cells we were tied up for nine hours. In the evening they came in and beat everyone in the cell."[29]

In concluding its editorial, *Haaretz* sounded the alarm, stating: "there is no justification for acting like animals toward Palestinians in state custody."

There are different accounts of treatment from Israelis who were taken hostage by the Hamas and related militants—most of these militants, by the way, are young men who had been orphaned by Israeli attacks over the years. Thus, a number of these hostages have given interviews saying that they were treated very humanely by these militants.

For example, eighty-five-year-old Yocheved Lifshitz, who was released along with another elderly female hostage early on in the conflict on humanitarian grounds, gave an interview saying that, while they were treated roughly while they were being taken captive, they were treated very well in captivity. As she explained,

> Once in Gaza, . . . she said her captors "treated her well," giving her and other captives "the same food they ate" and bringing in a doctor to provide medicine.

"They treated us gently, and provided all our needs," she said, when questioned about her reason for shaking the hand of one of her captors at the moment of her release.

"They seemed ready for this, they prepared for a long time, they had everything that men and women needed, including shampoo," she added.[30]

There is also the story of "78-year-old Ruti Munder [who] told Israel's Channel 13 television that she spent the entirety of her time with her daughter, Keren, and grandson, Ohad Munder-Zichri, who celebrated his ninth birthday in captivity."[31] Ruti, who was photographed smiling upon being released, reported that they were well-fed by their captors at least until the food started running out due to Israel's siege of Gaza. As the Associated Press (AP) reported, "'Initially, they ate 'chicken with rice, all sorts of canned food and cheese,' Munder told Channel 13, in an audio interview. 'We were OK.' They were given tea in the morning and evening, and the children were given sweets. But the menu changed when 'the economic situation was not good, and people were hungry."[32] As AP reported, "Munder, who was freed Friday, returned in good physical condition, like most other captives."[33]

This is not to say that these militants are angels or that they did not commit atrocities in the course of the October 7 attacks—atrocities that certainly should be condemned—but at the same time, they are not the barbarians that Israeli and US officials and pundits are trying to portray them as, and any criminal acts they committed pale in comparison to those committed by Israel with US backing.

One of the big lies told about October 7 has been the claim that Hamas and allied militant groups carried out mass rapes. These are reminiscent of the claims against Libyan leader Muammar Gaddafi in 2011 used to justify his murder and violent overthrow. At that time, US officials such as Hillary Clinton made the outrageous claim that Gaddafi was passing out Viagra to his troops in order to carry out this terrible crime. This claim was widely reported in the press. And, while this ended up being debunked, with human rights groups not finding even one person who could corroborate it and with US intelligence and military sources eventually admitting that there was absolutely no evidence of such a crime,[34] the damage had been done as NATO forces had already begun their eleven-month bombing of the country.

Similarly, while repeating the claims of rape against Hamas, sources such as the Israeli paper *Haaretz* ultimately reported on January 4, 2024—just shy of three months after the October 7 attacks—that the Israeli police, though desperate to find evidence to support these claims, could not find any victims or eyewitnesses to substantiate them.[35]

One of the more outrageous rape claims was made by French citizen Sandra Ifrah, who claimed that she found sperm from sixty-seven different Palestinian assailants in an Israeli hostage, suggesting that the hostage was raped by sixty-seven different militants. Ms. Ifrah would later recant and apologize for this claim, admitting that this was a false statement made up in an "emotional moment."[36]

Independent journalists such as those at the *The Grayzone* and *Electronic Intifada* have done deep dives dissecting the claims and demonstrating their lack of substantiation and the lack of credibility of those making them.[37]

Indeed, *The Grayzone* outed the *New York Times* for an embarrassingly bogus report it did on the alleged rapes of October 7.[38] As the *The Grayzone* related, "Exhibit A" of the *Times* report was the alleged rape of Gal Abdush, known as "the girl in the black dress." However, the story neglected a very important bit of information—that the family of the alleged victim, who was killed and therefore cannot speak for herself, are adamant that she was not in fact raped. Indeed, they did not even know the *Times* story was going to be about rape when they were interviewed; they thought it was going to be about their loved one's memory. *The Grayzone* explains that Gal Abdush's sister is now accusing the *Times* of "manipulating her family into participating by misleading them about their editorial angle. Though the family's comments have sparked a major uproar on social media, the *Times* has yet to address the serious breach of journalistic integrity that its staff is accused of committing."

What all of this demonstrates is that, as a number of commentators have pointed out, all of Israel's accusations against Hamas and the Palestinians in general are in fact confessions. That is, Israel projects its own crimes and sins upon the Palestinians. Israeli officials have accused the Palestinian militants, without good evidence, of rapes when it is in fact the Israeli forces, as discussed in depth above, who have been using rape as a weapon of war and occupation against the Palestinians since 1948. We will see such projection manifested time and time again.

One commentator detailing the accusations of Israelis as confessions is award-winning journalist Gareth Porter, and he does so in an article titled "How Israel Leverages Genocide with Hamas 'Massacres.'"[39] In this article, Porter details how Israeli officials manufactured stories of alleged Hamas atrocities and planted them in the mainstream media to impact public opinion, and specifically, to generate public support for the mass slaughter it had been preparing to carry out. Porter argues further that the atrocity stories were concocted to convince the Biden administration itself "to go along with the plan to reduce all of Gaza to a pile of rubble." And, the directive to come up with such stories came from the highest levels, Porter explains, with Netanyahu himself ordering "a special project of hasbara—the Israeli term for propaganda to reshape public opinion abroad—to ensure that both the US public and the Biden administration fully supported the Israeli position on Hamas's attack."

One of the big lies that Porter dissects is that of the alleged forty babies Israel claimed that the Hamas and related militants beheaded in the Kfar Aza kibbutz on October 7. Porter explains how this lie became truth as far as the media and the Biden administration were concerned. The source of this claim was originally General Major Itai Veruv who was quoted by CNN as stating, "I saw hundreds of terrorists in full armor, full gear, with all the equipment and all the ability to make a massacre, go from apartment to apartment, from room to room and kill babies, mothers, fathers in their bedrooms."

But, as Porter points out, Veruv did not even visit Kfar Aza until October 10—three days after the attacks and after the militants had either been killed or fled back to Gaza. As Porter notes,

> Veruv had not seen anything of the sort himself, but it was emblematic of the IDF manipulation of the Western press on the issue. When *Business Insider* contacted the IDF from New York about the story, spokesperson

Major Nir Dinar claimed that its soldiers had found the decapitated corpses of babies at Kfar Aza.

But when the Turkish Anadolu Agency and *The Intercept* sought confirmation of the claim of beheaded babies from the IDF on Oct. 10 and 12, respectively, the IDF couldn't back up the statement by Veruv.

Anadolu reported in a post on "X" that the IDF had "no information" confirming the allegations of beheaded babies.

And the IDF spokesperson told *The Intercept* that the military had not been able to independently confirm the claim.

Despite the absence of actual evidence for that propaganda claim, a cascade of such stories were aired by major US television networks and the BBC. It was a major triumph of deliberate Israeli deception by manipulating broadcast media eager for Hamas atrocity stories.

President Biden, so willing to exploit this story himself, would claim in October that he actually saw a photo of the beheaded babies. However, the White House would soon walk that claim back, making it clear that Biden was relying upon news reports and Israeli official claims for his ostensible knowledge about the incident.[40] Still, Biden would persist even after the story had been debunked, against falsely claiming in December that he had seen such photos.[41]

For most of the public, the story of the forty beheaded babies is probably still believed. Moreover, to the extent the story has been discredited in the minds of a portion of the public, the original lie did its dark magic—it created significant support for the slaughter to come, and indeed a slaughter that has already claimed thousands of Palestinian children. And that it was indeed the purpose of the lie.

A very good characterization of the October 7 attacks has been given by former US Ambassador Charles "Chas" Freeman, an individual with impeccable credentials, in a recent interview. As the introduction to this interview relates, Ambassador Freeman is "a retired career diplomat whose contributions have reshaped global diplomacy. From his pivotal role as Assistant Secretary of Defense for International Security Affairs during the post–Cold War era to serving as the US Ambassador to Saudi Arabia during Desert Shield and Desert Storm, Ambassador Freeman's career spans continents and historic moments. His work in designing a NATO-centered European security system, reestablishing defense relations with China, and mediating key African conflicts has left an indelible mark on international relations."[42]

In this interview, Ambassador Freeman sets forth the reasons behind and the nature of the October 7 attacks. As an initial matter, he describes the October 7 operations as "a spectacular jailbreak and rather like slave revolts in our own history in the United States." He contends that "Their objective was military. When they broke out of the Gaza concentration camp, which is the largest in the world, other groups and individuals came with them, followed them." As he explains, this latter group of non-militants were "people who sought revenge for the abuses that they've suffered for so very long."

Surprisingly, even the Rand Corporation—a long-standing defense contractor of the United States—similarly acknowledges the roots of the October 7 attacks, stating that they "grew out of Israel's decades-long failed strategy of 'mowing the grass' in Gaza—which attempted to both contain and deter Hamas in Gaza, while simultaneously not addressing any of the underlying economic and political conditions that had helped bring Hamas into power and keep it there. While Hamas's core supporters may not have changed, a more far-sighted Israeli policy could have at least undercut Hamas's popular support."[43]

The phrase "mowing the grass" or "mowing the lawn" refers to the IDF's policy of periodically inflicting disproportionate civilian casualties (the civilians being the "grass") in response to any attack by Palestinian militants. As *Foreign Policy in Focus* puts it well,

> Some Israelis refer to their periodic shelling of the Palestinian territory as "mowing the lawn." It is a disturbing metaphor because it is so indiscriminate. They don't talk about "weeding the garden" or "pruning the trees." A lawnmower cuts down everything in its path—grass, weeds, wildflowers. Also, a lawn needs constant mowing, suggesting that Israel plans to conduct bombing campaigns on a seasonal basis.[44]

Israel's current assault on Gaza constitutes an extreme version of "mowing the grass." While I address this issue in much more detail below, Ambassador Freeman references this when he condemns Israel's response to October 7, stating, "the Israeli response is essentially to conduct a genocide in Gaza. They are attempting to expel or murder all the Palestinians there, either murder them with bombing or murder them by starvation. This is a crime against humanity under international law."

In terms of the "underlying economic and political conditions" in Gaza referred to by the Rand Corporation, it is hard to conceive of more terrible conditions than those, it must be emphasized, Israel has intentionally created there.

As Ambassador Freeman also points out, a number of civilian deaths on October 7 that were originally attributed to Hamas and related militants ended up being the responsibility of the Israeli Defense Forces. Ambassador Freeman, discussing the deaths of Israelis at the "rave" festival not far from the Gaza border fences, relies upon reports specifically from the Israeli newspaper *Haaretz* to explain: "it turns out that at least some of those festival goers were killed by the Israeli army. So there is a video from a helicopter shooting on fleeing cars." Ambassador Freeman, having some choice words for the festival goers, further relates,

> the participants in this outlandish music festival, just think for a moment, they're having a music festival on the border of a concentration camp. And the people in the concentration camp can hear and see what's going on. This is outlandish to say the least. But the people who were killed there were largely killed, it appears, by hellfire missiles and by other undisciplined fire by Israeli forces who reacted in a chaotic manner to what had happened.

Many of the people who survived the attacks at the festival agree with Ambassador Freeman's assessment that the Israeli military has significant responsibility for the casualties there, with forty-two survivors of these attacks bringing a civil action against the Israeli military for negligence.[45]

Ambassador Freeman also notes that the Israeli military was also responsible for many of the civilian deaths at the kibbutz settlements that were attacked. As he relates,

Then they have the tanks that attacked the kibbutz houses, right? Where they blew the houses knowing that there are terrorists plus the inhabitants in there, right? Then I have seen videos where you virtually have hundreds of destroyed cars next to each other on this parking lot that can't be Hamas with their whatever RGBs or what they're having. They were not only burnt, they were like blown to pieces, right? So are those credible reports stating that actually for quite some degree the Israeli army might be responsible for the dead Israelis on October 7th? Yes, and there are two reasons for this.

The two reasons he gives for the Israeli military's killing of people in the kibbutz settlements are (1) the Israeli soldiers' lack of discipline and training; and (2) "something called the Hannibal Directive." As Ambassador Freeman explains, the Hannibal Directive stems from the fact that

> Israel has imprisoned thousands of Palestinian prisoners often with no charges, sometimes with fake charges, sometimes with a genuine judicial process conducted by military courts. But it has a huge number of hostages and many times in the past, Israeli hostages have been exchanged for Palestinian hostages in a vastly disproportionate ratio. So the Hannibal Directive basically says that rather than get into bargaining over a hostage exchange, you should just kill the Israeli hostages along with their captors. And that was also a factor here.

All of these assertions have been confirmed by Israeli news sources, such as *Ynet*, which—as summarized by journalist Max Blumenthal who has done more than anyone to expose the misinformation surrounding the October 7 attacks—found

- "Mass Hannibal" friendly fire orders;
- Seventy cars hit by Israeli helicopters, tanks or anti-tank missiles "and at least in some cases everyone in the vehicle was killed";
- Firing regulations abandoned.[46]

Further reporting, much of it being done by Israeli journalists, shows that the carrying out of the Hannibal Directive was indeed extensive and may have resulted in the majority of the civilian deaths on October 7. Thus, Asa Winstanley, writing for the *Electronic Intifada*, and summarizing the Hebrew-language reports of Israeli journalists "Ronen Bergman and Yoav Zitun, two journalists with extensive sources inside Israel's military and intelligence establishment," writes that interviews with Israeli helicopter pilots show

> that they had been ordered to "shoot at everything" moving between Israel's frontier settlements and Gaza.
>
> That Israeli article stated that "in the first four hours . . . helicopters and fighter craft attacked about 300 targets, most in Israeli territory."
>
> Bergman and Zitun's new article says that by the end of the day, drone squadron 161 alone (which flies Elbit's Hermes 450 drone) "performed no fewer than 110 attacks on some 1,000 targets, most of which were inside Israel."[47]

As Winstanley further explains, "The latest revelations confirm . . . that many—if not most—of the Israeli civilians killed that day were killed by Israel itself, not Palestinian fighters." Winstanley relates that, "It was also clear from the outset that hundreds of the dead were in fact Israeli soldiers. Hamas maintains that they targeted military bases and outposts, and that their aim was to capture rather than kill Israeli civilians, and to kill or capture Israeli soldiers."

Israeli forces would go on to kill three Israeli hostages in Gaza in December even though they were holding white flags and despite the fact that one even spoke Hebrew to try to make his case for not being shot.[48] Whether these killings were the product of panic and poor training, the Hannibal Directive in action or simply the rules of engagement of the Israeli forces in Gaza (i.e., one in which they are shooting at anything that moves) remains uncertain.

Bad training and the Hannibal Directive may not fully explain the killing of civilians by Israeli forces on October 7. As for the Hannibal Directive, Asa Kasher, the Israeli ethicist who wrote the IDF's Code of Conduct, has described the use of this on October 7 as "unethical, unlawful, horrifying," and it was so, as Kasher explains, primarily because this Directive was never meant to be, and should never be carried out, against civilians.[49] This raises the question as to whether this really was the Hannibal Directive in action, or something else. I would posit a third reason for these civilian killings—the intention to raise the civilian body count for the propagandistic purpose of ginning up domestic and international support for the massacres to come in Gaza.

In the end, whatever the reasons behind these "friendly-fire" killings, there is no doubt that whatever crimes Hamas and related militants committed on October 7, they pale in comparison to those carried out by Israeli forces against the Palestinians in Gaza and with bombs, supplied by the United States, amounting to multiple Hiroshimas and Nakasakis.

Incredibly, the militants' crimes on October 7 may even pale in comparision to Israel's crimes against its own people on that day.

CHAPTER 4

ISRAEL CARRIES OUT GENOCIDE, NOT SELF-DEFENSE, IN GAZA

Calling things by the wrong name adds to the affliction of the world.
—Albert Camus

If you fail to call this a genocide, it is on you. It is a sin and a darkness you willingly embrace.
—Munther Isaac, Lutheran pastor (Bethlehem)

While "The Case for Palestine" could have many meanings, at the time of this writing, it minimally means, "the case for allowing Palestine and the Palestinian people to exist and live." This case apparently must be made given the fact that Israel, with the full support of the US government and military, is currently attempting to wipe Gaza, and to some extent the West Bank as well, off the map. If this seems hyperbolic, consider the following.

In late October 2023, a number of media outlets, including the Associated Press (AP), reported that Israel has a written plan to ethnically cleanse all Palestinians from the occupied territory of Gaza and remove them into Egypt's Sinai desert. That is, Israel intends to force the fate visited upon the biblical nation of Israel upon the Palestinians—to wander in the Sinai desert as the Israelites themselves were condemned to do. As the AP explains:

An Israeli government ministry has drafted a wartime proposal to transfer the Gaza Strip's 2.3 million people to Egypt's Sinai Peninsula, drawing condemnation from the Palestinians and worsening tensions with Cairo.

Prime Minister Benjamin Netanyahu's office played down the report compiled by the Intelligence Ministry as a hypothetical exercise—a "concept paper." But its conclusions deepened long-standing Egyptian fears that Israel wants to make Gaza into Egypt's problem, and revived for Palestinians memories of their greatest trauma—the uprooting of hundreds of thousands of people who fled or were forced from their homes during the fighting surrounding Israel's creation in 1948.[1]

The AP's reference here to the Palestinians' "greatest trauma" is to the Nakba discussed in chapter 1. When considering the current events in Gaza, it is important to recognize that 70 percent of the residents of Gaza are refugees to begin with as a result of the displacement of the Nakba of 1948.[2]

The displacement happening now in Gaza is considered by many Palestinians as a second Nakba. And this is not just their subjective opinion. Indeed, as I write these words, an astounding 1.9 million Gaza residents (quickly nearing the entire population of Gaza) have already been displaced by the war, in many cases more than once since October 7.[3] This number of displaced is well over two times greater than the number of Palestinians displaced during the Nakba.

As well-explained by Josh Ruebner in a November 17, 2023 article in *The Hill*, "Israel is threatening a second *Nakba*, but it's already happening":

> "We are now rolling out the Gaza *Nakba*," Israeli security cabinet member and Agriculture Minister Avi Dichter declared on Saturday. "Gaza Nakba 2023. That's how it'll end."
>
> By referencing the Nakba, an Arabic word meaning "catastrophe," Dichter is rhetorically linking Israel's current attacks against 2.3 million Palestinians in the Gaza Strip—including 1 million children—with Israel taking over more than three-quarters of Palestine in 1948.
>
> This violent takeover involved the forced displacement of approximately 75 percent of indigenous Palestinians from their homes in what

became Israel and the new state's destruction of hundreds of Palestinian villages, towns and cities to prevent Palestinian refugees from returning.[4]

As Ruebner correctly relates, "Dichter's threat to inflict a new *Nakba* on Palestinians today is neither a bluff nor an understatement. In just a little more than a month, Israel already has killed more than 11,000 Palestinians, including more than 4,500 children. With thousands more Palestinians trapped under the rubble, including at least 1,500 children, and believed to be dead, Palestinian fatalities already have surpassed the number of those killed by Israel during the 1948–1949 Nakba, which historians estimate at 12,000."

That an Israeli official is acknowledging the first Nakba and threatening a second is a sea change, for Zionists have refused for years to admit that the first Nakba even happened, for this (1) implicitly concedes that there were hundreds of thousands of Palestinians living in this "land without a people" when Israel was created; and (2) is an admission of the brutality involved in the creation of Israel. The admissions of the Nakba, and the threatening of another, demonstrate just how much Israel is taking off the gloves in the current conflict. That is, the powers that be in Israel are not even trying to conceal the true barbarity of their actions in Gaza.

The details of this second planned Nakba are set forth in the leaked Israeli Intelligence Ministry document. The AP relates that the leaked document, dated October 1, 2023, "proposes moving Gaza's civilian population to tent cities in northern Sinai, then building permanent cities and an undefined humanitarian corridor. A security zone would be established inside Israel to block the displaced Palestinians from entering. The report did not say what would become of Gaza once its population is cleared out."

In order to accomplish this terrible feat, the document[5] details that Israel, through "Large Advertising Agencies," would engage in "dedicated campaigns **for Gaza residents themselves** to motivate them to accept this plan—the messages should revolve around the loss of land, making it clear that there is no hope of returning to the territories Israel will soon occupy, whether or not that is true. The image needs to be, 'Allah made sure you lose this land because of Hamas' leadership—there is no choice but to move to another place with the assistance of your Muslim brothers'" (emphasis in original).

According to this document, this would be accompanied by "a call for the evacuation of the non-combatant population from the combat zone of the Hamas attack," and then "operations from the air with a focus on the north of Gaza to allow aground invasion in an area that is already evacuated."[6] This would then be followed by a ground invasion of the evacuated northern region aimed at fighting against Hamas militants.

While this plan on its face is bad enough, and actually appears to be in the process of being carried out, there are a couple details of the actual operations that are even more reprehensible but not mentioned in the plan.

Thus, while Israel has in fact been publicly calling for civilians to evacuate from the north of Gaza, and while hundreds of thousands of Gazans are complying with this demand,[7] what many such Gazans have been surprised to learn is that Israel would fire upon them anyway even as they were fleeing or as they were sheltering after fleeing in refugee shelters, including those run by the United Nations.

For example, NBC News reported on October 14, 2023, that, following Israel's order for the one million residents of Northern Gaza to evacuate, "70 people—mostly women and children—were killed after Israeli airstrikes hit convoys of Palestinian evacuees heading south in Gaza."[8] In addition, as Al Jazeera reported on November 3, 2023[9]:

- Separate Israeli strikes in the north of Gaza . . . targeted a convoy of civilians seeking to evacuate via the al-Rashid road, killing at least 14; At least 20 were killed in an Israeli attack on a school hosting displaced people in the Saftawi neighbourhood.
- Amid the violence, the UN agency for Palestinian refugees has said it can no longer provide safety at shelters under the UN flag; UNRWA also said at least 38 people have died in UN facilities since the war began, with five facilities directly hit in bombardments.

It should be noted that at least 270,000 Palestinians have been sheltering at UNRWA facilities[10]—facilities UNRWA says cannot be kept safe from Israeli bombardment. Indeed, UNRWA has been unable to protect its own staff, with over one hundred such staff killed by Israel in less than the first two months of the war—the largest number of UN workers killed in any conflict in history as explained by Samantha Power, the Administrator of the USAID.[11] Samantha Power originally made a name for herself by writing, *A Problem from Hell*, a book decrying the West's history of failing to act to prevent genocide. Power won the Pulitzer Prize for this book, and this was the springboard for her stellar academic and diplomatic career. Ironically, Power is now part of an administration that is being accused, I believe quite rightly, of aiding and abetting one of the worst genocides we have witnessed in our lifetimes. She has remained silent about this just as the very people she criticized in her book did when confronted with genocides they could have stopped but ended up facilitating.

In addition to being killed while fleeing from the north as they were told, other Palestinians have been subject to other forms of abuse by Israeli forces. As the Geneva-based human rights group Euro-Med Human Rights Monitor relates, "While moving to the southern Gaza Valley region, displaced Palestinians were harassed and mistreated by Israeli forces, according to the human rights organization. Some of those who had been displaced testified that they had been stripped of all belongings, while others told of having been held as human shields and forced to cross on foot through raids, shelling, and explosions to get to the south of the Gaza Valley."[12]

Moreover, while Gazans were specifically told to flee to the south of Gaza, with the suggestion that the south would be safe haven for them, Israel has been attacking the south relentlessly as much as the north. In short, no part of Gaza is safe from attack. In another, earlier article from October 14, Al Jazeera explained,

> Thousands of Palestinians have fled to southern Gaza after Israel warned them to evacuate the north before a planned ground offensive against Hamas in response to its attack on Israel.
>
> However, those who fled to southern Khan Younis found no reprieve from Israel's bombardment, as warplanes struck a four-story building on

Saturday, killing and wounding several people. Dozens of Palestinians could be seen rushing to rescue people trapped in the rubble.[13]

This is reminiscent of both the Vietnam and Korean wars in which the United States, while purporting to be allied with the southern half of those countries, attacked civilians relentlessly there as well, sometimes even more so than in the north.

What is happening in Gaza is in fact beyond the ethnic cleansing signaled in the leaked Israeli planning document; it is in fact something worse—a genocide. And as an international law professor, I do not say this lightly.

To determine whether there is a genocide as a matter of law, we must first look to the language of the Convention on the Prevention and Punishment of the Crime of Genocide of 1948 (Genocide Convention)—the very first human rights convention agreed to by the international community after and indeed in response to World War II and the Holocaust.

The operative language of this Convention that defines genocide is brief and reads as follows:

> In the present Convention, genocide means any of the following acts committed with intent to destroy, in whole or in part, a national, ethnical, racial or religious group, as such:
> (a) Killing members of the group;
> (b) Causing serious bodily or mental harm to members of the group;
> (c) Deliberately inflicting on the group conditions of life calculated to bring about its physical destruction in whole or in part;
> (d) Imposing measures intended to prevent births within the group;
> (e) Forcibly transferring children of the group to another group.

As this language indicates, there are two essential requirements to establish genocide: (1) *any* one or more of the five prohibited actions enumerated above carried out with (2) the intent to destroy, in whole or in part, a certain protected group as such.

While there only needs to be one of the five prohibited actions present to establish a genocide, there are in fact at least three in this case. First of all, Israel is carrying out killings of thousands of members of the targeted national and ethnical group—Palestinians—and the vast majority of these are women and children.

As noted earlier, as of the time of this writing, "30,676 Palestinians have been killed during the Israeli attacks . . . , including 28,201 civilians. The death toll includes 12,040 children, 6,103 women, 241 health workers, and 105 journalists."[14] As the Geneva-based Euro-Med Monitor concluded, "about 4 percent of the total population of the Gaza Strip—more than 90,000 people—are now dead, wounded, or missing."[15]

According to the *New York Times*, the rate of killings in Gaza by Israel is unprecedented. As the *Times* explained on November 25, 2023:

> Israel has cast the deaths of civilians in the Gaza Strip as a regrettable but unavoidable part of modern conflict, pointing to the heavy human toll from military campaigns the United States itself once waged in Iraq and Syria.
>
> But a review of past conflicts and interviews with casualty and weapons experts suggest that Israel's assault is different.
>
> While wartime death tolls will never be exact, experts say that even a conservative reading of the casualty figures reported from Gaza shows that the pace of death during Israel's campaign has few precedents in this century.
>
> People are being killed in Gaza more quickly, they say, than in even the deadliest moments of US-led attacks in Iraq, Syria and Afghanistan, which were themselves widely criticized by human rights groups.[16]

In addition to the sheer number of killed, the *Times* further explains, the nature of the victims of the killings—70 percent women and children—is also without precedent in recent memory. The *Times* notes that in recent conflicts between Israel and Hamas, the figure was reversed, with 60 percent of those killed being men. The *Times* further relates that "more than twice as many women and children have already been reported killed in Gaza than have been confirmed killed in Ukraine, according to United Nations figures, after almost two years of Russian attacks."

The other thing that makes the carnage unique in this war against Gaza, the *New York Times* emphasizes, is the size of bombs being used by Israel. Thus, Israel is using 2,000-pound bombs against this densely populated area though "US military officials often believed that the most common American aerial bomb—a 500-pound weapon—was far too large for most targets when battling the Islamic State in urban areas like Mosul, Iraq, and Raqqa, Syria." The *Times* quotes Marc Garlasco, a former senior intelligence analyst for the Pentagon, for the proposition that one would "'have to go back to Vietnam, or the Second World War,'" to find the use of bombs of such tonnage against an urban population.

It must be emphasized that even while President Biden and other members of his administration were claiming that they were concerned about civilian deaths in Gaza and were cautioning Netanyahu about this, the Biden administration was also replenishing Israel with its supply of 2,000-pound bombs to continue the carnage.[17] Indeed, as the *New York Times* reported, the United States had sent Israel more than *5,000 of these 2,000-pound bombs* between October 27 and the end of December 2023.[18]

As the *Times* explained, Israel has "routinely used" these "2,000-pound bombs in an area of southern Gaza where Israel had ordered civilians to move for safety. While bombs of that size are used by several Western militaries, munitions experts say they are almost never dropped by US forces in densely populated areas anymore." Not surprisingly, the investigation of the *Times* "reveal that 2,000-pound bombs posed a pervasive threat to civilians seeking safety across south Gaza." And again, this seems to be the point.

For its part, the *Wall Street Journal* ran a story on how after October 7 the United States provided "Israel with large bunker buster bombs, among tens of thousands of other weapons and artillery shells," and how this, combined with Biden's refusal to call for a cease-fire, have undercut any ability of the United States to prevail upon Israel to protect civilians. As the *WSJ* wrote, in the most understated way possible,

The airlift of hundreds of millions of dollars in munitions, primarily on C-17 military cargo planes flying from the US to Tel Aviv, shows the diplomatic challenge facing the Biden administration. . . .

Some security analysts say the weapons transfers could undercut the administration's pressure on Israel to protect civilians.

"It seems inconsistent with reported exhortations from Secretary Blinken and others to use smaller-diameter bombs," said Brian Finucane, a senior adviser at the nonprofit International Crisis Group, and a former attorney-advisor at the State Department.[19]

The result of Israel's use of US-provided massive bombs is that—as I have heard from a number of Palestinians I know who have lost numerous relatives—entire families, entire bloodlines are being wiped out in an instant in Gaza.

The Associated Press (AP) ran a story on this tragic phenomenon on November 18, 2023, giving examples of individual Palestinians losing more than twenty family members in one swoop in Gaza. As the AP explained, "Entire generations of Palestinian families in the besieged Gaza Strip—from great-grandparents to infants only weeks old—have been killed in airstrikes in the Israel-Hamas war. . . . Attacks are occurring at a scale never seen in years of Israel-Hamas conflict, hitting residential areas, schools, hospitals, mosques and churches, even striking areas in southern Gaza where Israeli forces ordered civilians to flee."[20]

At a protest in Pittsburgh in front of the offices of US Senators Bob Casey and John Fetterman, Palestinian American Karim Alshurafa told of how he had already lost twenty family members in Gaza.

A terrible example of this phenomenon involves Issam al-Mughrabi, a UN Development Programme (UNDP) worker in Gaza City. As the *Guardian* reported, Issam, age fifty-six, was killed in a bombing along with seventy members of his immediate and extended family. A spokesperson for the UNDP stated in reaction to this terrible tragedy: "The UN and civilians in Gaza are not a target. This war must end. No more families should endure the pain and suffering that Issam's family and countless others are experiencing."[21]

The Secretary General of the UN, António Guterres, also commented on this, and the fact that "on average, one or two UN employees have died in Gaza each day of the war—more than 130 in total." According to Guterres, who Israel is demanding resign because of his criticisms of

Israel's treatment of the Palestinians, "that toll is something we have never seen in the history of the United Nations." Later, on December 22, 2023, Guterres posted a tweet, lamenting:

> 136 of our colleagues in Gaza have been killed in 75 days—something we have never seen in @UN history.
>
> Most of our staff have been forced from their homes.
>
> I pay tribute to them & the thousands of aid workers risking their lives as they support civilians in Gaza.

One gets the sense from this statement that Guterres, the head of the United Nations, is resigned to the killing of his people and that there is simply nothing that can be done about it. Up until the end of March 2024, the US vetoed every UN Security Council resolution that could have led to a cease-fire and/or the protection of civilians in Gaza. And then, when the US finally allowed a cease-fire to pass through abstention, the White House declared it "nonbinding." All we can do, apparently, is throw up our hands and "pay tribute" to these lost souls. What a terrible state of affairs, and one that, as discussed above, Hamas saw and took note of in deciding to carry out the October 7 attacks to begin with.

To get a sense of what the massive aerial bombings are like for the people of Gaza, the following description by the Euro-Med Human Rights Monitor of bombings by Israel on the night of November 6 is helpful[22]:

> In just a few hours of violent and intense air attacks on the Gaza Strip overnight, and amid a total blackout of communications and Internet services, Israel has committed its largest massacre since its establishment in 1948, the Euro-Med Human Rights Monitor reported today.
>
> Euro-Med Monitor estimated that Israel's overnight attacks, the scale of which is unprecedented since the start of its war on the Gaza Strip on 7 October, left more than 1,500 people dead or wounded as well as hundreds of homes destroyed, many with their residents trapped inside.
>
> The Euro-Med team received shocking testimonies from residents of Gaza City about the intense, bloody attacks, especially from the

Al-Fawaydah Harat Al-Rayes area of Gaza where scores of people were reportedly killed by hours of ceaseless bombardment.

Similar testimonies were given by residents of the Shati refugee camp, west of Gaza City, about a series of Israeli raids that destroyed entire residential blocks, burying dozens of inhabitants under the wreckage.

The collected accounts tell of hundreds of victims buried under the rubble, with corpses and dismembered body parts strewn throughout the streets by the morning hours.

Meanwhile, the work of ambulance and civil defense rescue teams was completely paralyzed due to last night's interruption of communications and Internet services, which lasted for more than 15 hours.

The Israeli army has declared it struck more than 450 targets last night, and continues its incitement against hospitals, with areas around several in Gaza City and its northern areas, including Al-Shifa Medical Complex, the Indonesian Hospital, the Eye Hospital, Al-Quds Hospital and the only psychiatric hospital in the Strip, targeted in an unprecedented and violent manner, according to Euro-Med Monitor. The Israeli army has claimed that hospitals are being used for military purposes without presenting any concrete proof.

Since the start of the ongoing Israeli war, 16 out of 35 hospitals and 51 primary care facilities (more than 75 percent) across the Gaza Strip have been unable to operate due to the intense Israeli raids or fuel shortages.

Euro-Med Monitor "confirmed that there are no safe corridors for displaced families or relief supplies amidst intense Israeli air and ground attacks on the Gaza Strip."

My sweet, dear friend Ola, who lives in Gaza City, told me on November 30, 2023, that she was alive but that death haunted her and everyone living in Gaza. She told me, "I walked the streets today. I was crying over the destruction. The smell in the streets is unbearable. We put on masks but that's even not enough." Her family, like many, have decided that if they must die, they will die together "with dignity in our house. Not on the streets to be eaten by stray dogs." A modest wish for the future indeed.

Israel has wounded—that is, caused serious physical harm to—over 61,000 Gazans as of January 18, 2024, and that number is rising by hundreds per day, with 326 Gazans wounded in just the twenty-four-hour period between January 17 and 18.[23] And I think it is fair to say that the devastation that Israel has visited upon Gaza has mentally scarred each of the 2.3 million people Palestinians, and especially the approximately one million children, living there.

Israel has also been "deliberately inflicting on the group conditions of life calculated to bring about its physical destruction in whole or in part" by cutting off water, food and medicines to the Palestinians in Gaza for weeks on end. At the time of this writing, it is unknown how many Palestinians have died as a result of this deliberate denial of materials necessary for human survival, but there is no doubt that it is substantial, and children are the most affected by the lack of such necessities, especially water.

As the *Guardian* explained on November 4, 2023, about a month into Israel's operations against Gaza, "*Palestinians who fled to southern Gaza, after warnings from Israel to leave their homes*, are standing in line for hours to get contaminated water they believe is making them ill. Long queues of people waiting to fill jerry cans are now ubiquitous across the territory as water becomes increasingly scarce, a result of restrictions on water and power imposed by Israel"[24] (emphasis added).

As the *Guardian* further related, "Gaza's water production capacity is a mere 5 percent of its usual daily output. Child deaths—particularly infants—to dehydration are a growing threat." And that output is 5 percent of extremely short water supplies already in existence *before* the beginning of Israel's current military operations. Thus, the *Guardian* relates that "Gaza has struggled with access to water since Israel imposed a blockade in 2007, with groundwater sources becoming polluted from overuse." Israel's flooding of the underground Hamas tunnels in Gaza with seawater is expected to destroy Gaza's aquifers, which the people there depend upon for drinking water.[25]

At the same time, Israel has been bombing food supplies in Gaza. As Euro-Med Human Rights Monitor detailed on November 5, 2023:

> As part of its ongoing war for the fifth week in a row, Israel has sharply increased in recent hours what can only be described as a war of starvation

against civilians in the Gaza Strip in an effort to deepen their difficult living conditions, which has reached catastrophic levels, Euro-Med Human Rights Monitor said in a statement issued on Sunday.

. . . The Israeli war of starvation has taken very dangerous turns, including cutting off all food supplies to the Northern half and bombing and destroying factories, bakeries, food stores, water stations, and tanks throughout the entire enclave. . . .

Euro-Med Monitor further noted that Israel's attacks also targeted the agricultural areas east of Gaza, flour stores, and fishermen's boats, as well as relief organizations' centers, including those belonging to the United Nations Relief and Works Agency for Palestine Refugees (UNRWA), the largest provider of humanitarian aid in the Strip.[26]

The result of all of this is a situation too horrifying to imagine. As Palestinian author Abdalhadi Alijla related on Twitter:

I had the opportunity to communicate with some members of my family. The situation is unbelievable. Hungry dogs are eating the remains of bodies buried under the rubble in Gaza City. The smell of decay pervades the city. There will be catastrophic health consequences. Food and clean water are scarce. One of my nieces was taken to the hospital because of lack of food two days ago. People are beginning to experience starvation in its most literal sense. They spend 7 hours in line to receive a single piece of bread for each member of the family. When food is found, it's exorbitantly expensive. If this continues before our very eyes, it will turn into a horrendous BLACK MOMENT IN HUMAN HISTORY.[27]

On November 26, 2023, Cindy McCain, the widow of the late Senator John McCain (R) and director of the UN World Food Program (UNWFP), told *Meet the Press* that Gaza by that time was already on the brink of famine.[28] She warned that "a life-threatening form of malnutrition in children could increase by nearly 30 percent in the territory," and with it would spread disease. For its part, the World Health Organization (WHO) warned around the same time that more people in Gaza would end up dying in Gaza from disease than from bombs because of the denial of food, water and medicine by Israel as well as Israel's destruction of critical civilian infrastructure.[29]

By December 23, 2023, "the United Nations Secretary-General Antonio Guterres . . . once again sounded the alarm on the dire humanitarian crisis in the Gaza Strip, lamenting that *four out of five of the hungriest people anywhere in the world are in Gaza*,'" and yet, Israel was continuing to block humanitarian aid from entering Gaza[30] (emphasis added). Then, in January 2024, *The New Yorker* ran the story "Gaza is Starving," in which it reported that 90 percent of Gaza was by then experiencing "acute food insecurity."[31] Citing a UN report, *The New Yorker* related that "'*This is the highest share of people facing high levels of acute food security' ever recorded 'for any given area or country*'" (emphasis added).

By January 16, 2024, the *Guardian*, quoting aid workers in Gaza, was reporting that there are already "pockets of famine" there. As the *Guardian* explained, "Doctors in Gaza said that children, weakened by lack of food, had died from hypothermia and that several newborn babies with mothers who were undernourished had not survived for more than a few days. 'We don't have the numbers but we can say that children are dying as a result of the humanitarian situation on the ground as well as due to the direct impact of the fighting,' said Tess Ingram, a spokesperson for UNICEF in Rafah."[32]

An article by Professor Devi Sridhar, the chair of global public health at the University of Edinburgh, predicts the catastrophic loss of life that may very well result from the preventable diseases Palestinians in Gaza will succumb to due to the intentional denial of food, water and medicines, and the destruction of critical civilian infrastructure. In her article titled, "It's not just bullets and bombs. I have never seen health organizations as worried as they are about disease in Gaza," Professor Sridhar ominously predicts, "Ultimately, unless something changes, the world faces the prospect of almost a quarter of Gaza's population of 2 million—*close to half a million human beings*—dying within a year. These would be largely deaths from preventable health causes and the collapse of the medical system. It's a crude estimate, but one that is data-driven, using the terrifyingly real numbers of deaths in previous and comparable conflicts"[33] (emphasis added).

Incredibly, this news was welcomed by some Israelis, with Retired Israeli General Giora Eiland writing in an op-ed in the Hebrew-language edition of *Yedioth Ahronoth*: "The international community is warning us against a severe humanitarian disaster and severe epidemics. We must not shy away from this. After all, severe epidemics in the south of Gaza will bring victory closer."[34] Again, remember that Israel had urged over a million Gazans to flee to the south of Gaza to find safe haven.

Further, what began as Israel's stated war on Hamas quickly became Israel's war on children and hospitals. While this claim may sound hyperbolic, the facts bear it out. Indeed, the staggering number of children being killed in Gaza at such a fast rate led the secretary-general of the United Nations, Antonio Guterres, to state that "Gaza is becoming a graveyard for children. Hundreds of girls and boys are reportedly being killed or injured every day."[35]

Similarly, French President Emmanuel Macron—even while a staunch supporter and defender of Israel, going so far as to ban pro-Palestinian protests in France[36]—would lament a little more than a month into the Gaza operations: "Today, civilians are bombed—de facto. These babies, these ladies, these old people are bombed and killed. So there is no reason for that and no legitimacy. So we do urge Israel to stop."[37]

For its part, the charity Save the Children related as far back as October 29, 2023:

The number of children reported killed in Gaza in just three weeks has surpassed the annual number of children killed across the world's conflict zones since 2019.

Since October 7, more than 3,257 children have been reported killed, including at least 3,195 in Gaza, 33 in the West Bank, and 29 in Israel, according to the Ministries of Health in Gaza and Israel respectively. The number of children reported killed in just three weeks in Gaza is more than the number killed in armed conflict globally—across more than 20 countries—over the course of a whole year, for the last three years.[38]

By December 26, 2023, the number of children killed in Gaza had climbed to over 10,000.[39] And in addition to these dead, more than 9,000 children have been seriously injured in the conflict, with many of these losing at least one limb.[40] Incredibly, by December 29, UNICEF was reporting that at least 1,000 children in Gaza had limbs amputated without anesthesia.[41]

On November 11, 2023, Reuters reported that children were being killed at a staggering rate of one every ten minutes.[42] And, as Reuters further explained, the destruction of Gaza hospitals has only been exacerbating this horrendous situation. As Reuters continued, World Health Organization Director-General Tedros Adhanom Ghebreyesus told the United Nations Security Council that "Gaza's thirty-six hospitals and two-thirds of its primary healthcare centers were not functioning and those that were operating were way beyond their capacities, describing the healthcare system as being 'on its knees.'" The lack of hospital and healthcare center functioning, moreover, is far from accidental. From the very beginning of Israel's assault on Gaza, hospitals, clinics, and ambulances have been a main target of Israeli defense forces. While Israel at first attempted to deny that it was targeting hospitals—this, after around 500 civilians were killed as the result of the bombing of a Baptist-run hospital early on in the operations—its intentions and actions became undeniable in short order.

First of all, as to the bombing of the Baptist hospital, the *Jordan Times*, in an article titled "Israel's war on Gaza hospitals continues unabated," would later state the obvious: "Israeli warplanes first bombed the courtyard of the Al Ahli Baptist Hospital, where 500 displaced persons were killed instantly. Most of these were women and children. Despite the fact that the Israeli army tried to say it was not its doing, all the fingers pointed in its direction because of its continual bombing operations and strikes of homes and population centers. Ever since, Israel has been bombing these hospitals with no compunction under the eyes of the international community."[43]

As a consequence of all of this bombing of hospitals, 278 health care workers, including over one hundred doctors, had been killed in Gaza by December 19, 2023.[44]

The most notorious hospital assault came later when Israel attacked the giant, five-building Al-Shifa hospital in Gaza. As the *Washington Post* explained:

The targeting by a US ally of a compound housing hundreds of sick and dying patients and thousands of displaced people has no precedent in recent decades. The march on al-Shifa caused the hospital's operations to collapse. As Israeli troops closed in and fighting intensified, fuel ran out, supplies could not enter, and ambulances were unable to collect casualties from the streets.

Before troops entered the complex, doctors dug a mass grave for as many as 180 people, the United Nations said, citing hospital staff. The morgue had long since ceased to function. Several days later, when WHO medics arrived to evacuate those still inside, they said the place of healing had become a "death zone." At least 40 patients—including four premature babies—died in the days leading up to the raid and its aftermath, the United Nations said.

In the weeks since, other hospitals in Gaza have come under attack in ways that mirror what happened at al-Shifa—making the assault not just a watershed moment in the conflict, but a vital case study in Israel's adherence to the laws of war.

The *Washington Post*, moreover, did a detailed study of Israel's claims that it attacked the Al-Shifa hospital because it was allegedly being used as a Hamas command center and that Hamas was utilizing tunnels underneath the hospital to carry out their operations. These were claims bolstered by the Biden administration, which was quick to echo them. However, the *Washington Post* concluded that these allegations were not supported by the evidence. Thus, the *Washington Post* concluded that

- The rooms connected to the tunnel network discovered by IDF troops showed no immediate evidence of military use by Hamas.
- None of the five hospital buildings identified by [IDF spokesman Daniel] Hagari appeared to be connected to the tunnel network.
- There is no evidence that the tunnels could be accessed from inside hospital wards.

While the *Washington Post* does not say so, it is also important to note that, to the extent that there are tunnels under the Al-Shifa hospital (or what is left of it now), it's because Israel itself built them. Thus, as reporter Jeremy Scahill reported in *The Intercept* on November 21, 2023, it is "well known that there are, in fact, tunnels and rooms under Al-Shifa. We know that because Israel admits that it built them in the early 1980s. According to Israeli media reports, the underground facilities were designed by Tel Aviv architects Gershon Zippor and Benjamin Idelson."[45]

Israel continued to destroy other hospitals and to kill more children, including more babies in incubators. Thus, CNN reported on the terrible scene at the Al-Nasr hospital in early December,

> The scene inside the Al-Nasr hospital ICU ward is chilling. The tiny bodies of babies, several still attached to wires and tubes that were meant to keep them alive, decomposing in their hospital beds. Milk bottles and spare diapers still next to them on the sheets.
>
> The video inside the hospital was filmed on November 27 by Mohamed Baalousha, a Gaza reporter for UAE-based news outlet Al Mashhad. He shared an unblurred version with CNN, which shows the remains of at least four infants.
>
> Three of them appear to be still connected to hospital machines. The bodies of the babies appear to be darkening and disintegrating from decay, with little more than skeletons left in some of the beds. Flies and maggots are visibly crawling across the skin of one child.[46]

It deserves pointing out that the death of the Palestinian babies in the incubators, in addition to being especially grisly and troubling, is an important example of the West's projection of its own crimes upon others; of the fact that all of the West's accusations are in fact confessions. Thus, in the run-up to the first Gulf War in 1990, one of the big lies the United States used to justify the invasion of Iraq was the claim that Iraqi troops had thrown Kuwaiti babies out of incubators on to a hospital floor, thereby killing them. This allegation, just as the later WMD claims made to justify the second invasion of Iraq in 2003, was later debunked. Indeed, the *Washington Post* would later refer to this as "The Kuwaiti Incubator Hoax."[47]

But as usual, the damage had been done and the wars proceeded. Fast-forward to 2023, and it was in fact Israel, with the aiding and abetting of the United States, which was really killing babies in incubators. And yet, there was not the same outrage expressed in the mainstream media for this real crime as with the false claim years before. In addition, as for the allegations that Iraq had weapons of mass destruction—including the allegation, famously made by Colin Powell at the UN, that Iraq had acquired matériel to create a nuclear dirty bomb—the truth is that the only country in the Middle East that has nuclear weapons is Israel, which is violating international law by refusing to officially declare these weapons of mass destruction. But this seems to be of absolutely no concern to the powers that be or obsequious press in the West. Instead, they panic about the alleged attempt of Iran to create nuclear weapons, with Israel periodically assassinating Iranian nuclear scientists, even though the two successive Supreme Leaders of Iran have issued religious fatwas against the creation, maintenance, or use of such weapons as an offense to God.

And, there are the deaths, indeed murders, of well over 10,000 children in Gaza as of the time of this writing. After October 7, Israeli officials claimed that the Palestinian militants had killed, by beheading, forty babies, and have continued to trumpet this claim in order to justify its brutal operations in Gaza. As an excellent article in *Slate* states, "Forty beheaded babies. Can you imagine such a thing? The problem is that no one is quite sure if it is true."[48] With the passage of time, it indeed appears that this story is not true.

However, as *Slate* rightly opines, this claim, also repeated by Joe Biden himself who lied about actually seeing evidence of these dead babies, has been a necessary piece of war propaganda to dehumanize the Palestinian people and justify their destruction. Specifically, it has been used to somehow justify the verifiable killing of literally thousands of Palestinian children, many who have actually been beheaded, if not completely obliterated, by 2,000-pound bombs supplied by Uncle Sam. Unlike the alleged dead Israeli babies, one has access to literally hundreds of photos and videos online of dead Palestinian babies, and they just keep coming. But this seems to have had little impact on the West's willingness to continue backing the Israeli slaughter of innocents in Gaza.

One certainly gets the impression from all of this, and indeed from every conflict the United States has ever fought in the Middle East, that Arab lives are valued at a very tiny fraction of the lives of white Westerners. In the instant case, it appears that the lives of white Israeli children, even assuming the story of the forty beheaded Israeli children to be true, are perhaps 250 times more valuable in the eyes of Western audiences than that of Palestinian children. The dehumanization of Palestinians—a process begun long ago—has worked its evil magic to pave the way for genocide. And while there is finally some rupture in this dehumanization process for the first time since 1948, largely thanks to social media and little thanks to the mainstream press, this may very well be too late in coming to save the people of Gaza.

Alas, this is the Orwellian world in which we live, and this is how wars are justified and prosecuted by the nations of the world that consider themselves to be the "civilized nations."

Israel also cannot claim that its massive attacks on hospitals, refugee shelters, housing, refugee camps, and other civilian buildings and areas are somehow accidental. This is because the United States has been providing Israel with intelligence on where such buildings and areas are. As Aaron Maté, a journalist and son of Holocaust survivor Gabor Maté, explains, this fact establishes both the Israeli culpability in serious war crimes as well as the US complicity in these crimes:

> The scale of US complicity in the carnage grows with each passing day. On top of providing weaponry and diplomatic cover, the US has given Israel the GPS coordinates of medical facilities and humanitarian groups that Israeli forces have ended up bombing, according to *Politico*. The US claims that this location data was shared to help Israel avoid hitting these sites; instead, it appears that Israel has seen them as targets. Aid officials also report that Israel is abandoning deconfliction practices that were previously used to protect humanitarian groups. Despite this, the Biden administration is loosening the already lax controls on US military support for Israel, according to *The Intercept*.[49]

As Maté also points out, the Biden administration seems much more concerned about the potential bad press from the Israeli bombing of civilian targets than about the human toll of this bombing as evidenced by the administration's expressed worries about Israel's agreeing to a humanitarian pause for the purpose of trading hostages. Maté explains, "According to *Politico*, 'there was some concern in the administration about an unintended consequence of the pause: that it would allow journalists broader access to Gaza and the opportunity to further illuminate the devastation there and turn public opinion on Israel.'" Maté continues:

> The Biden team's concern is understandable: the devastation that they have supported in Gaza is without precedent in recent memory.
>
> The United Nation's top aid official, Martin Griffith, describes Gaza as "the worst ever" crisis that he has witnessed. "I don't think I have seen anything like this before," Griffith remarked. "It's complete and utter carnage." Former senior Pentagon analyst Marc Garlasco likewise describes Gaza as "beyond anything that I've seen in my career." With so many large bombs hitting a small and densely populated area, a historical precedent could only be found "back to Vietnam, or the Second World War," Garlasco says. As the *New York Times* notes, after ordering hundreds of thousands of Palestinians to leave their homes in northern Gaza for supposed refuge in the south, "Israel has continued to carry out airstrikes across the south with large munitions: 1,000- to 2,000-pound bombs."

Israel itself shares Biden's concern that its brutality would be brought to light. In order to reduce the chances of this, Israel has engaged in the unprecedented killing of journalists in theater, killing eighty journalists and media workers, and arresting twenty-five others as of the time of this writing—the most journalists killed in a conflict since 1992 when the Committee to Protect Journalists began counting such deaths.[50] This figure may in fact be a great underestimate of this tragedy, with Palestinian authorities estimating that the number of journalists killed, as of December 23, 2023, was at least 100.[51]

There appears to be consensus that the death and destruction being leveled against Gaza is unprecedented. For example, as the Associated Press (AP) reported on December 21, 2023, even as the bombs continued to rain down on Gaza:

> The Israeli military campaign in Gaza, experts say, now sits among the deadliest and most destructive in recent history.

In just over two months, the offensive has wreaked more destruction than the razing of Syria's Aleppo between 2012 and 2016, Ukraine's
Mariupol or, proportionally, the Allied bombing of Germany in World
War II. It has killed more civilians than the US-led coalition did in its
three-year campaign against Islamic State group.[52]

In addition to the thousands killed in Gaza, the AP cataloged the following destruction:

> Israel's offensive has destroyed over two-thirds of all structures in northern
> Gaza and a quarter of buildings in the southern area of Khan Younis. . . .
> That includes tens of thousands of homes as well as schools, hospitals,
> mosques and stores. U.N. monitors have said that about 70 percent of
> school buildings across Gaza have been damaged. At least 56 damaged
> schools served as shelters for displaced civilians. Israeli strikes damaged
> 110 mosques and three churches, the monitors said.

The devastation has been so massive, AP relates, that the very texture of
Gaza now looks much different from space than it did before October 7.
Indeed, it appears to have the same surface as the moon: just dust, rocks
and craters.

The *Washington Post* reached similar conclusions from its own research
and analysis of the evidence, stating on December 23, 2023:

> The evidence shows that Israel has carried out its war in Gaza at a pace and
> level of devastation that likely exceeds any recent conflict, destroying more
> buildings, in far less time, than were destroyed during the Syrian regime's
> battle for Aleppo from 2013 to 2016 and the US-led campaign to defeat
> the Islamic State in Mosul, Iraq, and Raqqa, Syria, in 2017.
>
> The *Post* also found that the Israeli military has conducted repeated
> and widespread airstrikes in proximity to hospitals, which are supposed
> to receive special protection under the laws of war. Satellite imagery
> reviewed by *Post* reporters revealed dozens of apparent craters near 17 of
> the 28 hospitals in northern Gaza, where the bombing and fighting were
> most intense during the first two months of war, including 10 craters

that suggested the use of bombs weighing 2,000 pounds, the largest in regular use.

"There's no safe space. Period," said Mirjana Spoljaric Egger, the president of the International Committee of the Red Cross, who visited Gaza on Dec. 4. "I haven't passed one street where I didn't see destruction of civilian infrastructure, including hospitals."[53]

Other evidence of Israel's genocidal intent against the people of Gaza includes its use of prohibited munitions against the population, such as white phosphorus. Human Rights Watch confirmed early on in the conflict the use of white phosphorus by Israel and condemned this use, stating:

White phosphorus, which can be used either for marking, signaling, and obscuring, or as a weapon to set fires that burn people and objects, has a significant incendiary effect that can severely burn people and set structures, fields, and other civilian objects in the vicinity on fire. The use of white phosphorus in Gaza, one of the most densely populated areas in the world, magnifies the risk to civilians and violates the international humanitarian law prohibition on putting civilians at unnecessary risk.

"Any time that white phosphorus is used in crowded civilian areas, it poses a high risk of excruciating burns and lifelong suffering," said Lama Fakih, Middle East and North Africa director at Human Rights Watch. "White phosphorus is unlawfully indiscriminate when airburst in populated urban areas, where it can burn down houses and cause egregious harm to civilians."[54]

While I think it is clear that there are at least three of the five enumerated acts of genocide in this case, I think there is a case to be made that there are indeed four, with the fourth being the forcible "transferring children of the group to another group." Thus, as of the time of this writing, there are now around 25,000 Gazan children who have been orphaned by Israel's war on Gaza.[55] And, as Reuters explains, many of these are not only left without parents; they are also left without any close relatives at all.[56] It is certain that the number of such orphans will be much higher by the time this war is over. Where will those children end up? I suspect many, numbering in the thousands, will not end up with their "group" (Palestinians), but likely in an orphanage or family abroad of "another group."

I am not the only one concerned about the forcible transfer of Palestinian children. Indeed, Euro-Med Monitor, on January 2, 2024, reported that this may be happening in a very direct and intentional way. As Euro-Med detailed:

> The Israeli army has abducted Palestinian children and transferred them out of the Gaza Strip, Euro-Med Human Rights Monitor said, as part of its genocide against Gazans that has been ongoing since 7 October. The rights group called on Israel to return the children to their parents.
>
> In light of the horrific crime of kidnapping children, as well as the recent mysterious disappearance of hundreds of Palestinian detainees from the Strip, Euro-Med Monitor stressed that the international community must bear its responsibilities and apply pressure to Israel in order to ensure the safe return of all victims.
>
> The Geneva-based organisation also stated that it takes very seriously the information published by Israeli Army Radio on 1 January 2024 regarding the kidnapping of a Palestinian infant from inside her Gaza family home by Israeli officer Harel Itach, a commander in the Givati Brigade, after the killing of her family members. The incident's date was not revealed.
>
> Following the news that the Israeli officer died on 22 December 2023 from injuries sustained during fighting in Gaza, a friend of Itach's disclosed the kidnapping incident, and said that the little girl's whereabouts remain unknown. Euro-Med Monitor expressed its deep fear and concern that the incident involving the officer and the Palestinian baby is not an isolated case. Numerous testimonies that the rights group has received say that the Israeli army regularly detains and transfers Palestinian children without disclosing their whereabouts.
>
> Furthermore, Euro-Med Monitor has been receiving alarming reports from many Palestinian families who have lost contact with their children. It said that these reports are mainly from areas where Israeli ground incursions are occurring.[57]

In its genocide case against Israel before the International Court of Justice (ICJ), South Africa asserts that the fifth enumerated act is also being committed against the people of Gaza—that is, the prevention of births of the group. As the *Washington Post* summarized this claim by South Africa "accuses Israel of preventing Palestinian births by displacing pregnant people, denying them access to food, water and care, and killing them."[58]

The South African genocide complaint is truly a tour de force and something that is worth reading in full to get a sense of the gravity of the crimes being committed by Israel in Gaza. Even while Israel is vigorously defending itself against the genocide case against it, and as US officials dismiss the complaint is "meritless," the Israeli newspaper *Haaretz*, in an editorial board editorial, admitted that this case should be a wake-up call for Israel. In this candid editorial, *Haaretz* explains:

> The fact that Israel is led by the most extremist government in its history, whose members talk about "wiping out Gaza," openly discuss the idea of transfer and call to occupy the Gaza Strip and to build settlements on it; and the fact that the public dialogue within Israel normalizes the killing of 50,000 or 100,000 Gaza residents, the starvation of a population and the withholding of humanitarian aid as an instrument of pressure on Hamas are liable to help the court in The Hague to attribute to Israel genocidal intent.
>
> Israelis do not hear themselves. Since the war began, lawmakers and cabinet members have repeatedly made statements that could be seen as indicating an intention to carry out crimes against humanity. On Tuesday MK Moshe Saada of Likud said: "As it is clear to everyone today that the right was correct about the Palestinian issue, now it's simple, you go anywhere [and] they tell you 'destroy them.'"
>
> When Finance Minister Bezalel Smotrich says "If there are 100,000 or 200,000 Arabs in Gaza and not 2 million, the entire discussion on 'the day after' will be different"; when Minister Orit Strock blasts the IDF for pilots' alleged refusal to bomb civilians; when National Security Minister Itamar Ben-Gvir calls for "a project to encourage the emigration of residents from Gaza"; when Minister Amichai Eliyahu says "dropping

an atom bomb on Gaza is one way"—Israelis may dismiss these things as cheap populism, but the world takes them seriously.

Ultimately, I would contend, the manner in which Israel is prosecuting its assault on Gaza with US support—with the infliction of huge civilian body counts and casualties; the destruction of civilian infrastructure, including medical facilities; and the denial of water, food and medicine—provides sufficient evidence of genocidal intent. However, lest there be any doubt, numerous statements by Israeli officials, such as the ones cited by the *Haaretz* editorial, make clear such intent.

Indeed, the Center for Constitutional Rights (CCR) has sued the Biden administration for failing to prevent the genocide in Gaza—as the United States is explicitly required to do as a signatory to the 1948 Genocide Convention—and for actual complicity in this genocide through its material, intelligence, logistical, political, and diplomatic support for Israel's war efforts.

In its legal complaint, the CCR details a non-exhaustive list of public statements by Israeli officials that prove their genocidal intent. As the CCR explains in its complaint, "Evidence of Israeli government officials' specific intent to undertake and persist in undertaking . . . genocidal acts is significant and overt and sits on top of a longer history of Israeli dispossession and killing of Palestinians in Gaza as well as the West Bank. This evidence pronounced by senior Israeli officials, including the prime minister, the president and the minister of defense, belies any legitimate claim to 'self-defense.'"

The CCR continues, "Indeed, this evidence—that Israel also fails to distinguish between a civilian population and armed groups—reflects the kind of dehumanizing and totalizing rhetoric that genocide scholars and historians, including those opining in this action, recognize typically precede, accompany, and continue to fuel genocidal acts. It is designed to characterize victims as deserving of destruction, humiliation, and dispossession and correspondingly unworthy of elementary principles of humanity and foundational principles of international law."

And keep in mind that nearly half of the people Israeli officials are marking for "destruction, humiliation and dispossession" are children.

As the CCR details:

The statements . . . include: On October 7, Prime Minister Benjamin
Netanyahu ordered 2.2 million Palestinians in Gaza to "get out now" as
"[Israel] will be everywhere and with all our might." Two days later, the
Israeli Defense Minister announced, "I have ordered a complete siege on
the Gaza Strip. There will be no electricity, no food, no fuel, everything
is closed" and "We are fighting human animals and we are acting accord-
ingly." The next day, the Israeli Major General who heads the Coordinator
of Government Activities in the Territories ("COGAT") echoed him, stating, "Human animals must be treated as such. There will be no electricity
and no water [in Gaza], there will only be destruction. You wanted hell,
you will get hell." On October 10, the Israel Defense Forces spokesperson
announced dropping "hundreds of tons of bombs," as "the emphasis is on
damage and not on accuracy."

On October 12, when the Israeli military ordered the more than
one million Palestinians in northern Gaza to "evacuate" to southern
Gaza within 24 hours, the Minister of Energy and Infrastructure said,
"Humanitarian aid to Gaza? No electrical switch will be turned on, no
water hydrant will be opened and no fuel truck will enter until the Israeli
abductees are returned home." He later said "They will not receive a drop
of water or a single battery until they leave the world." On October 13,
Israeli President Isaac Herzog announced: "It is an entire nation out there
that is responsible. It is not true this rhetoric about civilians not being
aware, not involved. It's absolutely not true." Israeli Defense Minister
Gallant stated: "Gaza won't return to what it was before. We will eliminate everything." On October 15, as Israeli airstrikes killed over 2,670
Palestinian civilians, including 724 children, Prime Minister Netanyahu
stated that Israeli soldiers "understand the scope of the mission" and stand
ready "to defeat the bloodthirsty monsters who have risen against [Israel]
to destroy us."

On October 29, as the number of people killed by Israel in Gaza
rose to 8,000, Prime Minister Netanyahu invoked the story of Amalek
in the Bible to justify Israel's assault on Gaza, stating, "You must
remember what Amalek has done to you, says our Holy Bible, and

we do remember, and we are fighting." In the Bible, God commands the extermination of Amalekite men, women, children, and animals, and this commandment has been described by one scholar as "divinely mandated genocide."[59]

Other such statements, detailed by Common Dreams, include the Knesset member and former Public Diplomacy Minister Galit Distal Atbaryan stating in a Facebook post that "Israeli officials must invest all their energy 'in one thing: erasing all of Gaza from the face of the Earth.'"[60] In addition, "Former military officer Eliyahu Yossian said the IDF must enter Gaza "with the aim of revenge, zero morality, maximum corpses," and told Channel 14 in Israel on Monday that "there is no population in Gaza, there are 2.5 million terrorists."

For his part, Israeli journalist Zvi Yehezkeli, speaking to Tel Aviv–based Channel 13 . . . , said: "In my opinion, the IDF should have launched a more fatal attack, with 100,000 killed in the beginning" and then proceeded from there.[61] And then there is Amichai Eliyahu, ironically Israel's heritage minister, who celebrated the destruction in Gaza on Twitter, stating, "North Gaza, more beautiful than ever. Blow up and flatten everything, delightful. After we are done, allocate the lands of Gaza to the soldiers fighting and the settlers who lived in Gush Katif."[62] He was the same Israeli minister who earlier stated that Israel should consider just nuking Gaza into oblivion.

Tellingly, other such statements have been made even before the Palestinian militant attacks on October 7, 2023. As Common Dreams continues,

> Earlier this year [2023], Israeli Finance Minister Bezalel Smotrich said at an event in Paris, "There's no such thing as Palestinians because there's no such thing as a Palestinian people." He also said the West Bank town of Huwara should be "wiped out" by "the state of Israel," while Prime Minister Benjamin Netanyahu presented a map of what he called "The New Middle East"—without the illegally occupied West Bank, Gaza, or East Jerusalem—at the United Nations General Assembly just weeks before the onslaught in Gaza began.

It is important to note that, as explained by the *Washington Post* in "Welcome to the New, New Middle East," many reasonably believe that the October 7 attacks by the Palestinian militants were significantly motivated by Netanyahu's provocative presentation of the map to the UN of "The New Middle East"—a map that conspicuously and tellingly excluded all of Palestine.[63]

Netanyahu had presented this map as his vision of the future after the normalization of relations between Israel and other Arab states, mostly notably Saudi Arabia, with which he was in the process of negotiating at the time. The Palestinians correctly perceived this as Netanyahu's intention to literally wipe them off the map, and their attack was intended to disrupt this plan, though it may have ultimately provoked Israel into carrying it out quicker than scheduled.

I would also argue that the Israeli treatment of deceased Palestinians demonstrates an extreme level of dehumanization of Palestinians and is therefore further evidence of genocidal intent.

The Swiss-based Euro-Med Monitor details the grisly details of Israel's handling of Palestinian corpses during the current military operations, which Euro-Med itself refers to as a genocide:

> The Israeli army has been holding the bodies of dozens of Palestinians killed during its genocide in the Gaza Strip beginning on 7 October, and Euro-Med Human Rights Monitor has called for the creation of an independent international investigation committee into organ theft suspicions.
>
> Euro-Med Monitor has documented the Israeli army's confiscation of dozens of dead bodies from Al-Shifa Medical Complex and the Indonesian Hospital in the northern Gaza Strip, and others from the vicinity of the so-called "safe corridor" (Salah al-Din Road) designated for displaced people heading to the central and southern parts of the Strip.
>
> According to Euro-Med Monitor, the Israeli army also dug up and confiscated the bodies from a mass grave that was established more than 10 days ago in one of the Al-Shifa Medical Complex's courtyards. . . .
>
> Concerns about organ theft from the corpses were brought up by Euro-Med Monitor, which cited reports from medical professionals in Gaza who quickly examined a few bodies after their release. These

medical professionals found evidence of organ theft, including missing cochleas and corneas as well as other vital organs like livers, kidneys, and hearts. . . .

Israel has a long history of holding onto the bodies of dead Palestinians, Euro-Med Monitor said, as it holds the remains of at least 145 Palestinians in its morgues and approximately 255 in its "Numbers Cemetery," which is near the Jordanian border and off-limits to the public, in addition to 75 missing people who have not been identified by Israel. . . .

According to the human rights group, Israel has recently made it lawful to hold dead Palestinians' bodies and steal their organs. One such decision is the 2019 Israeli Supreme Court ruling that permits the military ruler to temporarily bury the bodies in what is known as the "Numbers Cemetery." By the end of 2021, the Israeli Knesset (or Parliament) had passed laws allowing the army and police to hold onto the bodies of dead Palestinians.

There have been reports in recent years of the unlawful use of Palestinian corpses held by Israel, including the theft of organs and their use in Israeli university medical school labs.

Israeli doctor Meira Weiss disclosed in her book *Over Their Dead Bodies* that organs taken from dead Palestinians were utilized in medical research at Israeli universities' medical faculties and were transplanted into Jewish-Israeli patients' bodies. Even more concerning are admissions made by Yehuda Hess, the former director of Israel's Abu Kabir Institute of Forensic Medicine, about the theft of human tissues, organs, and skin from dead Palestinians over a period of time without their relatives' knowledge or approval.

Israel is thought to be the biggest hub for the illegal global trade in human organs, according to a 2008 investigation by the American CNN network, which also revealed that Israel participated in the theft of organs from dead Palestinians for illegal use.

Euro-Med Monitor confirmed that Israel is the only country that systematically holds the dead bodies of those it kills and is classified as one of the world's biggest hubs for the illegal trade of human organs under the pretext of "security deterrence" and in total violation of international charters and agreements.[64]

At the end of December 2023, a number of news outlets, including the progressive Jewish website *Mondoweiss*,[65] reported that eighty Palestinian bodies taken by Israelis from graves and morgues in Gaza were returned to Gaza with organs missing, and that it was presumed that these organs had been harvested.

This reminds me of what my friend Fadia Barghouti told me about an incident that happened way back in 1999 when she was a high school student growing up in a village in the West Bank. Thus, she told me that a classmate of hers was killed by Israeli forces inside the school at that time. His body was then taken away by the Israelis in a helicopter. When the body was returned to the family, it showed a giant incision in the torso from the chest to the waist where it appeared organs had been removed, and the boy's eyes were replaced with glass marbles. As Fadia explained, this devastated the boy's mother who would never emotionally recover.

All of the above has led a number of experts to conclude that Israel is in the process of carrying out genocide in Gaza. Thus, both Israeli Holocaust Scholar Raz Segal and UN official Craig Mokhiber—who has studied genocide for decades and who resigned from the New York Office of the UN High Commissioner for Human Rights over the UN's failure to protect the people in Gaza—referred to Israel's assault on Gaza as a "textbook case of genocide."[66]

For his part, Raz Segal, an associate professor of Holocaust and genocide studies and endowed professor in the study of modern genocide at Stockton University in New Jersey, wrote an illuminating op-ed for the *LA Times* in which he details his reasons for concluding that Israel's military operations against Gaza constitute genocide. In this article, he explains:

> Now, Israeli politics, society and media are awash with annihilatory language against Palestinians in Gaza, from the dehumanizing language of Defense Minister Yoav Gallant's "total siege" order, where he referred to Palestinians as "human animals," and journalists who have called to turn Gaza "into a slaughterhouse," to banners on bridges in Tel Aviv that call "to annihilate Gaza." Israeli state leaders, ministers in the war cabinet and senior army officers—people with command authority—have used such language dozens of times since Oct. 7 in a way that constitutes clear

"intent to destroy," according to the United Nations Convention on the Prevention and Punishment of the Crime of Genocide.[67] (Emphasis in original.)

Significantly, Raz Segal argues eloquently against the accusation that the criticism of Israel and its mistreatment of Palestinians is somehow anti-Semitic. As Mr. Segal writes:

> I spoke about this last weekend at Kol Tzedek, my Jewish congregation in Philadelphia, from my perspective as an Israeli and Jewish Holocaust and genocide studies scholar. I noted that Israel's mass violence against Palestinians stems from a new Jewish identity, tied to the creation of Israel in 1948: Jewish supremacy. I also noted that white supremacists in Europe and the US find Israeli state practices of Jewish supremacy inspiring even as they hate Jews in Europe and the US deeply. While Israel and its allies strive to portray any criticism of Israeli policies and violence against Palestinians as antisemitism, some of Israel's greatest supporters, such as American white supremacist Richard Spencer or Hungarian Prime Minister Viktor Orbán, are fierce antisemites. . . .
>
> Imagining possible futures, beyond Israel's Jewish supremacy, then, is for me a political act rooted in Jewish histories and Jewish identities that are not far removed from us. They point to the urgent need to forefront Palestinian voices and experiences, to humanize Palestinians in the face of attempts to demonize and silence them, to call for a cease-fire and the return of all the hostages held in Gaza and the political prisoners held in Israel and to insist on truth, justice and equality for everyone between the Jordan River and the Mediterranean Sea.[68]

These words are critical at this time when those demonstrating against the racist/genocidal treatment of Palestinians are themselves grotesquely labeled as somehow racist.

Seven UN Special rapporteurs warned that "The situation in Gaza has reached a catastrophic tipping point," noting the "dire need for food, water, medicine, fuel, and essential supplies and the risk of looming health hazards."[69] These rapporteurs further stated, "We remain convinced that the Palestinian people are at grave risk of genocide," and "The time for action is now. Israel's allies also bear responsibility and must act now to prevent its disastrous course of action."

The question then arises why the United States, under a Democratic administration that often professes concern for human rights and international law, is not only failing to stop this genocide, but why it is actively aiding and abetting it by, for example, planning to send an emergency $14 billion to Israel—a figure over three times higher than the United States sends to Israel in a year—to prosecute the war.

It appears that the reasons for this have nothing to do with religion or with lofty goals such as democracy and human rights, but instead are very typical geopolitical concerns involving the control of the most precious resource in the Middle East—energy—and the goal to ensure that the US's adversaries (most notably Russia and China) do not gain control over it. As has been the case for over seventy-five years, Israel is a key to advancing such geopolitical interests.

A major interest the United States, and other Western nations, have in the current conflict is the major natural gas reserves recently discovered off the Mediterranean coast of Gaza. And Hamas and the Palestinian people themselves are huge obstacles to control over these reserves.

The independent muckraking journal, *The Canada Files*, explains that the US Geological Survey estimates

> that the Levant Basin Province contains 'a mean of 1.7 billion barrels of recoverable oil and a mean of 122 trillion cubic feet of recoverable gas.' The northern end of the Levant Basin lies near the Syrian port of Tartus, runs down the coastlines of Lebanon, Israel, and the Gaza Strip (part of the occupied Palestinian territory), and west towards Cyprus. This means that the Eastern Mediterranean will be one of the most important areas in the world for the production of natural gas over the decades to come, which is why Israel chose to attack and seal off Gaza [in 2007] in order to steal, extract and sell natural gas which belongs to the Palestinians.[70]

Canada Files further explains that the siege of Gaza that began in 2007 and the subsequent Cast Lead operations by Israel against Gaza in 2008–2009 were motivated by the fact that the newly elected Hamas government was a threat to the control of Israel, the UK, and the United States over the Palestinians' gas reserves off the coast of Gaza.

As *Canada Files* relates,

> In 1999, Yasser Arafat gave a permit to a British consortium to extract the natural gas. This would have given 10 per cent of the proceeds for the sale of the gas to the Palestinian Authority. This would have been used to develop the Palestinian economy and government programs. Israel blocked the proceedings.
>
> Thanks to Tony Blair, who was Prime Minister of the UK at the time, a new deal was prepared with Israel, which eliminated three-quarters of future royalties owed to the Palestinians, shifting their reduced share to an international account controlled by Washington and London. However, after having won the 2006 election in Gaza, Hamas refused to accept this new Israel-UK-US deal. The Hamas government denounced it as thievery and demanded that it be renegotiated. That was the cue for Israel to attack Gaza.

And attack Gaza it did, with Israel carrying out the 2008 Cast Lead Operations detailed in the Introduction to this book.

Lest one believe this analysis to be just another conspiracy theory, on November 20, 2023—weeks into the conflict that began on October 7— the Israeli newspaper *Haaretz* reported that President Biden had sent Amos Hochstein, President Biden's energy security advisor, to Israel to discuss the urgency of developing the natural gas fields off the coast of Gaza. As *Haaretz* explained, "Israel gave preliminary approval for the development of a gas field off Gaza's coast in June [2023], stressing it would require security coordination with both the PA [Palestinian Authority] and Egypt. The Gaza Marine field, nearly twenty miles off Gaza's coast, has remained undeveloped despite holding an estimated 1 trillion cubic feet of natural gas."[71]

While Hochstein is quoted in the article as saying that the gas reserves belong to the Palestinians and should be used for the development of the Palestinians' economy, these appear to be empty words. This is so because if Israel gets its way in displacing all of the Palestinians from Gaza and into

Egypt's Sinai desert and Israel takes over Gaza for itself, the gas reserves will effectively become Israel's. And, the fact that, as *The Intercept* reported, Biden was working behind the scenes to remove any limits—including human rights and humanitarian limits—on Israel's access to US weapons and ammunition reserves even before Hochstein was sent to Israel to talk about developing the gas fields, it appears that the United States is more than prepared to help Israel obtain its goals in Gaza at all costs, even if this means ethnic cleansing and genocide.

Indeed, *The Intercept* cited experts who made it clear that Biden's efforts to lift the arms and munitions restrictions would remove nearly all ability of the US government to curb Israel's ongoing crimes in Gaza. Thus, *The Intercept* explained:

> Biden is looking to lift virtually all the meaningful restrictions on the stockpile and the transfer of its arms to Israel, with plans to remove limitations to obsolete or surplus weapons, waive an annual spending cap on replenishing the stockpile, remove weapon-specific restrictions, and curtail congressional oversight. . . .
>
> "The Biden administration's supplemental budget request would further undermine oversight and accountability even as US support enables an Israeli campaign that has killed thousands of children," said [John Ramming] Chappell, of Center for Civilians in Conflict. . . .
>
> "Taken as a package," said William Hartung, an arms expert at the Quincy Institute for Responsible Statecraft, "it is extraordinary, and it will make it much harder for Congress or the public to monitor US arms transfers to Israel, even as the Israeli government has engaged in massive attacks on civilians, some of which constitute war crimes."[72]

The other, related interest that both the United States and Israel share is the desire to complete the long-planned Ben Gurion Canal through Israel—a Canal that would run right through Gaza and would be used for the shipment of cherished commodities, most notably oil. As commentator Sekarsari Sugihartono wrote in the online journal *Modern Diplomacy* on November 24, 2023, "Many allegations are focused on the Israeli attack on Gaza and this is certainly bigger than just revenge for the alleged Hamas attack. One of them is Israel's motivation in launching their long-term project, namely the Ben Gurion Project. This project is a long-planned canal construction project from the 1960s, initiated by David Ben-Gurion. If this project is successfully built, the potential of this canal will be very high, competing with the Suez Canal."[73]

As Sugihartono relates, the Suez Canal brings in over $9 billion of revenue to Egypt every year and has long been a source of conflict between Egypt—which has close ties with Russia and is poised to join the BRICS alliance—and the West, which has coveted control over this canal just as the United States coveted control over a canal through Panama in the late nineteenth and early twentieth century, and as the United States still covets control over a possible canal through Nicaragua to this very day.

As Sugihartono explains, "The idea of The Ben Gurion Canal Project has been around for a long time, but it emerged again in the Abrahamic Accords between Israel and Morocco, Sudan, Bahrain, UAE. On April 2, 2021, Israel stated that they would start this project in June 2021. This has not been successfully implemented and the existence of the Gaza Strip could be one of the main reasons. . . . Many parties speculate about the connection between the construction of this project and the IDF attack on Gaza. If Gaza is leveled and all the Palestinian people have been allocated, then the construction of this project will save more costs and shorten the route."

The importance of such trade routes, particularly for the transport of oil and other energy products, cannot be overemphasized. Indeed, recall that one of the motivations behind the Balfour Declaration of 1917 was the desire of the Western imperial powers, and especially Britain, to create a friendly state in the Middle East that could take control of the Suez Canal. In 1956, Israel then went to war with Egypt in furtherance of this goal to control the Suez Canal—a canal to which it is now trying to build an alternative. In the 1970s, President Jimmy Carter, the "human rights President," went on to announce what would later come to be known as the Carter Doctrine—a doctrine pursuant to which the United States reserves to itself the right to militarily intervene at any time to protect its national interests (i.e., control over crude oil) in the Persian Gulf.

And at present, what is the major concern that President Biden seems willing to go to war over in the Middle East? Certainly not protecting the

Palestinians. Rather, his priority has been in trying to militarily protect access through the Red Sea in the face of Yemen's successful attempt to prevent any ships from traveling to or from Israel through that route. The result of Yemen's actions has been a general deterrence of all shipping through the Red Sea. Yemen is now attempting to prevent shipping through the Suez Canal as well. As of the time of this writing, the United States, betraying its true priorities, has engaged in sixty bombing raids against Yemen to the end of protecting shipping lanes and commerce.

It must be noted that Yemen's act of solidarity with the Palestinians is truly remarkable given that Yemen has been the victim of a US-backed Saudi War since 2015 that led to the greatest humanitarian crisis in the world in Yemen—a crisis now certainly eclipsed by the crisis in Gaza. And Yemen has made it clear that it is doing this in order to fulfill its obligation under Article 1 of the Genocide Convention, which places the obligation upon all nations to prevent and stop genocide.

That Yemen, one of the poorest countries in the region to begin with, has the wherewithal to act in this noble manner, even as it is still suffering from brutal war—a war Biden had promised at the outset of his presidency to stop supporting, but which he never did—puts to shame the rest of the world's nations, which have barely lifted a finger to stop the genocide in Gaza.

In short, the United States and Israel have practical reasons for carrying out the ethnic cleansing and genocide of the Palestinians living in Gaza. And it is important to note that, as a legal matter, these practical reasons do not detract from the finding that a genocide is being carried out in Gaza. This is so because it is well-settled in international law that if a party has genocidal intent—that is, the intent to destroy in whole in part a national, ethnical, or religious group, as such—genocide is still established even if that party has other, more mundane motives for its violence against this group. And indeed, it is the usual case that such dual motives exist in the mind of the genocidaire who is often motivated by both racial hatred as well as practical concerns, such as gaining and holding on to political power by scapegoating certain racial or ethnic groups, or simply gaining coveted territory.

CHAPTER 5

GENOCIDE IN THE WEST BANK

To understand the Palestinian-Israeli conflict, look at who cultivates the olive tree, and look at who destroys it.
                                                            —Palestinian saying

There are two kinds of people in the world—those who love and create, and those who hate and destroy.
                                    —José Martí, Cuban poet and revolutionary

The other half of current-day Palestine is the West Bank that is currently ruled by the Palestinian Authority (PA)—a government that, it can fairly be said, cooperates closely with Israel, including in the repressive security arrangements in the West Bank. Hamas is not the governing party in West Bank and has little influence there. And yet, this has not spared the West Bank from the escalation of violence by Israel against the people there since October 7. This is further evidence, I would submit, of Israel's genocidal intent. That is, as far as Israel is concerned, the problem with the people in the West Bank is the same with the people in Gaza—it's because they are Palestinian; not because they are associated with Hamas. Or, in the words of my friend Fadia Barghouti from the West Bank: "It is not our resistance that they oppose; it is our existence."

I decided to visit the West Bank during the post-October 7 hostilities, and so flew to Amman, Jordan on November 30, and then traveled by land across the Dead Sea to the West Bank.

As I was planning my trip, I communicated with a few of my friends there, including my former student Yara who I became friends with while she was in Pittsburgh. During the COVID-19 pandemic, Yara was stuck in Pittsburgh for a few months while waiting to return home, and we would sometimes go out to Ritter's—Pittsburgh's historic, sixty-year-old diner—to chat, enjoy their great omelets, and pass the time. Yara would later tell me that she couldn't stand most American food, but she loved Ritter's.

Before my travels, I excitedly sent Yara a photo of a painting I have by a Palestinian artist named Maysaa Ghazi of the Dome of the Rock in Jerusalem—one of the most iconic sites in the Holy Land and located on the Al Aqsa Mosque compound. I've been buying paintings from Maysaa for almost two years, and I absolutely love them. My buying paintings from her has supported her and her big family in Gaza, and it has given me paintings that enrich my home and indeed my life. Maysaa's sister Heba Zegout was also a painter who I got to know.

I say "was" because Heba, along with two of her four children, were sadly killed early on in Israel's post-October 7 operations against Gaza when the IDF bombed her home. Heba had direct messaged me on Facebook Messenger just before being killed. She sent me a photo of her children cowering in a dark room along with two photos of a tower of smoke rising up in the distance outside her apartment window. Along with this, she wrote, "We are sitting with the children. There is bombing. I feel afraid." I never heard from Heba again.

I found out shortly after on social media of Heba's death. Maysaa would tell me about the death of Heba's two children and the fact that her two remaining children were now orphans seeking shelter in a school somewhere. Maysaa had no way of reaching these two children because of the war. Maysaa and I have remained in touch. She and her family have gone from place to place to find shelter from the bombings, with Maysaa becoming increasingly desperate and despairing about the situation. I often don't know what to say in response to Maysaa's obvious pain except that she remains in my thoughts and prayers. This seems wholly inadequate to the situation, but I don't know what else to say. Maysaa and her family, like all other Gazans, have virtually no way of leaving Gaza, though she desperately wants to. They are all trapped, simply waiting to die or to survive in some postapocalyptic hellscape.

I told Yara that I wake up to Maysaa's painting of the Dome of the Rock every morning and that I was excited to be able to see it for real. Her response really shocked me. Yara told me that she had never visited it before even though she lives in the West Bank. This is because of the draconian restrictions on travel that Israel, with the cooperation of the PA, imposes upon Palestinians in their own territory. Because she holds a green pass, instead of a blue one, she cannot travel to one of the most important holy sites in her religion.

As Al Jazeera explains, the pass system Israel created back in 1967 after the Six-Day War—a war in which Israel displaced 300,000 Palestinians in what is known as the Naksa (defeat), gained significant land from the Palestinians and significant control over the land they still have—is still in place to this day in both Gaza and the West Bank.[1]

Those with blue passes—Palestinians living in East Jerusalem and Israel—have relatively full freedom of movement through, and to and from, the Palestinian territories, while the remainder of the Palestinians in Gaza and the West Bank have green passes that greatly restrict their movement. As Al Jazeera also points out, it is the Israeli military that issues these passes, though in the West Bank the PA, playing a purely administrative/secretarial role, prints theses passes out for the Palestinians. As Al Jazeera further explains, all Palestinians must have their IDs with them at all times for internal travel, "due to the check-points interspersed within the territory. This system has drawn comparisons to the [passbook] laws in apartheid South Africa designed by whites to control the movement of blacks and mixed-race people and to keep them in inferior positions."

Israelis, of course, have full freedom of movement. In planning my trip, I was told that an Israeli car with a yellow plate would pick me up on the Israeli/Palestinian side of the bridge that crosses to Jordan, and that I would therefore not have to stop through the many Israeli checkpoints within the West Bank to get to my destination.

Yara, with her green pass, has never been able to travel to Jerusalem, with the sole exception being the time she was allowed to go there to obtain her visa from the US Embassy (newly moved from Tel Aviv) to travel to Pittsburgh to study. Even then, she had to leave Jerusalem by 6 p.m. She said that, ultimately, she was able to walk around the Old City for ten minutes, and then went home. Given new rules that Israel has imposed, it is doubtful that Yara would even been able to step foot in the Old City today.

Yara kindly ordered me a cab with the coveted yellow, Israeli tag to pick me up on the Israeli side of the King Hussain Bridge that connects Jordan to Israel/Palestine. First, I had to get through Israeli Customs. I was told by a number of others who have visited Israel/Palestine that this can be a very frustrating process. Some of my friends have in fact been deported by Israeli Customs before ever entering, and others, though allowed in, had to endure long hours of questioning beforehand. I myself had no trouble at all. I told the customs official that I wanted to visit the Holy Land during Advent, and this seemed to do the trick. I was immediately let in. Another American behind me, a gray-haired, kindly looking African American man, was not as lucky. He was told to take his passport and sit down with others waiting for interrogation by customs. I immediately left and don't know what ultimately happened to him.

When I recounted this story to some friends in the West Bank later, they opined that the fact that the other American was Black probably was why he was stopped for questioning while I was allowed to enter without hassle. They indicated that racial profiling is the norm at Israeli check-points and border crossings.

While it is impossible to know if this was the case in my fellow American's case, it is certainly possible. Indeed, Jews in Israel from African countries, most commonly Ethiopian, are treated disparately from white Jews. Thus, they have been given the worst land in the desert region of northern Israel. In addition, as *Haaretz*, an Israeli newspaper, has reported, Israel has admitted to sterilizing Ethiopian Jews against their will in order to keep their numbers down. And, apparently, this has worked. As *Haaretz* explains in the article, "Israel Admits Ethiopian Women Were Given Birth Control Shots," on an Educational Television program journalist Gal Gabbay revealed the results of interviews with 35 Ethiopian immigrants. The women's testimony could help explain the almost 50-percent decline over the past 10 years in the birth rate of Israel's Ethiopian community. According to the program, while the women were still in transit camps in Ethiopia they were sometimes intimidated or threatened into taking the injection. "They told us they are inoculations," said one of the women interviewed. "They told us people who frequently give birth suffer. We took it every three months. We said we didn't want to."[2]

It should be noted that such a practice is a clear case of genocide, violating Article II (d) of the Genocide Convention, which forbids "imposing measures intended to prevent births within" a national, ethnic or racial group in order to destroy in whole or in part that group (here, Ethiopians). Clearly, this was the intent, and indeed the result of these forced birth control measures.

In addition, Israel has (quite illegally) sent planeloads of Jewish asylum seekers from various African countries to Uganda for the same reason they have sterilized Ethiopians—to keep the proportion of Blacks in Israel at comfortably low levels.[3]

This is a good segue for discussing one of Netanyahu's possible plans for the ethnically cleansed of Gaza—to send thousands to the Democratic Republic of the Congo (DNC). As the *Times of Israel* explained in discussing this plan for what Israeli officials euphemistically call a "voluntary migration" plan, "Congo has high levels of inequality, and 52.5 percent of the population lives below the poverty line according to the World Food Programme,"[4] meaning that this would hardly be a hospitable place to send any immigrants and would further strain the DRC's resources for providing for the Congolese. It also should be noted that the DRC has been the scene of one of the most terrible genocides in world history, with over six million Congolese being killed in a bloodbath carried out with Western, and in particular US, backing since the mid-1990s. Famously, the violence in the DRC has been marked by mass rapes at an unprecedented level. This is but another reminder of the West's hollow concerns about human rights and genocide.[5] And the fact that Israel would consider sending Palestinians into such a situation shows how little it regards the lives of Palestinians.

Craig Mokhiber—the head of the New York office of the UN High Commission for Human Rights (UNCHR) who quit in response to the failure of the UNCHR and other UN bodies to adequately respond to what he saw as a "textbook case" of genocide in Gaza after October 7, 2023—explained to *Electronic Intifada* that he began to warn about the impending genocide against the Palestinians back in early 2023 in light of pogroms that were being carried out then in the West Bank by Israeli settlers.[6]

Many of these pogroms—a term most commonly associated with the mob violence against Jews in Europe in the late nineteenth and early twentieth century—have been carried out against the Palestinian shepherding communities (the Bedouins) who can be seen in the desert area along the highway between the King Hussein bridge and Jerusalem and Ramallah. These communities invariably have ramshackle homes made of tin and a big water tank used for drinking, bathing, and livestock. Sometimes, Israeli settlers will intentionally pollute even these meager water supplies.[7]

As the Israeli Information Center for Human Rights in the Occupied Territories (Center) explains in a recent report titled "The pogroms are working—the transfer is happening," "In the past two years, at least six West Bank communities have been displaced" as a result of the pogroms. As the Center relates,

> Dozens of Palestinian shepherding communities are scattered across the West Bank. Because Israel considers these communities to be "unrecognized," it does not allow them to connect to the water and power grids or the road system. Israel also considers all structures built in these communities—homes, public buildings and agricultural structures—"illegal" and issues demolition orders against them, which, in some cases, it executes. Some structures have been demolished and rebuilt several times.
>
> In recent years, settlers have built dozens of outposts and small farms near these communities with the aid of the state, and since then, violence against Palestinians living in the area has increased, reaching new heights

under the current government. These violent attacks, which have become a terrifying daily routine, include settlers driving Palestinian shepherds and farmers out of pasturelands and farm fields, physically assaulting residents of the communities, entering their homes in the middle of the night, setting fire to Palestinian property, scaring livestock, destroying crops, theft and road closures. Palestinian residents have also reported water tank valves being opened and settler flocks being led to drink in Palestinian water reservoirs.[8]

As some have pointed out, these pogroms look a lot like the acts of American settlers during the early years of the Republic that involved organized mob violence against the Indigenous population. They also look a lot like the orchestrated mob attacks against predominantly Black towns in the United States, most famously the Tulsa race massacre of 1921. And indeed, it is ironic that many of the settlers now carrying out these pogroms are Americans. As Dr. Brian Feeney, writing in the *Irish News* put it colorfully, "There are over 500,000 American colonists living in Israel, some of them the most racist, aggressive, and violent in killing Palestinians and stealing their land. They seem to think they're in the Dakotas in the 1870s or Oklahoma in 1890 exterminating Sioux and Cherokee."[9]

These pogroms are not merely directed against the shepherding communities. Rather, they have been occurring throughout the West Bank, and on a regular basis.

Writing in July 2023, Amos N. Guiora, a retired lieutenant colonel in the IDF's Judge Advocate Generals Corps., wrote an op-ed for *The Hill* in which he decried these pogroms. As Guiora wrote, these pogroms "are becoming a daily occurrence, unfortunately, with the proverbial 'nod and wink' approval of a complicit government whose condemnations are merely rhetorical."[10] As Guiora lamented, "The word "pogrom,' which cuts deep for Jews, is correctly used to describe the actions of the Jewish settlers. I am convinced, based on both my IDF experience and academic research, that the settlers committing the pogroms are terrorists and must be held accountable. As widely reported in the press, this is not happening. That is an anathema to the rule of law." Guiora went so far as to say that the United States should reconsider its assistance to Israel in response to this state-supported violence against the Palestinians in the West Bank.

As noted elsewhere in this book, Israel, and indeed the collective West, have decided to punish the Palestinians for the crimes of Nazi Germany, and to even impose the guilt for these crimes upon them. What's more, Israel has decided to punish the Palestinians for these crimes of others by doing unto them many of things done to Jews back in Europe, including the carrying out of pogroms against them, imprisoning them in concentration camps and ghettos, and subjecting them to genocide.

One of the worst cases of pogrom violence was in the town of Huwara in the West Bank. CNN did a report on this incident "in which hundreds of Israeli settlers rampaged through Huwara and surrounding Palestinian towns in the occupied West Bank on February 26, [2023] leaving at least one Palestinian man dead and hundreds of others injured."[11] As CNN explained, "What unfolded was violence so brutal that the Israeli military commander for the West Bank called it a 'pogrom,'" but still, as CNN found, the IDF did nothing to protect the Palestinians from this violence. And this should not be surprising, for the anti-Palestinian hatred of the settlers—hatred that clearly rises to the level of genocidal animus—is shared by Israeli officials at the highest ranks.

Thus, as another CNN piece explains, "While carrying out this violence, some of the settlers screamed 'death to Arabs, we will wipe out Huwara.' Three days after settlers tried to do exactly that, far-right Israeli Finance Minister Bezalel Smotrich, himself a settler leader, repeated the phrase on stage at a media conference. 'I think the village of Huwara needs to be erased' he told a reporter. . . . 'I think the State of Israel needs to do this, and not—God forbid—private citizens.'"[12]

And, this violence, both by settlers as well as the IDF, has only accelerated after October 7, 2023. As Al Jazeera explained in a Christmas-day article, in addition to Israeli forces killing hundreds of Palestinians in the West Bank since October 7, attacks by Israeli settlers have also increased there. Al Jazeera further reported:

At least 700,000 Israeli settlers live in illegal, fortified, Jewish-only settlements across the West Bank and East Jerusalem, the majority of which were built either entirely or partially on private Palestinian land.

Painting of Heba Zagout, by permission of her family.

Deena Eldahour, a Palestinian American, speaks at a protest in Pittsburgh. She has lost seventy family members in Gaza since October 7.

Fadia Barghouti points to the plaque bearing her family name on the ancient palace in her village of Deir Ghassan.

Yahya Reemawi (now eighteen) at his home in the village of Beit Reema after being released from his months of imprisonment for reasons still unknown to him.

The family of Malek Barghouti stand at their home in front of a banner with his image. Malek had been killed just a week before, his death killing the dreams of the family with him.

The birthplace of Jesus Christ at the Church of the Nativity in Bethlehem.

Refugee camp just south of Bethlehem.

Part of the endless separation wall in Ramallah.

Dome of the Rock at the Al-Aqsa compound, Old City, Jerusalem.

Uri Davis, who generously took me to Bethlehem.

My friend Abir at the Sabra and Shatila refugee camp in
Beirut, Lebanon, where she was born.

My friend Amal shows me a map of a Palestine in 1948 before the Nakba.

Beautiful Maaloula, Syria, one of the last cities in the world where Aramaic, the language of Jesus, is spoken. I was surprised to learn that Hezbollah helped save this Christian city from the Western-backed Free Syria Army.

Attacks, which have increased exponentially over the past three months, include shootings, stabbings, rock throwing and beatings, as well as arson and serious damage to homes, vehicles and agricultural land.

The United Nations noted that "in nearly half of all incidents, Israeli forces were either accompanying or actively supporting the attackers."[13]

The first city one sees when crossing the King Hussein Bridge into the West Bank is the walled city of Jericho—the oldest continuously-inhabited city in the world. It is mostly inhabited by Palestinians and indeed is under the Palestinian Authority as per the Oslo Accords. Still, Jericho contains ancient Jewish synagogues that remain undisturbed and which have been well-maintained. Jericho is also at the lowest land elevation in the world at over 500 meters below sea level. Jericho is known for its pure water, which is even mentioned in the Bible as the product of a miracle, and it is thought to have healing properties to this day. Most of the water I drank on my stay in the West Bank was bottled in Jericho.

At the time I was visiting the West Bank, the Israeli government was warning tourists not to visit Jericho because of increased hostilities there. These hostilities were being caused by illegal incursions of Israeli troops into the city. On December 23, 2023, for example, it was reported that "several [Israeli] military vehicles stormed the city and its [refugee] camps, broke into homes in both camps and roamed the streets, sparking protests."[14]

The first person I met in the West Bank was Fadia Barghouti, an amazing woman from the village of Deir Ghassana, one of the oldest villages in Palestine. Fadia met me at a cafe in Ramallah and would later host me in Deir Ghassana and the adjacent village of Beit Reima, which together form the municipality of Bani Zaid. Deir Ghassan is one of twenty-four feudal villages (known as Thrown Villages) going back centuries.[15]

The story of the Barghouti's is emblematic of the story of Palestine. The Barghouti's are a clan of Bani Zaid, "a Bedouin tribe . . . who came from Saudi Arabia in the eleventh century. Some of them took part in Salah Eddin al-Ayyubi's campaign to conquer Jerusalem against the Crusaders. After winning, Salah Eddin decided to reward this tribe and convince them to stay in Palestine, so he gifted 'Bani Zeid' the territory of Deir Ghassanah, Beit Rima, and other neighboring villages."

While in Deir Ghassana, Fadia showed me an old castle, the Palace of Saleh Al-Barghouti, which bears her family name. A Palestinian tourist guide describes this palace as follows:

> One of the oldest and most powerful clans of the Bani Zeid tribe was the wealthy noble family of al-Barghouti. The clan consisted of nine branches whose collective power extended beyond the Bani Zeid sheikhdom to the coastal plain of Palestine.
>
> In 1602, they built their one-floor palace at the centre of Deir Ghassanah as a sign of their power. Two hundred fifty years later, Sheikh Saleh al-Barghouti, at the top of his power, renovated the palace and enlarged it.[16]

Fadia explained to me that Israelis have stolen part of the village and even antiquities from the village. She even pointed out a beautiful, ornate door of the palace, decorated with stars, which the Israelis tried to steal. Fadia joked, "They think anything with a star on it is theirs."

Once a royal family, the Barghoutis are now one of many Palestinian families who suffer periodic arrests and killings at the hands of the Israelis who now dominate their daily life. Indeed, while at the palace, Fadia pointed out a graffiti painting on the palace wall of one of her relatives, Nasir Barghouti, who had been unceremoniously gunned down by Israeli forces just one month before.

While Fadia lives in Deir Ghassana, she works in Ramallah, which is only fifteen miles south of Deir Ghassana. However, because Israel has totally enclosed her village with a fence, allowing for only one way in and out, Fadia's commute has gone from a mere twenty minutes to now over an hour. She said that if the Israelis close the gate to her village, which they periodically do, people cannot even leave to go to the hospital. Many women have given birth at the gate, in a car or at home, and sometimes the baby has died.

Fadia, who has a master's in English as a Second Language, is a supervisor of English language instruction for the Palestinian Authority (PA) Ministry of Education. She observes, teaches, and trains English language teachers and has done so for thirty years. Fadia was nominated to run in legislative elections in 2021 before these elections were canceled by Israel and the PA.

Fadia is a mother of three boys and one girl. At one time or another, her two older sons have been arrested by Israeli forces. Currently, both her husband and son Basel are in Israeli prisons.

Her husband, Mahmoud (age 56), was arrested eighteen months ago. He is an accountant and Hamas political member. Fadia made a point to tell me that he is not in the military wing. Mahmoud is still being held even though an Israeli judge concluded that he is not a threat and should have been released months ago.

Fadia's son Amro now lives in Dubai. He had been arrested by the PA and Israel as the result of his student activism at the university. When he was released, he fled the country.

Her son Basel (age 22) was arrested on October 23 for demonstrating and for his membership in the Islamic Gathering, a Hamas youth group. Basel had been in his last year at college where he was studying computer engineering. He was arrested at home at 3 a.m.—a typical time for such arrests to be made. Twenty Israeli soldiers broke down the door of their family home in Deir Ghassana. They entered the home shouting, grabbed Basel, and threw him on the floor. They ransacked and destroyed the home. They took Basel's phone, computers, and USB.

An Israeli intelligence officer entered and said, "all of you should be punished. Hamas will be smashed." He turned to Fadia and said, "women like you should be raped like Hamas raped women. When you were in Gaza, you should have been bombed." He also said Hamas is just like ISIS. He proceeded to break a framed photo of her husband and posted a photo of the broken picture on his Facebook page.

Basel was ultimately put into administrative detention. They claim he is a "security danger." They have a secret file on him that can only be looked at by the judge.

Before October 7, Fadia visited her husband once a month. She has not seen her husband since October 7, and she has not seen her son even once. There is no writing or calling. Her husband and son are not even meeting with their lawyers for fear that they could be beaten or killed on the way to seeing them. These fears indeed seem well-founded.

Fadia explains that three of her female friends have been released as part of the prisoner exchange in November. All three were beaten in prison. They only received two meager meals a day. As Fadia explains, she has heard other prisoners report of rapes and sexual assaults while in Israeli jails.

Fadia mentioned to me the case of Mohammed Nazzal (age eighteen) who had both of his wrists broken by Israeli prison guards just before being released in the prisoner exchange. The BBC reported on this case shortly thereafter as well as other reports of prisoner abuse. As the BBC explained, they spoke with six former prisoners, all of whom said they were beaten in prison in the weeks following October 7. In addition, one female prisoner reported being threatened with rape. Also, the BBC reported: "The Palestinian Prisoners Society says some guards are alleged to have urinated on handcuffed prisoners. And that six prisoners have died in Israeli custody in the past seven weeks."[17]

While together, Fadia and I spoke generally about the situation of Palestinians under occupation. She explained very calmly and seemingly without anger about the plight of her people. She related that the Israelis "stole the best land and still fight us for a bunch of rocks. They won't even leave us in peace with the little we have." Still, she explains, while Israelis are given many incentives to live here, many still leave, while the Palestinians who live here under terrible conditions continue to stay.

For Israelis, "we are the others," Fadia laments, "who can be mistreated as if not even human. One Israeli official even said it is unfair to animals to compare us to them."

She told me about the Paris Agreement between the PLO and Israel that gave Israel incredible economic concessions and control over the water and other resources. She believes that the Oslo and Paris accords have led to a situation worse than the Nakba for the Palestinian people. A number of Palestinians I have talked to share this opinion. And indeed, it was only after Oslo and Paris that the walls and fences and gates were built by the Israelis; it was only after these agreements that the system of apartheid was reinforced and perfected with concrete and steel. And it was only after these agreements that Gaza and the West Bank, only a half hour drive from each other at one point, were cut off from each other.

Fadia made it clear who the Palestinians' main antagonist is. As she said, echoing the opinion of many Palestinians, *"We are not fighting Israel; we are fighting the United States."*

Fadia, who appeared to be the matriarch of her village, and indeed the surrounding villages as well, took me around to meet as many people as possible so that I could get a sense of what the Palestinians were going through at that time. The only break we had was for lunch. She had a huge lunch prepared for me, which consisted of two main dishes and rice. She slow-cooked the meal as we were going about our day. There is no way that a Palestinian would let me go through the day without a home-cooked meal.

The first family we met was that of Malek Barghouti—yes, another Barghouti. Apparently, there are about 30,000 Barghoutis throughout Palestine.

As we approached the home, we could see a giant banner of Malek hanging at the front of the house. Malek had just been killed by Israeli forces the week before. Malek is just one of hundreds of Palestinians killed in the West Bank since October 7. As the *Wall Street Journal* explained on January 19, 2024,

> Since Israel launched its response to the deadly Hamas-led Oct. 7 attack, 357 Palestinians, of whom 90 were children, have been killed across the West Bank, including East Jerusalem, according to the United Nations. Five Israelis, including four members of the security forces, have been killed in the West Bank over the same period, the U.N. said.
>
> Israeli security officials refer to the West Bank as a third front in the war, after Gaza and the country's northern border with Lebanon, where Israeli forces clash routinely with Hezbollah fighters and Palestinian militants.[18]

These figures are worth contemplating—357 Palestinians killed (ninety of them children) to five Israelis (four of whom were security forces). While Israel claims ad nauseum that it is at eternal risk of existential violence—indeed of a second Holocaust—at the hands of the Palestinians, somehow it is always the Palestinians who are doing the lion's share of the dying at the hands of the Israelis. Again, Israel's accusations are in fact confessions.

Malek's family of seven, consisting of three boys (including Malek) and two girls, invited us into their home and served us coffee and candies. They then explained what happened to Malek.

Malek was seventeen years old and in his last year of high school. He played football and was a sweet and kind boy who everyone loved. He dreamed of becoming a police officer for the PA. His dream was to get married and move in next door to the family. The family was waiting for him to become an adult and to change their lives with more financial support and grandchildren. His death killed their dreams of happiness, they explained.

Malek was killed at 4:00 in the morning of November 28, 2023. He was at home when he heard a disturbance outside. He just went to see what was happening. He did not throw stones, they emphasized. Israeli soldiers had arrested a Palestinian in the village. While Malek was simply watching this arrest, the soldiers shot him four times with banned "butterfly bullets" even though he was just a bystander standing 100 to 200 meters away. This is typical that Palestinians are killed at long range, they explained. They shot him, took away their captive (Nasim Barghouti) and then immediately withdrew. They made sure Malek was dead and never called for medical help. They just left his body in the street.

Red Cross and human rights groups came, but they did nothing, the family complained. No one was ever punished, and no one ever will be. As Malek's father said, "This is the daily life for Palestinians. The act of killing is continuous. The message is that any resistance will exact a price." As an example, the father mentioned the case of the man with special needs who was killed in Hebron on December 5—a death I had heard about in the news.

The next person we visited was the mayor of Kafr Al-Dik, Mohammad Naji. Israeli settlers had invaded this village earlier in the year as reported by the Palestinian News and Information Agency. As the agency reported on July 1, 2023:

> Extremist Israeli settlers attacked Palestinian farmers today while they working in their own lands in the town of Kafr Al-Dik, in the occupied West Bank province of Salfit, according to local sources.

Abdullah Al-Dik, a local Palestinian resident, told WAFA that armed Israeli settlers brutally assaulted his father and uncle after raiding their agricultural lands on the outskirts of the town.

He said an Israeli army force later arrived at the scene, and instead of arresting the attacking settlers, they opened fire in the air and arrested his father, Ahmad Al-Dik, and assaulted his uncle, Mahmoud.[19]

Naji explained that 6,500 people (all Palestinians) live in the village of 15,500 acres. As he related, 13,500 acres are considered to be under the authority of Israeli forces (in what is known as Area C). In Area C, the Palestinians are not allowed to make any improvements to the land. They cannot pave roads or remodel buildings. They can't even cut down trees on their own property.

The remaining 2,000 acres are in Area B, which means that Israeli forces can technically only enter here with good cause and with advance notice. Of these 2,000 acres, only 1,800 can be used for building homes by Palestinians. Four Israeli settlements and an Israeli industrial zone have been built above the village on the top of the hills. These settlements are growing and are taken from the land of the village.

All of the sewage of the industrial sector rolls down into the village. This is clearly deliberate, Naji explains. The Israelis could manage this differently if they wanted, but they have chosen to pollute the village. Some people are suffering cancer due to the waste, and the soil and water supply are being destroyed.

As Fadia explained about her village, Israelis can close the gates of Kafr Al-Dik whenever they want and lock them in.

Three Palestinian homes in the village were recently demolished by the Israeli authorities, including the home of Naji's son. The homes were built without permits from the Israelis, but the Israelis never give them the permits. Naji twice helped his son apply for a permit and twice was inevitably denied.

In the village, there are 2,000 acres of olive trees, Naji explained. This year, Palestinians were prevented by Israelis from harvesting the olives. The Israelis shot at them if they tried. As Fadia explained to me, some of these olive trees are ancient, dating back to the Roman Empire. Indeed, such trees, which continue to bear olives, are called "Romans." The olive trees are a staple of Palestinian life and culture and have been so for centuries. Knowing this, the Israelis have destroyed around 800,000 olive trees, many of them ancient, since 1967 when Israel began to occupy Gaza and the West Bank.[20]

In considering the case for Palestine, the protection of the land, the environment, the agriculture, and especially the olive trees weighs strongly on the side of a free and independent Palestinian state.

The next family we visited was that of Yahya Reemawi in the village of Beit Rima. At least six Palestinians (including two brothers) have been killed by Israeli forces in this small village since October 7, 2023. Two of these killed were children.

Yahya is eighteen years old. He was seventeen when he was arrested, and in his final weeks of high school—a very typical time for young men to be arrested as this is a way to interrupt their studies. Yahya was in administrative detention for eight months and was released shortly before my visit on December 7. He was clearly still in shock from the experience as his mother noted.

Yahya was arrested for allegedly "planning for terrorist action" and "trying to build resistance groups." According to his family, he is a mild-mannered, peaceful student. Because of his secret file, he doesn't even know what the factual basis for his arrest was, and he most likely never will.

Once arrested, the Israeli troops made him walk eight miles to the base up the mountains. They handcuffed him and beat him as he walked. They then took him to an isolated area for two days where he was put into solitary confinement. He was interrogated for fifteen minutes, and then sent to prison.

He was brought before a judge, but the proceedings were in Hebrew and were not translated. He had no idea what they were saying.

Before October 7, the conditions were not too bad, Yahya explained to me. However, after October 7, "special troops" as he called them came in and took everything from them—radios, TVs, fans, brooms, all of their clothing except what they wore on their backs. They took their pillows, mattresses, and bedding, leaving them with only one blanket. They were allowed to wash five minutes every four or five days. They had no hot water and no electricity for anything but the lights. The lights were on from 6 p.m. to midnight. They had to drink from the sink of the filthy bathrooms.

After October 7, the prison cells went from six prisoners in a cell to twelve or thirteen. They then received only one plate of rice and white beans per cell to share among them, plus some water. They were literally starving. In the morning, they got a little yogurt and a little piece of bread. If they ever got meat, which was seldom, it was poorly cooked, and they would not eat it. They received no medication, with the exception of one Advil tablet.

From time to time, the special troops came in with sticks, guns with rubber bullets, and stun guns. They would then pick one cell at random and beat everyone inside.

When they were brought to court for interrogation, they were beaten the whole time en route. They were also tortured when transferred from one prison to another.

The guards attacked a Gazan prisoner with dogs and sticks. They could often hear the Gazan prisoners, who were generally treated much more brutally than the West Bank prisoners were, screaming.

Yahya could meet with his family only after the first three months of imprisonment. After that, they visited him once a month. But after October 7, there was no contact at all.

He was finally released a week ago. When he was cleared for release, they did not tell him so at first. They pulled him out and told him he was being interrogated. They had him remove all of his clothes. They told him that if there is a Hamas flag at his family's celebration at home, or any "wrong people," he would be punished and sent back to jail. They threatened to tear down his home. Also, they confiscated all of his identification documents, so he cannot move around.

Yahya's brother Mubtasem (age twenty-two) remains in jail. Mubtasem was arrested as they were all sleeping. He had been living in Jordan and was arrested while visiting for their other brother's wedding. Their grandfather had died in prison. This family experience is, sadly, typical for Palestinians in the West Bank.

While in the West Bank, I spent a day in Jerusalem, which is one of the most troubled areas right now because of Israel's attempts to take full control of that city, including East Jerusalem, which is legally considered occupied Palestinian territory.

I set out for Jerusalem from Ramallah in a taxi bearing the Israeli yellow license plate. While the distance between these two cities is nominal—about eight miles—it took me almost two hours and $100 to get there that day. This is because the closest checkpoint between the two cities—Qalandia—was shut down due to an IDF incursion into the nearby Palestinian refugee camp. I would find out only later what that was all about.

My host in Jerusalem was Zakaria Odeh, a Palestinian human rights activist who is also a resident of Jerusalem. Zakaria has spent a short time in jail because of his human rights advocacy.

Zakaria seemed tired and stressed, and was being weighed down by the constant indignities and pressure of the occupation in Jerusalem that he is advocating against. Still, he was incredibly generous with his time and even canceled a meeting at the last minute so he could spend more time with me in Jerusalem.

Incredibly, though Zakaria is a Jerusalem resident and was even born there, he is not allowed into the Old City—the area with some of the most important religious sites (Muslim, Christian, and Jewish) in the world. While we viewed the Old City, at least from afar, and saw some of the holy sites—the Mount of Olives, Golgotha where Jesus was crucified and died, and the Tomb of the Blessed Virgin—most of our tour was unorthodox, focusing on how Israel is attempting to ethnically cleanse Palestinians from Jerusalem and gain dominion over the city.

Zakaria showed me numerous Palestinian homes and neighborhoods that had been demolished or were now slated for demolition. As Zakaria explained, these demolitions have accelerated greatly since October 7, and the main pretext for demolitions is that the homes were not built with the required permit. But as he explains, the Israelis charge $40,000 for such a permit, which is simply impossible for most Palestinians to pay, and that is the point.

When a Palestinian home is demolished, the Palestinians living there must either demolish the home themselves or be forced to pay the Israelis to do it for them. This reminds me of the "bullet fee" levied by dictatorial states such as Nazi Germany in which the families of people accused of being traitors and sentenced to death were required to pay for the bullets used in the execution.

Zakaria also pointed out a number of homes Israelis had stolen from Palestinians. Most of these are easily identified with Israeli flags hung from the homes in order to ostentatiously show the transfer of ownership. Many of us recall watching in horror what is an all-too common occurrence in Jerusalem when a video surfaced of a man from Brooklyn who came to take the home from a Palestinian family in East Jerusalem who had lived there for generations. The man raised his hands in exasperation when the family protested, saying, "If I don't steal your home, someone else will."[21]

By now, as Zakaria explained, 200,000 Israeli settlers now live in East Jerusalem, which used to be exclusively Palestinian as of 1967 when Israel began its occupation of the West Bank and Jerusalem.

No real tour of Jerusalem would be complete without seeing the giant walls that Israel has erected since the Oslo Accords of 1993 to (1) segregate Israelis from Palestinians; and (2) to maintain demographic dominance in Jerusalem. As for the latter goal, Zakaria explained to me, for example, how a wall was built to change the boundaries of Jerusalem in order to remove 160,000 Palestinian Jerusalem residents from the city limits. At the same time, Israel has also expanded the boundaries of Jerusalem into some areas, creating "Greater Jerusalem," in order to bring over 150,000 Israelis into Jerusalem. In other words, Israel is engaged in a demographic gerrymandering of Jerusalem.

In addition, some of the walls have been built *between* Palestinian communities in Jerusalem, cutting off families from each other. Now, it can take two hours for families once living next door to each other to visit each other.

CHAPTER 6

THE UNITED STATES, ISRAEL, AND THE MODERN-DAY PERSECUTION OF THE CHRISTIAN CHURCH

Creative destruction is our middle name, both within our society and abroad. We tear down the old order every day, from business to science, literature, art, architecture, and cinema to politics and the law. Our enemies have always hated this whirlwind of energy and creativity, which menaces their traditions (whatever they may be) and shames them for the inability to keep pace. Seeing America undo traditional societies, they fear us, for they do not wish to be undone. . . . We must destroy them to advance our historic mission.[1]

—Michael Ledeen, US neocon

The most exciting day I had on my trip to the West Bank was my journey to Bethlehem, which took place just as Advent was beginning. As someone raised Catholic who still has connections, though a bit conflicted, to the faith, I was excited to see the birthplace of Jesus. However, I was told by a number of people that getting to Bethlehem would be very difficult if not impossible given the number of Israeli checkpoints on the way and the increased vigilance of the Israeli security forces after October 7.

When eating dinner with new friends in Ramallah on my first night there, I said in an offhand way that I would like to go to Bethlehem but that this was probably not possible. One of my companions, Uri Davis, upon saying goodbye for the night, said that he would take me. Uri, who is a seventy-eight-year-old dual citizen of Israel and Great Britain, and whose family heritage in Palestine goes back many generations, said that he has been doing this for fifty years and knew how to get me there.

During our dinner, Uri gave me a lot of information about and many insights into the Israeli/Palestinian conflict. One thing he urged me to look into, and which I had never heard of before, was the Kafr Qasim massacre of 1956.

Kafr Qasim is within the boundaries of Israel and sits on the border just east of the West Bank (at that time, a protectorate of Jordan). While this is a city populated by Palestinians, the Palestinians there are Israeli citizens. Palestinians say that a town like Kafr Qasim is "in 1948," meaning that it is a Palestinian town outside the borders of Gaza and the West Bank—the small areas now officially designated for Palestinians—but within the borders of what was Palestine before the founding of Israel in 1948.

The Interactive Encyclopedia of the Palestinian Question (Interactive Encyclopedia) explains that, as of 1956, "Israel's Palestinian citizens (whose population numbered 160,000) were subjected to military rule and suffered a range of restrictions, including repeated pressures to leave their homeland. A number of Israeli leaders were waiting for an opportunity (for instance, a new round of war with Arab states) to trigger a mass exodus. The 1956 massacre—which was perpetrated during the Tripartite Aggression against Egypt—was deliberate, planned at the highest levels, and aimed at terrorizing the population . . . so that they would flee. However, this goal was not achieved; residents did not leave."[2]

The Interactive Encyclopedia describes the massacre as follows:

On Monday, 29 October 1956, the Israeli government and military decided to impose a curfew on the Arab villages near the border with Jordan. At 4:30 p.m. that day, a border police sergeant informed the mayor of the village of Kafr Qasim that a curfew would be imposed starting at 5 p.m. that evening. Hundreds of villagers who had left home in the morning to go to work had no way of knowing about the curfew until they returned home. The soldiers tasked with carrying out the order in

Kafr Qasim were informed that they "should shoot to kill at any person seen outside their home after 17:00, making no distinction between men, women, children and those returning from outside the village." When villagers returned to their homes after 5 p.m., border police stopped them on the western side of the village. Soldiers made them get out of their vehicles and cars, or off their bicycles, and began shooting at them at close range. They killed forty-nine residents of Kafr Qasim (including children) in cold blood in just one hour.

When the Israeli government and military command learned that such a huge number of villagers had been killed, including men, women, and children, they used a variety of tactics to attempt to cover up the horrific massacre. But slowly, news spread that a massacre had been carried out by soldiers in their military uniforms and under clear orders from the high military command to fire on citizens returning home. Journalists, activists, communist members of the Knesset, and others went to the village (despite the presence of military checkpoints) to investigate and inform the public. This forced the Israeli government to bring the perpetrators to court. However, instead of bringing the high command to trial, the soldiers in the field were put on trial and given light sentences only.

As the Interactive Encyclopedia explains, "By 1960, all the soldiers had been released from prison after their sentences were reduced or they had received pardons. Members of the cabinet, including the prime minister, expressed solidarity with the killers, and 'compensated them' for their time in prison by giving them official appointments, including to positions of responsibility over Arab citizens in the city of Lydda and elsewhere."

In short, this episode demonstrates that, for all of its claims of being a democracy, Israel is in fact not a democracy for its Palestinian population that is treated as second class citizens, with their very lives being expendable.

Uri and I set out toward Bethlehem from Ramallah at just after 8:00 a.m. two days later. The driving distance between these two cities is a mere eighteen miles, meaning that it should take no longer than a half an hour in normal circumstances, but nothing in Palestine is normal. To bypass some checkpoints, and especially those that Uri knows have computers with which our backgrounds could be checked, we took a circuitous path. Bethlehem is almost due south from Ramallah, and it would seemingly make most sense to drive into Bethlehem through its northern gate. Instead, we drove all the way around the ugly walls of Bethlehem—walls erected by Israel to cut the city off from Israeli settlements nearby and to control entry and exit—and entered at the most southern gate.

Uri and I saw a procession of young men carrying the draped corpse of a slain Palestinian on the way. This was in the refugee camp located near the Qalandia checkpoint between Ramallah and Jerusalem. The day before, the military had entered this camp and ended up killing one young man (most likely the individual we saw being carried through the streets) and injuring several others. They also threw away food being sold by vendors there. This was all caught on video.

In total, five Palestinians had been killed by the Israelis in the West Bank that day. And, on the day we traveled to Bethlehem, there were more fatalities. Indeed, we had planned to go to Hebron as well that day but were prevented by the fact that Israelis had invaded the city that very morning, killing a special needs person at point-blank range. The Israeli military also clashed with Palestinians in Bethlehem the night before we visited there.

While we crossed three checkpoints on the way to the southern gate, none of these were manned—a lucky break for us. When we reached the southern gate, we were greeted by a giant red sign with white lettering that reads, in Hebrew, Arabic, and English:

> THIS ROAD LEADS TO AREA "A"
> UNDER THE PALESTINIAN AUTHORITY
> THE ENTRANCE FOR ISRAELI
> CITIZENS IS FORBIDDEN,
> DANGEROUS TO YOUR LIVES
> AND IS AGAINST THE ISRAELI LAW

The designation of cities and villages as Area A (where Israelis may never pass), B (where Israelis may only pass if necessary and then with notice) and C (which are under Israeli security authority) was agreed to between the Israeli government and the Fatah Party as part of the Oslo Accords. As the sign clearly indicates, cities in Area A are forbidden for Israelis, including Israeli troops, to enter. However, that law is now a dead letter, with Israeli troop and Israeli settlers entering any area they wish at any time to cause mayhem.

Uri was indeed the person to take me to Bethlehem. First, because he is an Israeli citizen, he has the yellow license plate, which allows him to travel freely throughout Israel/Palestine. However, because he has a British passport, he can enter Area A despite being an Israeli. And also, like me, he is white as the driven snow, and as Uri explained to me, the Israeli guards at the gates usually utilize "racial profiling" to decide who goes in. And sure enough, when we got to the southern gate, the Israeli guards, seeing two white guys with white hair, waved us in without even checking our documents.

All told, it took around three hours total (excluding a brief stop in Jerusalem to meet with one of Uri's lawyers—Lea Tsemel, an Israeli and a Jew who has bravely spent her entire legal career defending Palestinian political prisoners) to travel the eighteen miles from Ramallah to Bethlehem. But in truth, we were lucky to get there at all. This is so because, for all Uri has going for him, he has strong negatives.

Thus, while he is a Jew, an Israeli, and a Brit, he is also a high-ranking member of the Fatah Party—the party of Yasir Arafat and of the governing Palestinian Authority. Uri, who was born in this land before 1948 and whose family has lived here for much longer wrote a book back in 1987 accusing Israel of being an apartheid state. As Uri told me, he owes loyalty to no state; his only loyalty is to the Universal Declaration of Human Rights. Uri himself was nervous as we came to every guard post, reminding me of the story we were to tell if we were questioned—that we were pilgrims going to see the birthplace of Christ. The benefit of this story was that it happened to be true.

For Palestinians without the yellow license plate (generally, only Palestinians born in Jerusalem would have this) this would be an impossible trip. And even if they had the coveted yellow tag, their skin color and Palestinian background could easily get them harassed, turned around or worse, for every interaction they have with armed Israelis can result in arrest, physical assault, or even death. If it is not obvious already, I as a foreign tourist traveling on a foreign passport have more freedom of movement (indeed, nearly total) than Palestinians whose families have lived on this land for centuries.

Because Uri is so essential to my story, and really the story of Israel and Palestine, and because he was key to my ability to visit Bethlehem, I'll allow him to speak for himself so you, dear reader, can get a sense of this amazing man; of his intellect and his irreverent sense of humor. Following is a letter he sent to King Charles III in May 2023 that gives one a good sense of who Uri is. Uri kindly gave me permission to reprint this here:

I write in my capacity as a concerned human being of Jewish and of European origins born in Jerusalem in 1943 who happens to be a dual citizen of apartheid Israel and the (lacking) constitutional Monarchy of the United Kingdom of Great Britain and Northern Ireland. At the outset I wish to add that I am fully aware that as a constitutional Monarch, Your Majesty (as a Defender of Faiths) does not intervene in any political or personal disputes.

Though it may seem prima facie that the Subject of this letter, the footnotes below and my life-time journey (Summary Biographical Note 2023, enclosed) are quintessentially political, in retrospect I recognize that all of such strategic choices as I made throughout my life-time have been guided by the voice of my conscience and by the quintessentially civil values of the UN Universal Declaration of Human Rights/UDHR (as clearly distinct from the domain of the political). Specifically, I propose to frame this letter in terms of Articles 13 through 17:

Article 13
1. Everyone has the right to freedom of movement and residence within the borders of each state.
2. Everyone has the right to leave any country, including his own, and to return to his country.

Article 14
1. Everyone has the right to seek and to enjoy in other countries asylum from persecution.

2. This right may not be invoked in the case of prosecutions genuinely arising from non-political crimes or from acts contrary to the purposes and principles of the United Nations.

Article 15

1. Everyone has the right to a nationality.
2. No one shall be arbitrarily deprived of his nationality nor denied the right to change his nationality.

Article 16

1. Men and women of full age, without any limitation due to race, nationality or religion, have the right to marry and to found a family. They are entitled to equal rights as to marriage, during marriage and at its dissolution.
2. Marriage shall be entered into only with the free and full consent of the intending spouses.
3. The family is the natural and fundamental group unit of society and is entitled to protection by society and the State.

Article 17

1. Everyone has the right to own property alone as well as in association with others.
2. No one shall be arbitrarily deprived of his property.

Given the above, I hope Your Majesty is able to accept my assertion that underpinning the apartheid Israel/indigenous Palestinian-Arab conflict there are a fundamentally humanitarian civil issues of justice and equality of rights (with political implications) notably property rights, specifically the property rights of Dr Kholoud al-Ajarma, in respect of which, as a constitutional Monarch, Your Majesty may—nay, ought to intervene as distinct from political issues (with humanitarian civil issues of justice and equality of rights implications).

Your Majesty as a concerned successor of H M George V and I as a concerned British citizen are not guilty of the war-crimes perpetrated by the British Mandate in Palestine—but Your Majesty (as a Defender of Faiths and as successor Monarch) and I (inter alia as a concerned British citizen of Jewish origin) have a responsibility (on a UDHR civil humanitarian basis) not to turn our back when a specific case is brought to our attention, namely: The case of the property rights of Dr Kholoud al-Ajarma in the apartheid Israel ethnically cleansed Palestinian village of 'Ajjur, the ruins of which are veiled by a park named "The British Park", planted and developed as a gift of the Jewish National Fund of Great Britain.

To my understanding, the right to property as defined in the UDHR is a fundamental civil human right (regardless of its political implications). In this connection, I wonder whether Your Majesty would consider applying Your Majesty's prerogative as the Sovereign of the United Kingdom and Northern Ireland (as well as the Monarch and Head of State of the Commonwealth realms) and engage with the JNF with the view to removing the sponsorship of the UK from the JNF park in question and suspending Your Majesty's response to the Invitation extended to you by the President of apartheid Israel so long as the fundamental civil inheritance rights of Dr Khoulud al-Ajarma in her family land in the said ethnically cleansed Palestinian village of 'Ajjur are officially recovered and registered with the Israel military occupation Land Registry (otherwise known as Tabu).

In this connection, notwithstanding my ambivalence in respect of political systems based upon the undivided sovereignty or rule of a single person . . . I cannot but express my respect for your late mother, H M Queen Elizabeth II, who throughout her long reign refrained from visiting apartheid Israel. As reported in the report in *The New York Times*, "Following her visit to Jordan in 1984, the queen raised some alarm among British Jews" due to "sympathetic comments she had made about the plight of the Palestinians and her seeming disapproval of Israeli actions. . . ."

With all good wishes
Sincerely
Dr Uri Davis

Uri refers in the letter to Israel as an apartheid state, and indeed, he wrote a book back in 1987 with the title, *Israel: An Apartheid State*. This makes Uri a very early proponent of this idea. Uri drops a footnote in the letter explaining briefly why he believes Israel is an apartheid state, and indeed that it is a more extreme version of an apartheid state than South Africa was. As he succinctly argues, "To my reading, Israel is an apartheid State (at core) if only due to the fact that just over 90 percent (approximately +/-93 percent) of the 1948 territory of the State of Israel (within the 1949 armistice line, the so called "Green Line") is reserved in law and in practice for one section of the population under its sovereignty, namely: For "Jews" only (exceptions notwithstanding). Note that in former apartheid South Africa just under 90 percent of the territory of the Republic (approximately +/-87 percent) was reserved in law and in practice for "Whites" only (exceptions notwithstanding)."

While defenders are quick to accuse proponents of the idea that Israel is an apartheid state of being anti-Semites, it seems hard to refute this apartheid claim. South Africa was the model for what apartheid is during most of the twentieth century. South African apartheid, moreover, was heavily influenced by the legal and systematic form of racial segregation in the United States in the Jim Crow South—a system firmly in place at the time of the 1917 Balfour Declaration, which the United States then backed.

Postapartheid South Africa, now ruled by the Black majority that had been oppressed so long under apartheid and knows better than anyone else what apartheid is, itself recognizes Israel as an apartheid state.

And it is very telling that Israel was one of the few countries in the world to support apartheid South Africa, though quietly, until the bitter end. In what was a pattern for Israel, it did so even after it was too embarrassing for the United States, one of the world's other holdouts in supporting the regime, to continue doing so. Indeed, the Israeli paper *Haaretz*, though trying to desperately downplay this support, acknowledged in the article, "Why Israel Supported South Africa's Apartheid Regime," that "Israel, starting in the 1970s, [had] become a friend of the apartheid regime, to such an extent that by 1986 it was the only Western nation that did not take part in sanctions imposed on South Africa."[3] I would argue that this was a case of birds of a feather flocking together.

There is a very important caveat to this. Thus, while Israel supported apartheid South Africa, many Jews around the world and in South Africa itself did not; and indeed, individual Jews were some of the staunchest allies and friends of Nelson Mandela and the ANC against apartheid. This is why Mandela, though deeply committed to Palestinian liberation and also aware of Israel's support for the state that oppressed him, was nonetheless quite forgiving of Israel. As the *Times of Israel* wrote upon Mandela's death in 2013:

> Nelson Rolihlahla Mandela had close friendships and alliances with many Jews, but his relationship with the Jewish state was complicated. While always courteous and never hate-filled, the South African icon's dealings with Israel were overshadowed by Jerusalem's staunch support for his tormentors and, even more so, his ironclad loyalty to the Palestinian cause.
>
> In the name of reconciliation, he made no ongoing issue of Jerusalem's strong long-term partnership with the apartheid regime after he was released from a lengthy prison sentence and became South Africa's first black president in 1994. He professed the legitimacy of Zionism as Jewish nationalism and, upon receiving the 1993 Nobel Peace Prize, he said Yitzhak Rabin deserved it more (Rabin was co-honored the following year).[4]

This says a lot about the great man that Mandela was, but the point that must be made here is that, as Mandela himself correctly recognized, not all Jews are in line with Israel, Zionism, or their values, and indeed many are critical of them. To the extent that defenders of Israel attempt to equate Judaism with Zionism and Israel, they themselves are playing a racist and deceptive game because it is they who are making generalizations and caricatures about the Jewish people that simply are untrue and could never be true. Mandela—who the United States incredibly labeled a "terrorist" until 2008, again saying more about the accuser here than the accused—understood this from experience and from his infinite wisdom.

A number of human rights groups have finally come around to acknowledging the apartheid nature of Israel. One of these groups includes Human Rights Watch (HRW), which I view to be a very conservative, pro-Western organization. HRW, in a 2021 report,[5] details why it has reached this conclusion.

While it is worth reading the whole report, here are some of HRW's findings. As HRW summarizes,

> About 6.8 million Jewish Israelis and 6.8 million Palestinians live today between the Mediterranean Sea and Jordan River, an area encompassing Israel and the Occupied Palestinian Territory (OPT), the latter made up of the West Bank, including East Jerusalem, and the Gaza Strip. Throughout most of this area, Israel is the sole governing power; in the remainder, it exercises primary authority alongside limited Palestinian self-rule. Across these areas and in most aspects of life, Israeli authorities methodically privilege Jewish Israelis and discriminate against Palestinians. Laws, policies, and statements by leading Israeli officials make plain that the objective of maintaining Jewish Israeli control over demographics, political power, and land has long guided government policy. In pursuit of this goal, authorities have dispossessed, confined, forcibly separated, and subjugated Palestinians by virtue of their identity to varying degrees of intensity. In certain areas, as described in this report, these deprivations are so severe that they amount to the crimes against humanity of apartheid and persecution.

HRW further explains:

> In the OPT, which Israel has recognized as a single territory encompassing the West Bank and Gaza, Israeli authorities treat Palestinians separately and unequally as compared to Jewish Israeli settlers. In the occupied West Bank, Israel subjects Palestinians to draconian military law and enforces segregation, largely prohibiting Palestinians from entering settlements. In the besieged Gaza Strip, Israel imposes a generalized closure, sharply restricting the movement of people and goods—policies that Gaza's other neighbor, Egypt, often does little to alleviate. In annexed East Jerusalem, which Israel considers part of its sovereign territory but remains occupied territory under international law, Israel provides the vast majority of the hundreds of thousands of Palestinians living there with a legal status that weakens their residency rights by conditioning them on the individual's connections to the city, among other factors. This level of discrimination amounts to systematic oppression.

In Israel, which the vast majority of nations consider being the area defined by its pre-1967 borders, the two tiered-citizenship structure and bifurcation of nationality and citizenship result in Palestinian citizens having a status inferior to Jewish citizens by law. While Palestinians in Israel, unlike those in the OPT, have the right to vote and stand for Israeli elections, these rights do not empower them to overcome the institutional discrimination they face from the same Israeli government, including widespread restrictions on accessing land confiscated from them, home demolitions, and effective prohibitions on family reunification.

The fragmentation of the Palestinian population, in part deliberately engineered through Israeli restrictions on movement and residency, furthers the goal of domination and helps obscure the reality of the same Israeli government repressing the same Palestinian population group, to varying degrees in different areas, for the benefit of the same Jewish Israeli dominant group.

Of course, this was written before October 7, 2023. Now, even worse than being accused of being an apartheid state, Israel stands accused of committing genocide. Appropriately, it is South Africa that has put Israel in the dock for this crime, having filed a case against Israel before the International Court of Justice under the Genocide Convention.

After crossing the southern gate of Bethlehem, Uri and I drove about another half an hour through very poor Palestinian neighborhoods until we reached Bethlehem. I thought to myself at the time that the Holy Family would have felt at home in these neighborhoods. Our first stop was at a youth center for a Palestinian refugee camp south of Bethlehem to meet with Saleh, the director of the center, who was waiting to give us a tour of the area.

First, Saleh showed us around the youth center, proudly pointing to the many trophies the children had won in various competitions and the music learning room with the different instruments available to aspiring musicians. He then took us to a room where we were able to chat. As is the custom among Palestinians, he offered us coffee and cookies as refreshments.

Saleh explained that, like many of the 16,000 residents of the refugee camp served by the youth center, he was born in this refugee camp, his family having fled the Nakba in 1948. At first, he explained, the camp was as one might envision it, lined with tents in which people lived. And then, with the help of the newly formed United Nations Relief and Works Agency for Palestine Refugees in the Near East (UNRWA), one-story housing units began to be erected for the residents. He would later show us how, due to lack of space, residents have begun building additional levels upon these structures, which is dangerous given that they were not originally designed with a foundation to support multiple stories.

Saleh then gave us a tour of the refugee camp itself, which now looks more like a little city with concrete housing, shops, restaurants, and barber shops. I asked if there was much crime in the camp, and he said, much to my surprise, that there was virtually none. He attributed this to the fact that the camp was very left-wing and had a developed working-class ideology and a strong sense of solidarity that prevents people from criminalizing each other. The left-wing nature of the camp was evident to me upon entering the youth center and seeing a poster of the Marxist revolutionary Ernesto Che Guevara.

Saleh said that the only real crimes committed were by Israeli troops when they periodically and illegally invade the camp to arrest young men, sometimes killing someone in the process. Indeed, we walked by a number of paintings of young martyrs that adorn the walls of the refugee camp. Along the way, we met a middle-aged man who volunteered that his youth had been stolen when he was arrested and jailed for a few years when he was in his early teens. Saleh himself has spent time in Israeli prison as well. And so has Uri for that matter. Indeed, it seemed to me that there were few Palestinians I met who hadn't been in prison at one time or another.

The latest, and quite recent, crime by the Israeli forces had involved the youth center itself, which they violently entered and then proceeded to steal computers and even thousands of dollars in cash from the safe.

Saleh explained that, since the war started on October 7, one-third of the residents have become unemployed. He said that it is very hard for people to obtain enough food these days.

After touring the refugee camp, Saleh led us into Bethlehem itself, which is a quaint and beautiful little city with stunning stone architecture dating back centuries. As Saleh related to us, about 40 percent of Bethlehem residents are Palestinian Christians. Indeed, Palestinians were the very first Christians and count Jesus, Mary, and Joseph as Palestinians. Every Palestinian I have met, including Muslim and Jewish Palestinians, are very proud of this heritage. Uri himself, though Jewish, often goes to the Church of the Nativity to attend the Christmastime Masses.

As the *Washington Post* recently explains, "Palestinian Christians belong to the world's oldest Christian communities, rooted in the historic cradle of Christianity. But they are diminished in number, at least in proportion to their neighbors of other faiths, and are represented in greater strength in the Palestinian diaspora around the world. Palestinian Christians comprise some 2 percent of the overall Palestinian population in the West Bank, concentrated mostly around Ramallah, Bethlehem, and Jerusalem, and less than 1 percent of the population in Gaza."[6]

As an article in Al Jazeera puts it, Palestine's "Christian legacy stretches right back to the days when the faith was a persecuted sect promising salvation to the downtrodden. . . . Palestine's Christians, totaling 50,000 across the occupied territories, are sometimes referred to as 'living stones,' a metaphor first invoked by Peter the Apostle, the ex-fisherman called upon to be a disciple of Jesus, to describe the role of believers in building the spiritual house of God. Today, the term harks to their special status as custodians of a faith born on their land."[7]

While some challenge the notion of Jesus as a Palestinian, what is most important is that the Palestinians claim him as one of their own and that this is very important to the Palestinian identity. Israel, intent on wiping out all of Palestinian identity, wishes to destroy this crucial aspect of that identity. Moreover, sources like the *Encyclopedia Britannica* state definitively that he was.[8] As *Britannica* explains, Jesus was from "Jewish Palestine"—of course, he was Jewish himself—which, at the time of Jesus's birth and life, was under Roman domination.

Nowadays, as Uri explained to me, Israeli tour buses take many tourists to Bethlehem and other holy sites, but stay only during the day, taking the tourists back to Jerusalem hotels run by Israelis. This is killing the

Palestinian-run hotels in Bethlehem and other such tourist spots. Indeed, a number of these Palestinian-run hotels in Bethlehem were completely shuttered when I was there.

The other notable thing about Bethlehem at the time I visited—at the beginning of Advent—was that there were absolutely no Christmas decorations in the town: no Christmas lights, no Christmas trees, nothing. And this was by design. Thus, the patriarchs of the Christian churches in Bethlehem announced publicly that there would be no Christmas celebrations this year due to the carnage happening in Gaza. In essence, they announced that Christmas was canceled.

In addition, all of the Christian patriarchs in Bethlehem signed a letter addressed to President Biden and delivered personally to the White House by three representatives, decrying what is happening in Gaza. This letter dated November 27, 2023, reads in full:

We bring you greetings on behalf of the Christian community in Bethlehem, the city of our Lord and Savior Jesus Christ, the Prince of Peace.

Next week, we were supposed to begin our advent and Christmas season. This should have been a time of joy and hope. This year, it is a season of death and despair. This year, Christmas prayers are the only moment of hope in the middle of this human catastrophe caused by the war. There will be no manifestation of joy for the children. This year, Christmas celebrations are cancelled in Bethlehem.

We write to you in deep sorrow and pain. We are devastated by the images of death and destruction we see in our land, regardless of the victim. We lament the death of all peoples, Palestinians and Israelis. We pray for freedom for all. We affirm that every human being is created in the image of God and is worthy of living in a dignified life and "a life more abundant". We hold firm the truth that all humans, regardless of their religion or nationality, have the right to live in dignity and justice. We lament the death of all peoples and condemn the killing of all innocent civilians. We pray for peace and prosperity for all.

Yet at the same time, we are broken because this war could have been avoided. For years, as followers of Jesus, we have called for peace that is based on justice. It is time everybody can live with dignity in this land. The Palestinian and Israeli children deserve to live, hope and dream.

Dear Mr. President: There can be no peace and security without justice and equality. There can be no peace and security without equal rights for all. Siege, violence and war cannot bring peace and security. A comprehensive and just peace is the only hope for Palestinians and Israelis alike.

We are writing to plead with you to help stop this war. God has placed political leaders in a position of power so that they can bring justice, support for those who suffer, and be instruments of God's peace. We want a constant and comprehensive ceasefire. Enough death. Enough destruction. This is a moral obligation. There must be other ways. This is our call and prayer this Christmas.

As followers of Jesus, we find our comfort and consolation in the son of our Bethlehem. He is the way, the Truth and the Life. He is the Prince of Peace. From Bethlehem, from the midst of pain, we send a message of peace and life to all humanity.

Respectfully,
Leader of the Christian Community in Bethlehem[9]

In Bethlehem's Lutheran church, a crèche was set up with Jesus in a Palestinian Kafiya sitting atop rubble resembling the rubble of buildings destroyed in Gaza. Reverend Munther Isaac of the church was quoted as saying, "If Christ were to be born today, he would be born under the rubble and Israeli shelling. This is a powerful message we send to the world celebrating the holidays."[10]

Due to the long time it took to get to Bethlehem, and the fact that Uri at nearly eighty years old and having suffered a recent heart attack moved a bit slow, we arrived at the Church of the Nativity, which houses the place of Jesus's birth, just as it was closing. Indeed, the priest there was already turning off the lights. However, I went up to him and said that I had come all the way from the United States to see Christ's birthplace, and I begged him to give us a few moments to see it. I also asked if he could turn the lights back on so I could take some photos. While he grimaced momentarily, he quickly obliged and gave in to my beseeching. I had the joy of being able to see where Jesus was born and where he was laid to sleep. There was an Indian family leaving as we entered. Though Hindi, as they explained to me, they came to pay their respects. I took the opportunity to say one quick prayer—that peace be brought to Gaza and to all the Palestinian people.

As I first learned from a Palestinian refugee in Caracas, Venezuela who was in Bethlehem at the time and attempted to defend the Church of the Nativity, the Israelis laid siege to and attacked this church, and indeed all of Bethlehem, for over a month in the spring of 2002 when 200 to 250 Palestinians sought sanctuary there. This, despite the fact that, as discussed above, Bethlehem is designated "Area A," meaning that it is under the control of the Palestinian Authority and Israelis are not even allowed to enter.

The *Middle East Monitor* explains the background of this event. As it explains, on March 29, 2002, Israel launched its biggest military operation since the 1967 Six-Day War in order to put down a Palestinian uprising in the West Bank, which was provoked when "then Israeli opposition leader Ariel Sharon stormed into Al-Aqsa Mosque protected by heavily armed Israeli police and soldiers."[11] The *Monitor* continues:

> Israel's assault on Jenin, where the occupation forces remain accused of carrying out a massacre, began a day before the siege on the Church of the Nativity. Israeli soldiers killed at least 52 Palestinians in the Jenin refugee camp and enforced a total lockdown that lasted for weeks. The Israeli government, meanwhile, banned journalists and human rights observers from the Palestinian city in the occupied West Bank.
>
> Palestinian civilians had very few places to seek shelter from the advancing Israeli army and its indiscriminate violence. Trapped in the center of Bethlehem by the incoming Israeli troops, approximately 200 Palestinians, most of them civilians and policemen, along with Palestinian Christian priests and nuns and a few resistance fighters from local Fatah militias, took refuge in the Church of the Nativity, which Christians revere as the birthplace of Jesus.

According to Anton Salman, a member of the Antonius Society humanitarian group in Bethlehem, "the Palestinians facing the advancing Israeli army 'saw their mosque, Masjid Umar, on the other side of the square from the Church of the Nativity, bombed. They were afraid, and they looked for a place to be secure. So they found the only way; they ran to the church and found a place to stay.'"[12]

While spokespeople for the Israeli government claimed that Israeli forces were under strict orders not to attack the Church of the Nativity—an incredibly important holy site for Christians dating back to 326 years after the birth of Christ—this order, if really given, was not followed. Thus, Israeli snipers shot into the church at anyone in view. In addition,

> Israeli forces shelled the Church of the Nativity sporadically in an attempt to force the Palestinians inside the historic building to surrender. The bell ringer of the church, Samir Ibrahim Salman, was killed by Israeli fire. Being pinned down in one of the holiest sites in Christendom did not guarantee safety from the Israeli siege. The occupation forces destroyed the southern gate of the church and several Israeli soldiers moved into its southern courtyard. A week into the siege, Israeli soldiers opened fire at the church, resulting in a fire in the room of one of the priests who lived there. An Armenian monk was shot and wounded by an Israeli soldier. Israeli snipers killed seven more Palestinians and injured another 40.[13]

The Vatican condemned this as an "'indescribable act of barbarity.'"

In addition, as the Israeli paper *Haaretz* explained during the siege of the church, the Vatican, in a statement that could have been written today, while critical of alleged terrorist attacks by Palestinian militants, focused criticism on Israel's terrible treatment of the Palestinians, which leads to such attacks. As *Haaretz* related at the time:

> The Vatican sharply criticized Israel for imposing "unjust conditions and humiliations" on the Palestinians and also denounced acts of terrorism against the Jewish state. In a strongly worded statement, the Vatican said it had called in the Israeli and US ambassadors to the Holy See to discuss the crisis in the Middle East. Although it condemned acts of terrorism, in apparent reference to a recent wave of Palestinian suicide attacks, the statement included a list of criticisms of Israel. It said Pope John Paul II "rejects

unjust conditions and humiliations imposed on the Palestinian people, as well as the reprisals and revenge attacks which do nothing but feed the sense of frustration and hatred."[14]

Most recently, Israel chose Christmas Day, 2023, to launch a raid and arrest Palestinians in Bethlehem, along with other West Bank cities.[15]

There is a strong sense among many Christians in the West Bank, including Jerusalem, that Israel is intentionally persecuting Christians and has been doing so since the very founding of Israel. Award-winning journalist Jonathan Cook has been writing about this persecution for years, and explained in 2020:

> For decades Israel has pointed to the steady decline of the Palestinian Christian community as proof of a supposed clash of civilizations in which it is on the right side. The gradual exodus of Christians, it argues, is evidence of the oppression they suffer at the hands of the Palestinians' Muslim majority. Claiming to represent Judeo-Christian values, Israel supposedly stands as their sole protector.

However, as Cook relates, Palestinian Christians are fleeing Israeli repression—not Muslim repression. He explains that the Israeli repression "began with the country's creation in 1948 and the events Palestinians call their *Nakba*, or Catastrophe. Christians, who lived historically in Palestine's main cities, were among the first targets of the new Israeli army's ethnic cleansing operations. Since then, those in the West Bank, Jerusalem, and Gaza have sought to escape from decades of occupation, while those belonging to a Palestinian minority living as citizens in Israel have tried to break free from the institutionalized discrimination they face in a self-declared Jewish state."[16]

The feelings among Christians in the West Bank that they are a victim of anti-Christian discrimination and persecution came to the fore in the spring of 2023 when Israeli police greatly restricted the number of Christian Pilgrims going to the Church of the Holy Sepulcher in Old Jerusalem—the church in which Jesus was buried—from 10,000 to 1,800 to attend the annual, 2,000-year-old Holy Fire Ceremony before

Orthodox Easter. The Israeli police set up barricades and checkpoints to limit the number of faithful and ended up attacking scores of worshippers attempting to attend and physically attacking some Coptic Christian priests in front of the church.[17]

The president of the National Christian Coalition in the Holy Land, Dimitri Dilani, stated at the time that Israel's actions "flagrantly violate the most basic human rights."[18] He further called upon the world to "express deep concern about the racist nature of the Israeli occupation authorities, which manifests these days in religious persecution against anyone who is not Jewish. The National Christian Coalition calls for protecting the rights of all, including Muslims and Christians, in Palestine."[19] As the *Arab News* further explained, in advance of the Holy Fire ceremony, "The churches said they would refuse to cooperate with the police restrictions, which they see as part of long-standing efforts to push out the local Christian community. Some church leaders have voiced concern over what they describe as an environment of impunity in the face of rising acts of violence and vandalism targeting Christians and their properties in Jerusalem."[20]

Armenian Christians have also suffered attacks in the West Bank. Indeed, just three days after Christmas, 2023, thirty masked men invaded the Armenian Quarter of the Old City of Jerusalem and engaged in a concerted attack against Armenian Christians, throwing rocks and other objects at Armenian Christian clergy. While the identity of these attackers has not yet been revealed, the Armenian Patriarchate has stated publicly that he believes the attackers are associated with George Warwar, "a Jaffa man thought to be involved in a controversial and now cancelled deal to acquire a plot of land in the Armenian neighborhood ostensibly to build a luxury hotel by Jewish investors."[21] This deal was known to be linked to "the extremist Israeli settler movement."[22]

And this is not an isolated incident, with similar attacks taking place recently, including last month when, "on two separate occasions, private security guards and Israeli and Jewish settlers burst into the Armenian Quarter accompanied by two bulldozers."[23] The Armenian Patriarchate issued a desperate plea referring to this most recent, violent attack "as an 'existential threat,' stating that 'Bishops, Priests, Deacons, Seminarians and indigenous Armenians are fighting for their very lives,'" and calling upon international authorities to investigate the incident and to provide protection to the Armenian Church in the West Bank.[24] (A complete copy of the Armenian Patriarchate's message is included in the Appendix). It is worth noting that, as reported in an October 5, 2023, AP story, Israel is militarily supporting Azerbaijan in its conflict with Armenia and in its ethnic cleansing of Armenians from the breakaway republic of Nagorno-Karabakh that sits between those two countries.[25]

As I was told while in the West Bank, it is also very common for Christians to be harassed on the street, with Israelis even pulling off the crosses from around the necks of Christians. A recent thread on Twitter contains videos of such anti-Christian harassment of (including spitting upon) both Palestinians as well as Christian pilgrims in the West Bank.[26] Lest one believe these to be isolated instances, Israel's Minister of National Security, Ben Gvir, recently stated, and proudly, that spitting on Christian priests and churches is in fact an "ancient tradition."[27]

Israel has not contained its attacks on Christians to the West Bank. Thus, it has also aimed at the Church in Gaza as well. The most blatant of such attacks was the bombing of the Greek Orthodox Church of St. Porphyrius, the third-oldest Christian church in the world, on October 20, 2023. Palestinian Christians were taking shelter in the church at the time, and eighteen Palestinian Christians were killed, and at least twenty others were wounded.

As an op-ed in the *LA Times* lamented, "The Christian community had to hold a mass funeral to bury dead outside of the Church of St. Porphyrius, followed by a mass baptism service for the children of the community in case they, too, may soon die."[28] This op-ed explains that there were around 1,000 Christians remaining in the Gaza Strip at the time that Israel's military operations against Gaza began after October 7. The op-ed related that "While most Palestinian Christians in the Occupied Territories reside in the West Bank, the number of Christians in Gaza, and across Palestine/Israel, has been dwindling to less than 2 percent of the overall Palestinian population. Most members of these communities have migrated to Europe and North America seeking economic stability and peace of mind."

According to the op-ed, "Palestinian Christians, descendants of the oldest Christian communities, feel largely abandoned by the world—particularly by other Christian communities in Western countries—who seem indifferent or even hostile to the Palestinian struggle for freedom and human rights."

For its part, the *Washington Post* explained recently that the Christian community in Gaza, "small but prominent, *is in the midst of a potential extinction event.* There are roughly fewer than 1,000 Christians in Gaza, who have lived there without much problem despite the de facto takeover of the territory in 2007 by Hamas. But Israeli airstrikes destroyed or damaged almost all the community's homes in Gaza City while also hitting Gaza's oldest active church, where some were sheltering. The vast majority of the Christian community in Gaza are now homeless" (emphasis added).[29] In stating that the Christian community in Gaza "is in the midst of a potential extinction event," the *Washington Post* is acknowledging another type of genocide that is happening in Gaza—the quite successful genocide specifically against Palestinian Christians.

In addition to targeting Christians and historic Christian churches, Israel has generally been destroying important historic sites in Gaza with reckless abandon. As an NPR report explains, the devastation to history itself has been catastrophic. Thus, since October 7, there has

> been tremendous losses to the region's ancient and globally significant cultural heritage. The region was a hub for commerce and culture under Egyptian, Greek, Roman, and Byzantine rule. It remained influential for centuries thereafter.
>
> A recent survey by the group Heritage for Peace details the damage done so far to more than 100 of these landmarks in Gaza since the start of the present conflict.
>
> The casualties include the Great Omari Mosque, one of the most important and ancient mosques in historical Palestine; . . . a 2,000-year-old Roman cemetery in northern Gaza excavated only last year; and the Rafah Museum, a space in southern Gaza which was dedicated to teaching about the territory's long and multi-layered heritage—until it was hammered by airstrikes early on in the conflict.[30]

As for the Rafah Museum, NPR quotes the director in relating that "There were priceless items from coins, precious stones, copper plates, clothes" that now lay among the rubble. Tellingly, the president for Heritage for Peace is quoted in the story as saying, "If this heritage be no more in Gaza, it will be a big loss of the identity of the people in Gaza." And indeed, I would submit, this is the very point of such targeted destruction—to destroy even the memory of Palestinian history. Indeed, while Israeli officials has oft tried to compare Hamas to ISIS, it is Israel that is acting like ISIS, or the Taliban in Afghanistan, in wantonly destroying historic sites and antiquities.

The targeting of Christians in Gaza has continued into the Israelis' operations there, even triggering the ire of the Vatican. Thus, as CNN reported, on December 16, 2023, Israeli snipers shot Christians sheltering in the Holy Family (Catholic) parish in Gaza City, killing two women (an elderly mother and her daughter) and wounding seven other individuals.[31]

CNN quoted a report by the Latin Patriarchate in Jerusalem who oversees Catholic churches throughout the region as saying, "No warning was given, no notification was provided. . . . They were shot in cold blood inside the premises of the parish, where there are no belligerents." The Latin Patriarchate reported that "Israel Defense Forces tanks also targeted the Convent of the Sisters of Mother Theresa, which houses fifty-four disabled people and is part of the church's compound. The building's generator, its only current source of electricity, as well as its fuel resources, solar panels, and water tanks were also destroyed." According to the Patriarchate, "IDF rockets had made the convent 'uninhabitable.'" Pope Francis, during his weekly Angelus Prayer in Rome, denounced these attacks against unarmed civilians as "terrorism."

For his part, Hamman Farah, a psychologist now living in Toronto and a relative of Nahida and Samar who were murdered in the Holy Family Parish, was quoted as saying: "This is a targeted death campaign during the Christmas season on the world's oldest Christian community."[32]

And indeed, the facts appear to back up Farah's claim. Thus, a report in *Politico* exposes the fact that the Israeli Defense Forces (IDF) knew exactly what they were targeting when they attacked the Holy Family Parish and the Convent of the Sisters of Mother Theresa. This is without a doubt because Israel was informed of these sites, and the need to protect them, by none other than staffers of the US Senate. As *Politico* explains, emails

> dated Oct. 14 through Oct. 26, show that Catholic Relief Services sent the coordinates of a number of buildings to Senate staffers, who forwarded them to the Israeli military. The congressional aides confirm in the messages that Israel received the list of coordinates for four buildings, including the two that were later struck, but the Israeli officials told them they "can't guarantee" the safety of the dozens of civilians inside.
>
> The emails shed light on the cracks in the international system through which aid organizations attempt to protect their buildings and staff from getting hit. They also raise questions about the alleged Israeli strikes given the IDF confirmed to the staffers that it had located the positions of the facilities on the list, including the two that were hit.[33]

In short, the IDF knew full well that they were targeting Catholic sites that US Senate staffers asked them to make sure that they did not strike, and they struck them anyway.

This terrible story does not end in the West Bank and Gaza. Thus, Israel has also been targeting historic Christian sites in neighboring Lebanon, just as it had during its assault on Lebanon in 2006. Indeed, just one day before Christmas Eve, 2023, Israel bombed the historic Deir Mimas Monastery (originally built in 1404 AD)—a monastery Israel had completely leveled in 2006, and which had been rebuilt with the help of Qatar starting in 2008. As the *Doha News* concluded, this attack, along with the attack on Christian and other historic sites in Gaza, signaled "a broader pattern of Israeli aggression against religious sites and civilian sanctuaries" and "highlight[s] a disregard for the sanctity of religious spaces by the apartheid regime, and the lives of those who seek refuge within their walls."[34] The *Doha News* stated that "with Byzantine-era churches destroyed," as well as 192 mosques (some very ancient) destroyed since October 7, 2023, "Israel is erasing the Strip's religious and cultural history."

The whys and wherefores of such wanton destruction was revealed recently by a sick joke, at the Palestinian people's expense, in the form of a book that quickly shot to number one in Amazon's "Middle East History" category before being pulled from the website. This book, *A History of the Palestinian People: From Ancient Times to the Modern Era,* by Israeli "author" Assaf Voll, purported to be "the comprehensive and extensive review of some 3,000 years of Palestinian history."[35] This book consisted of 120 blank pages—a cruel joke attempting to demonstrate that the Palestinians have no history. In my view, the book, and its popularity, presumably among Zionists, shows that Israel is not content to merely wipe out the Palestinian people, but is also bent on destroying their cultural heritage, even going so far as to claim that the Palestinians have no heritage or history of their own to begin with.

This intention was recently manifested in Israel's destruction and looting of Gaza's Hall of Records. As one commentor explains, "Israel erased the civil registry in Gaza, destroyed it completely, destroyed the libraries and stole tens of thousands of ancient records, Palestinians now have no proof of their assets, the degrees they earned at the university or even the birth certificates of their children."[36] In short, Israel literally wiped out any documentation of the Palestinians' very existence. And, in the process they have made the Palestinians who survive in Gaza non-people who lack any papers to be able to travel or work.

And, while Israel is extinguishing the very memory of Palestine, its history, culture, and technology, the United States is doing the very same to Arabs in much of the Middle East.

All of this paves the way for the expansion of Western hegemony in the Arab world, which the West hopes will be entirely forgotten by history, and for the accompanying expansion of unfettered capitalism—an economic system that has no need for, and indeed that finds anathema, ancient cultural heritage and more communal forms of living and exchange promoted both by some forms of Islam as well as the earlier forms of Christianity.

The Greater Assault upon Liberation Theology

This attack on Christianity has not been limited to the Middle East. Indeed, the United States and Israel have been collaborating on the destruction of what is known as liberation theology throughout the world, and especially in Latin America, since the early 1960s. And the United States and Israel have willingly partnered with some of the worst, right-wing governments to carry out this project.

Liberation theology is a strain of Catholicism that harkens back to the early days of Christianity before it became the official church of the Holy Roman Empire and when its focus was on serving the poor and oppressed—this "preferential treatment for the poor" representing an afront to capitalist system being promoted by the West. It should be noted that Islam also has its own version of liberation theology, and indeed, the country that claims to live by this Theology is none other than one of the greatest enemies of both the United States and Israel—Iran.

As Noam Chomsky has been arguing for years, the numerous US military campaigns in Latin America since 1962

> were in substantial measure a war against the Church. It was more than symbolic that it culminated in the assassination of six leading Latin American intellectuals, Jesuit priests, in November 1989, a few days after the fall of the Berlin wall. They were murdered by an elite Salvadoran battalion, fresh from renewed training at the John F. Kennedy Special Forces School in North Carolina. As was learned last November, but apparently aroused no interest, the order for the assassination was signed by the chief of staff and his associates, all of them so closely connected to the Pentagon and the US Embassy that it becomes even harder to imagine that Washington was unaware of the plans of its model battalion. This elite force had already left a trail of blood of the usual victims through the hideous decade of the 1980s in El Salvador, which opened with the assassination of Archbishop Romero, "the voice of the voiceless," by much the same hands.
>
> The murder of the Jesuit priests was a crushing blow to liberation theology, the remarkable revival of Christianity initiated by Pope John XXIII at Vatican II, which he opened in 1962, an event that "ushered in a new era in the history of the Catholic Church, . . ." Inspired by Vatican II, Latin American Bishops adopted "the preferential option for the poor," renewing the radical pacifism of the Gospels that had been put to rest when the Emperor Constantine established Christianity as the religion of the Roman Empire.[37]

As Noam Chomsky has further explained, one of the advertising points of the US Department of Defense's School of the Americas, now based in Columbus, Georgia, is that it "helped defeat liberation theology, which was a dominant force, and it was an enemy for the same reason that secular nationalism in the Arab world was an enemy—it was working for the poor."[38]

Israel has always been willing to lend a hand to the unholy US campaign against the Church in Latin America, sometimes even stepping in to assist a brutal dictatorship when the United States was too embarrassed to do so itself.

One of the best examples of this is Israel's support for the brutal military dictatorship in Guatemala in the 1980s that killed 200,000 of its own people in what is now commonly accepted as a genocide. During this genocide, Catholic clerics and laity associated with the Christian communes set up by the Mayans of Guatemala—the victims of the genocide—were especially targeted for assassination. As a report by Open Democracy explains, by the late 1960s,

> The military began to indiscriminately persecute Catholic priests and laymen . . .
>
> In 1976, the army killed William Woods, a priest of the American Catholic order Maryknoll. Woods was helping the Maya take control of their northern forest home. In 1978, Father Hermógenes López was shot dead. He had denounced the military's seizing of water and the conscription of children. This was part of the larger wave of repression to which members of the cooperatives, Indigenous mayors and trade unionists were subjected, and was the situation immediately before the murder of the ten Catholics in Quiché.
>
> The murder of priests were the first signs of the coming storm. Between 1980 and 1982, the Guatemalan army razed the villages considered red bastions. Many of them had at least three decades of organizing with Catholic Action and cooperatives.[39]

By 1977, the Carter administration, which prided itself on upholding human rights standards throughout the world, was unwilling to keep supporting the Guatemalan dictatorship. However, the cause of brutal repression was not all lost, for, "Within months, Israel had stepped in to fill the void with President Ephraim Katzir signing an agreement for military assistance. According to the Stockholm Institute for Peace, Israel supplied Guatemala with $38 million worth of arms during the civil war period. . . . Israel also utilized its shadowy arms industry to avoid embarrassing the US, often shuttling arms to Guatemala through intermediaries, normally retired generals and 'securocrats' with dual nationalities."[40]

However, the worst and most brutal years of the Guatemalan genocide occurred under the leadership of General Ríos Montt, who took power in 1982. It should be noted that Ríos Montt, who was later convicted of genocide and crimes against humanity, was inspired by the example of Israel in brutalizing the indigenous Palestinians. As *TRT World* magazine explains, "The Israeli military's scorched earth campaign against the Palestinians inspired the Guatemalan right-wing military to replicate the tactic against the country's rebellious indigenous Maya population through a brutal process of their 'Palestinianisation' with its forced 'integrated nationalism.'"[41]

But Israel, now in concert with the Reagan administration, which was not embarrassed to support a brutal regime, provided more than just inspiration to the Ríos Montt dictatorship. Thus, as *TRT World* explains:

In the early 1980s, the Guatemalan military under General Jose Efrain Ríos Montt, who came to power via a military coup in 1982, backed by former US President Ronald Reagan, conducted a village massacre in Dos Erres, killing everyone except four.

In 1999, a UN-sanctioned Truth Investigation Committee found that "All ballistic evidence recovered (from the village scene) corresponded to bullet fragments from firearms and pods of Galil rifles, made in Israel."

Montt was also thankful to the Israel military for its training of Guatemalan soldiers for the success of his military coup, which was central to the conduct of the genocide against the Maya population. Experts have pointed out that "at least 300 Israeli advisers" were in Guatemala during the coup.[42]

Guatemala would later pay its thanks to Israel for its support in its geno-cidal war when its right-wing, evangelical president Jimmy Morales—who had himself been a death-squad leader during the genocide—joined the United States in moving Guatemala's embassy from Tel Aviv to Jerusalem.[43] This was a highly provocative act given the Palestinians' legally supported claim to East Jerusalem as its capital.

The other brutal regime that Israel supported was in Colombia, South America, which may hold the world record for state-murdered Catholic clergy, with over eighty such clergy murdered from 1984 to 2013.[44] As in the case of Guatemala in the late 1970s, Israel was willing to do something in Colombia that the United States was not willing to do directly—to train and arm the brutal death squads organized into the paramilitary umbrella group known as the AUC and led by infamous leader Carlos Castaño.

The AUC, which worked very closely with the right-wing Colombian military that the United States did support directly, was responsible for the torture and deaths of tens of thousands of Colombians and some of the grisliest crimes in that country. The goal of the AUC's terror campaign has been the suppression of individuals and groups advocating for pro-gressive social change, including Catholic clergy advocating for the poor. Carlos Castaño, the most infamous death squad leader in Colombian his-tory, was trained in Israel in both "terrorism and counterterrorism," and Castaño once declared, "I learned an infinite amount of things in Israel and to that country I owe part of my essence, my human and military achievements."[45]

In addition to training Castaño and his troops, both inside and out-side Israel, Israel also found a way to provide the AUC with thousands of AK-47s with which to carry out its reign of terror in which it was kill-ing an average of thirteen civilians per day. As longtime journalist Jeremy Bigwood explains:

> As the paramilitaries expanded, continuing to absorb other paramilitary organizations, it needed arms, and probably had several sources for them, one of which came to light last May. It should come as no surprise to the reader that the major suppliers were Israelis. Israeli arms dealers have long

had a presence in next-door Panama and especially in Guatemala. While some of the details of this particular deal have been contested and are still sketchy, one thing is clear: by a series of misrepresentations, GIRSA, an Israeli company associated with the IDF and based in Guatemala was able to buy 3,000 Kalashnikov assault rifles and 2.5 million rounds of ammunition that were then handed over to the paramilitaries in Colombia through a Colombian port controlled by a US banana company.[46]

The US banana company mentioned here was Chiquita, then based in Cincinnati, Ohio. I personally talked to Colombia's former attorney general, Mario Iguarán, in his office in Bogotá about the support that Chiquita gave to the AUC paramilitaries (I didn't know then that this was with the crucial assistance of Israel), and he said that this support led directly to the deaths of thousands of Colombians and was crucial in helping the AUC take over huge swaths of Colombian territory—control the AUC and its successors continue to maintain to this very day.

As Bigwood concluded in 2003, "there can be no doubt that Israeli interests share some blame for the many years of ongoing bloodbath in Colombia, which kills as many as twenty people a day—some 70 percent or more of which is attributed to the paramilitaries, totaling tens of thousands over the last decade—most of whom are killed for merely being suspected of sympathies to the insurgency, not for being actual combatants. Unfortunately, in other new places around the world, we can expect the training of right-wing paramilitary groups to continue, as the Israeli state and its agents gleefully continue to undertake operations that are deemed too distasteful for its US counterparts."[47] Indeed.

Incredibly, Israel even supported fascist dictatorships in Latin America that, in addition to persecuting Catholic clerics associated with liberation theology, were also openly neo-Nazi and anti-Semitic. This was most notable in the case of Israel's support of the right-wing dictatorship of "Nazi sympathizer Alfredo Stroessner, whose thirty-five-year dictatorship is known as the *stronato* (1954–1989). In addition to entrenching an oligarchy that still rules the country to this day, Stroessner's government committed genocide against the Indigenous people of Paraguay, repressed campesino organizations that opposed the concentration of land in the hands of the elite (Paraguay still has the most unequal distribution of land in the world), engaged in systemic torture and killing of political opponents, and abducted 1,000 girls to be raped by military and government officials."[48]

As a report by *Canada Dimension* about Israel's support for such regimes over the years explains:

> Stroessner's Paraguay was an open haven for Nazi war criminals, including Hans-Ulrich Rudel, an unrepentant Nazi colonel who represented numerous West German companies across Latin America, and Josef Mengele, the infamous "Angel of Death" of Auschwitz. His regime was also a key ally of the US, Britain, and West Germany during the Cold War. Throughout his rule, the US government denied that Stroessner was perpetrating genocide and continued providing him with military aid.
>
> Despite its fascist character and the Nazi sympathies of its leadership, the Stroessner regime was deliberately courted by the Israeli government in the late 1960s. Israel's Ambassador to Paraguay, Benno Weiser Varon, claimed that the Israeli state considered leftism first, and Arab nationalism second, to be Israel's two main enemies, and as a result they viewed Stroessner's government as an admirable model. Varon insisted that Stroessner's Nazi tendencies were irrelevant, stating in his autobiography that Israel was "under steady attack from the Communist world" and therefore "the enemy of our enemy had to be our friend."[49]

The other right-wing regime and haven for World War II–era Nazis was the Argentine junta of the early 1980s. Israel had no problem arming this regime even as it was murdering Jews, and Catholics as well, including two priests who were friends of the cleric who would later become Pope Francis. Again, *Canada Dimension* explains, "In the early 1980s, the military dictatorship in Argentina imported large amounts of Israeli weapons and military advisors even though the dictatorship was openly antisemitic and specifically targeted the country's Jewish population for imprisonment and persecution. To this day, many Argentine Israelis are still petitioning the Israeli government to release all documents pertaining to its security collaboration with the military junta."

For its part, the Israeli magazine *+972* also did a report on the fact that "Israel, according to many testimonies, maintained ties with the dictatorship, aiding it with weapons and military training," and that a number of Argentine Jews, such as journalist Shlomo Slutzky, are still lobbying the Israeli government to this day for a full accounting about this.[50]

The Argentine Junta was not merely fascist, but even neo-Nazi. As the Jerusalem Center for Public Affairs explains,

> Tragically, while Argentinian Jews represented between 0.8 and 1.2 percent of the population in the 1970s, they accounted for 5 to 12 percent of the disappeared persons. Of the 8,961 victims documented in *CONADEP*'s 1984 report, *Nunca Mas*, or Never Again, 1,117 were Jewish. Once in captivity, Jewish prisoners were singled out for especially harsh treatment. This is a consequence of the "Nazi ideology that permeated the military and security forces during the country's dictatorship." *DAIA* reporting shows that "just as in the Nazi concentration camps, political prisoners in Argentina were assigned numbers, stripped of their names and humiliated, and that after they were killed, their bodies were hidden." Furthermore, recordings of Hitler's speeches were played during torture sessions.[51]

The Jerusalem Center for Public Affairs further explains that

> "Jews were subjected to an especially cruel and sadistic form of torture," including incessant beating, painting swastikas on their bodies, and the infamous "rectoscope," which consisted of inserting a tube with a rat crawling through it into a prisoner's anus. . . . The barbaric treatment of Jews by the military is a harrowing and dark memory for the Jews of Argentina. Nazi influences were evident in the ideology and actions of the regime. These frightful episodes reminded Jews of the horrors of the Holocaust and gave them a sense of how it might have felt to be a prisoner in an SS camp.

But again, none of this was an impediment to Israel's military support of this brutal regime. This is so because the interests of the State of Israel are preeminent for Zionists, even over and above the well-being of individual Jews. Indeed, Israeli forces regularly harass, beat, and arrest ultra-Orthodox Jews in Israel who support Palestine and openly protest the Israeli state as anathema to the Jewish faith.[52]

In addition to supporting these openly neo-Nazi regimes, Israel also provided military support to the Brazilian military dictatorship that came to power in 1964 in a US-backed coup, which, as Noam Chomsky has explained,[53] represented the first US government overthrow aimed at destroying the burgeoning liberation theology movement, as well as the Chilean fascist dictatorship of Augusto Pinochet.[54]

There will be some who respond to this discussion about Israel's persecution of Christianity with the retort that Israel has much-welcome support from right-wing evangelical Christians who support Israel. These Evangelicals offer such support because they believe, from a tortured interpretation of the Book of Revelation—a strange and riddle-like book of the Bible that, in my view, is open to pretty much any interpretation people wish to give it—that if and when Israel gains full dominion over the Holy Land, including over the Al-Aqsa Mosque, this will bring about the Apocalypse in which the good will be taken body and soul into Heaven and the bad are killed in an inferno of fire.

It is true that Israel is supported by such Christians who seem to be eagerly awaiting, and indeed wish to quicken, the end of the world and see Israel as a vehicle of bringing it about. They also believe that Jews, who have not accepted Jesus as their Savior, will not be a winner in God's separation of the wheat from the chaff in this event.

If any response to this need be given, I would simply say that I view the apocalyptic fantasies and desires of these Evangelicals as heretical nonsense, which has nothing to do with the notion of Christianity and Jesus that I understand from the teachings of the Gospels—teachings that are, above all, about love, forgiveness and redemption and not the fiery destruction of humanity and the world. In short, I see this as bad religion aimed at and inevitably leading to bad ends.

And this does not make me anti-Christian. Indeed, I do not view this as having anything to do with real Christianity, which I do indeed value. Similarly, one is not anti-Jewish, or an anti-Semite, because they are critical of Zionism—a belief-system rooted in the worship of a state and the belief in the superiority of one people over another. Many Jews, and I as well, view this belief-system as anathema to the very spirit of Judaism, which involves the worship of one God, forbids the worship of false idols (including a state) and whose prophets were indeed invariably critical, and many times martyred, by the states in which they lived.

Moreover, being critical of the State of Israel is more analogous to being critical of the Holy Roman Empire that had adopted Christianity as its state religion, or the Islamic Republic of Iran that has adopted Islam as its state religion. No one would seriously make the claim that a critique of the Holy Roman Empire is somehow anti-Christian or anti-papist, or that a critique of the Islamic Republic of Iran is somehow anti-Muslim. Similarly, I would submit that the claim that being critical of Israel (for example, for supporting neo-Nazi regimes) is somehow anti-Semitic is an equally silly one.

It is worth emphasizing that one very positive attribute of the United States is its founding principle of separation of state and church—something that most Americans value greatly. And indeed, most Americans are deeply suspicious and critical of nations that merge state and church, rightly believing that this naturally leads to the repression of non-state religions. Israel stands alone in getting a pass from such skepticism, with the worst feared outcomes of its one-religion state now manifesting themselves.

I end this chapter with the words of Bethlehem-based Father Munther Isaac who spoke of the false "state theology" that describes both the Zionism of Israel as well as the accompanying bad religion of American Exceptionalism, a dogma that holds that the United States is a unique, indispensable nation that is entitled to dominion over the world:

> The South African Church taught us the concept of "The state theology," defined as "the theological justification of the status quo with its racism, capitalism and totalitarianism." It does so by misusing theological concepts and biblical texts for its own political purposes.
>
> Here in Palestine, the Bible is weaponized against our very own sacred text. In our terminology in Palestine, we speak of the Empire. Here we

confront the theology of the Empire. A disguise for superiority, supremacy, "chosenness," and entitlement. It is sometimes given a nice cover using
words like mission and evangelism, fulfillment of prophecy, and spreading
freedom and liberty. The theology of the Empire becomes a powerful tool
to mask oppression under the cloak of divine sanction. It divides people
into "us" and "them." It dehumanizes and demonizes. It speaks of land
without people even when they know the land has people—and not just
any people. It calls for emptying Gaza, just like it called the ethnic cleansing in 1948 "a divine miracle." It calls for us Palestinians to go to Egypt,
maybe Jordan, or why not just the sea?

The full text of Father Isaac's "Christ in the Rubble" homily that he gave
on December 23, 2003, and of which the above was a part, is attached at
the end of the book as Appendix A.

THE CASE FOR PALESTINE

I am all for freeing the hostages; ALL of the hostages: the 240 Israelis being held hostage and the 2.3 million people of Gaza who have been held hostage for twenty years.

—Norman Finkelstein, author, professor and
descendant of Holocaust survivors

We must use terror, assassination, and intimidation. We must steal their land and eliminate every social service to free Israel from its Arab population.

—David Ben-Gurion, founding father and first
prime minister of Israel

The curtain has been pulled back. The veil has been ripped away. The mask has been discarded. There is no law applicable to the west. They never really believed in human rights, humanitarian law, or even the prohibition of genocide. It was all about controlling the other.

—Craig Mokhiber, former head of the New York Office
of the UN High Commission for Human Rights

As I write these words, the war on Gaza is still raging. Around 1.4 million Gazans, out of 2.3 million, are living in tents in Rafah along the border of Egypt, and it is winter there and cold. They have little to no access to food.

In terms of water, their choice is between drinking salty sea water or filthy water from the ground. More and more people are succumbing to hunger, thirst, and disease. I saw one report that "children in Gaza are dying from cardiac arrest because they haven't slept in two or three months & the constant bombardment by IOF [Israeli Offensive Forces] has caused their bodies to continuously release adrenaline, which is damaging their hearts."[1] Israel has begun bombing Rafah and is now threatening a full-scale ground invasion into this city—an invasion that all agree will bring about possibly the greatest mass slaughter yet seen in the conflict.

Peace does not seem close at hand. While there have been cease-fire talks being brokered by Qatar and Egypt, these seem to be a dead end, at least for now. And, while the Western press seems to blame Hamas for this impasse, and Biden has called Hamas's counterproposal to Israel's cease-fire "over the top," this does not appear to be fair. Thus, while not reported widely, Hamas has made an offer that seems eminently reasonable and intended to protect the well-being of the hostages as well as the people of Gaza.

In short, this proposal called for a three-phase exchange of hostages during a 135-day cease-fire during which time the parties would negotiate a final end to hostilities.[2] In addition, the proposal called for "at least 500 humanitarian aid and fuel trucks to be allowed into Gaza daily. It has asked for the provision of 60,000 temporary homes and 200,000 tents and has stipulated that displaced Palestinians in Gaza must be allowed to freely return to their homes, with no barriers, in the context of a mutual, temporary truce."[3] And ultimately, it called for Israel to rebuild that which it had destroyed.[4] Israel quickly rejected this counterproposal out of hand.

I pray that, by the time you read this book, the current war on Gaza is over. But whether it is or not, there is no doubt that Gaza and the people still living there will be in utter misery, with virtually no civilian infrastructure left—no functioning hospitals, no universities, and just a few schools. As for universities, many of us have watched in horror the video showing the last of the universities in Gaza still intact blown up in an act of surgical demolition by Israeli forces who set 315 mines at the foot of it and brought it down into rubble and dust.[5]

And this was not an isolated instance of demolition carried out with cold calculation by the Israeli forces in Gaza. Indeed, such demolitions—to my knowledge never carried out in any other armed conflict—is standard operating procedure for the IDF. As the *New York Times* detailed, in the article "Israel's Controlled Demolitions Are Razing Neighborhoods in Gaza,"

> The damage caused by Israel's aerial offensive in Gaza has been well documented. But Israeli ground forces have also carried out a wave of controlled explosions that has drastically changed the landscape in recent months.
>
> At least 33 controlled demolitions have destroyed hundreds of buildings—including mosques, schools, and entire sections of residential neighborhoods—since November, a New York Times analysis of Israeli military footage, social media videos and satellite imagery shows.[6]

In short, the IDF is surgically dismantling the entire civilian architecture of Gaza in a nihilistic and unprecedented act of violence. And the fact it is able to do so in such a slow and methodical manner shows how the IDF's assault on Gaza is not so much a war as it is a turkey shoot, which has always been the case with regard to Israel's "military" actions.

In addition to bringing down buildings such as universities and schools, the Israelis have also been killing professors and students in Gaza at an alarming rate in what some have referred to as a calculated act of "educide."[7]

First of all, it must be noted when making the case for Palestine that Palestinians value education and intellectualism highly, and despite all of the obstacles presented to them, are some of the most educated people in the world. As Anne Irfan writes in the Columbia University Press blog,

> In September 2018, a report from the Palestinian Central Bureau of Statistics found that Palestinians have one of the highest literacy rates in the world. The finding chimed with the Palestinians' long-running reputation as the world's "best-educated refugees"—a claim often made by international organizations as well as regional actors. Particularly but not exclusively in the Middle East, Palestinians have long had a reputation as high-performing graduates, often proficient in at least two languages, and

frequently going on to pursue successful careers in engineering, business, or medicine. At the same time, the Palestinians are the world's largest refugee population, with the longest-running case of protracted displacement. How did it happen, then, that a large-scale refugee population, many of whom survived for decades in refugee camps, became so highly educated?[8]

The main answer to this query is that the Palestinians go to great lengths to educate themselves and their children even in extremely adverse circumstances. The Israelis, hell-bent on wiping out Palestinian society, are doing their level best to destroy this culture of education.

On January 30, 2024, the British Society for Middle Eastern Studies (BRISMES), which was founded in 1973 and describes itself as the "largest national academic association in Europe focused on the study of the Middle East and North Africa," sounded the alarm in an open letter to UK Prime Minister Sunak and other officials:

> The education system in Gaza is made up of over 625,000 students and about 22,500 teachers and professors, all of whom have been impacted by the war. As documented by the Palestinian Ministry of Education and the Euro-Mediterranean Human Rights Monitor, since the beginning of the war, 4,327 students have been killed and 7,819 others injured, while 231 teachers and administrators have been killed and 756 injured during the ongoing attacks. The Israeli army has also killed 94 university professors. The number of students and educational staff killed in such a short period is unprecedented in the region's history.
>
> The destruction of educational infrastructures is also unprecedented. During the war's first 16 weeks, 345 out of Gaza's 737 schools were destroyed or damaged, and as we write about 30 percent of school buildings will be out of service even after a ceasefire is implemented. Consequently, hundreds of thousands school children who have already been deprived of education for several months will not have a school to return to once the Israeli forces' attacks subside.[9]

BRISMES also explained that "Higher education infrastructures have also been heavily targeted. The Geneva-based independent Euro-Med Human

Rights Monitor has documented *Israel's systematic destruction of every university in Gaza*" (emphasis added).

BRISMES noted with particular concern the fact that "On January 17, 2024, Israel circulated images of the complete destruction in a controlled detonation of Israa University, the last remaining major university in the Gaza Strip." If this were not all, BRISMES related that "Alongside the wholesale decimation of the physical infrastructure of higher education in the Gaza Strip, including, for example, the looting of 3,000 rare artifacts by Israeli soldiers who occupied Israa University before they demolished it." In addition, "Israeli forces have killed many members of Gaza's academic community, including numerous internationally respected scholars, who comprised part of the region's intellectual leadership."

BRISMES does not mince words about what it believes is going on here: "The systematic indiscriminate targeting of the Palestinian education system is a war crime and a crime against humanity, as defined by the 1998 Rome Statute, and appears to be an integral part of the broader pattern of elimination emphasized in South Africa's application to the International Court of Justice." That is, this "educide" is part and parcel of Israel's genocidal campaign in Gaza.

In the West Bank, Israel's attacks against the Palestinians continue unabated. And nothing and no one will be off limits. For example, on February 16, 2024, it was reported that the hundredth child had been killed by Israeli Forces in the West Bank since October 7. The *New Arab*, citing The Defense of Children International—Palestine, reported that the hundredth victim, Neehel Ziad Mohammad Bregheith, "was shot as he and other students were leaving school on Wednesday during a raid by Israeli forces on the town. Ten Palestinians were reportedly injured during the attacks. In February alone, Israeli forces shot dead five boys aged between fourteen and seventeen. In two of these cases, they confiscated the bodies and are indefinitely withholding them from the families."[10] One child who was killed in February, Mohamad Ahmed Khadour, was a Palestinian American, having been born in Washington state.[11]

On February 13, 2024, it was reported that Israeli forces had arrested 7,000 Palestinians in West Bank since October 7.[12]

My friend Firas Sarhan, who now lives in London, told me of the destruction of a charitable institution he had taken years to help build in the Nur Shams refugee camp in the West Bank.

This institution, a center for children with physical and learning disabilities, was invaded by IDF forces who ransacked it and left it in a shambles. Firas sent me the press release announcing this tragedy. The release reads, in pertinent part, "'They ransacked the building, destroying equipment, damaging all the rooms including the new sensory room,' [the Center's Manager] Nehayah reported today. Essential paperwork for the 250 children who receive treatment at the centre was also destroyed, with IDF also taking food and winter clothing for children, the ink from the printer and throwing walking frames, mattresses, and beds out on the street. Windows were peppered with shots and, although snipers took positions on the building's rooftops, fortunately no one was injured. Nehayah's house was also searched and partly destroyed. She continues; 'Thank God no one was injured at the Centre. There is no fresh food and nowhere for people to go,' she added. 'I helped to build the Centre from zero, my own soul has been broken.'"

Another despicable act carried out in the West Bank was in the Ibn Sina hospital in the Jenin refugee camp. On January 30, 2024, armed Israeli soldiers—dressed as medical staff and civilians, with some pretending to carry babies—entered the hospital and murdered three young men while they were sleeping.[13] One of the men killed was eighteen years old and paralyzed. While Israeli officials claim that these men were terrorists who were themselves planning an attack, it is clear that they could have apprehended these individuals and tried them upon such allegations. Instead, the IDF terrorized the occupants of the hospital and carried out a cold-blooded killing. The terror was all part of the plan as it has been since 1948. Can you imagine what outrage would have been expressed if Hamas militants carried out a similar attack in an Israeli hospital? The outcry would be deafening. Instead, a collective yawn was heard from the Western press, which just assumes that the assassination of Palestinians is justified upon mere allegations of terrorism.

Another aspect of Israel's attack against the West Bank that is intensifying is the systematic theft and killing of sheep being raised by the Bedouin community, sheep being the lifeblood of the Bedouin.[14] The sheep of the Bedouin are indeed akin to the bison of many indigenous communities of North America which were also targeted for destruction by the colonial settlers in order to cut off their lifeline.

Sadly, this is just another day in the life for Palestinians living under Israeli occupation.

The International Court of Justice has issued a preliminary ruling on South Africa's genocide charges against Israel. Thus, on January 26, 2024, the ICJ concluded that it is at least "plausible," given the facts known about the assault on Gaza, that Israel is carrying out a genocide against the Palestinians and that Israel is therefore required to take a number of "protective measures" to stop and prevent such a genocide from occurring.[15] In pertinent part, the ICJ wrote:

> The Court takes note . . . of the statement made by the United Nations UnderSecretary-General for Humanitarian Affairs and Emergency Relief Coordinator, Mr Martin Griffiths, on 5 January 2024:
> "Gaza has become a place of death and despair.
> . . . Families are sleeping in the open as temperatures plummet. Areas where civilians were told to relocate for their safety have come under bombardment. Medical facilities are under relentless attack. The few hospitals that are partially functional are overwhelmed with trauma cases, critically short of all supplies, and inundated by desperate people seeking safety.
> A public health disaster is unfolding. Infectious diseases are spreading in overcrowded shelters as sewers spill over. Some 180 Palestinian women are giving birth daily amidst this chaos. People are facing the highest levels of food insecurity ever recorded. Famine is around the corner.
> For children in particular, the past 12 weeks have been traumatic: No food. No water. No school. Nothing but the terrifying sounds of war, day in and day out.
> Gaza has simply become uninhabitable. Its people are witnessing daily threats to their very existence—while the world watches on."

The ICJ also took into consideration the statement of a representative of the World Health Organization (WHO) who stated, "An unprecedented

93 percent of the population in Gaza is facing crisis levels of hunger, with insufficient food and high levels of malnutrition. At least one in four households are facing 'catastrophic conditions': experiencing an extreme lack of food and starvation and having resorted to selling off their possessions and other extreme measures to afford a simple meal. Starvation, destitution, and death are evident."

In addition, the ICJ cited the UN agency in charge of providing humanitarian assistance to Palestinians, UNRWA, which had stated the following:

> It's been 100 days since the devastating war started, killing and displacing people in Gaza, following the horrific attacks that Hamas and other groups carried out against people in Israel. It's been 100 days of ordeal and anxiety for hostages and their families.
>
> In the past 100 days, sustained bombardment across the Gaza Strip caused the mass displacement of a population that is in a state of flux—constantly uprooted and forced to leave overnight, only to move to places which are just as unsafe. This has been the largest displacement of the Palestinian people since 1948.
>
> This war affected more than 2 million people, the entire population of Gaza. Many will carry lifelong scars, both physical and psychological. The vast majority, including children, are deeply traumatized. Overcrowded and unsanitary UNRWA shelters have now become "home" to more than 1.4 million people. They lack everything, from food to hygiene to privacy. People live in inhumane conditions, where diseases are spreading, including among children. They live through the unlivable, with the clock ticking fast towards famine.
>
> The plight of children in Gaza is especially heartbreaking. An entire generation of children is traumatized and will take years to heal. Thousands have been killed, maimed, and orphaned. Hundreds of thousands are deprived of education. Their future is in jeopardy, with far-reaching and long-lasting consequences.

Note that, in addition to describing the abhorrent conditions of life created for the people of Gaza by Israel, UNRWA also condemns what it describes at the outset of its statement "the horrific attacks that Hamas and other groups carried out against people in Israel." We shall return to UNRWA and this denunciation shortly.

In addition, I note UNRWA's reference to the fact that "thousands" of children in Gaza have been "orphaned" as a result of the current conflict. As of the time of this writing, it is estimated by UNICEF that there are around 17,000 children in Gaza who are now "unaccompanied"—that is, without any family or friends to take care of them.[16] One must ask, what will become of these children?

The ICJ considered the death and destruction resulting from Israel's assault on Gaza in combination with the litany of genocidal language coming from Israeli officials. In terms of this language, the ICJ relied, in pertinent part, on the observations "of the United Nations Human Rights Council, in which they voiced alarm over 'discernibly genocidal and dehumanizing rhetoric coming from senior Israeli government officials.' In addition, on 27 October 2023, the United Nations Committee on the Elimination of Racial Discrimination observed that it was 'highly concerned about the sharp increase in racist hate speech and dehumanization directed at Palestinians since 7 October.'"

In light of the foregoing, the ICJ concluded "that the plausible rights in question in these proceedings, namely the right of Palestinians in the Gaza Strip to be protected from acts of genocide and related prohibited acts identified in Article III of the Genocide Convention and the right of South Africa to seek Israel's compliance with the latter's obligations under the Convention, are of such a nature that prejudice to them is capable of causing irreparable harm," and that "provisional measures" were therefore required to prevent such harm pending a full trial on the matter.

It is important to note that, on January 31, 2024, the US District Court for the Northern District of California, in the Center for Constitutional Rights (CCR) case against President Biden for aiding and abetting genocide in Gaza, reached the same conclusion as the ICJ, thus writing,

The undisputed evidence before this Court comports with the finding of the ICJ and indicates that the current treatment of the Palestinians in the Gaza Strip by the Israeli military may plausibly constitute a genocide in violation of international law. Both the uncontroverted testimony of the Plaintiffs and the expert opinion proffered at the hearing on these motions as well as statements made by various officers of the Israeli government indicate that the ongoing military siege in Gaza is intended to eradicate a whole people and therefore plausibly falls within the international prohibition against genocide. . . . It is every individual's obligation to confront the current siege in Gaza.[17]

While the US District Court ultimately held, reluctantly it made clear, that the "political question" doctrine prohibited it from exercising jurisdiction in the case—that is, because the Constitutional separation of powers prevented it from interfering in the foreign policy decisions of the Executive Branch—it nonetheless stated, "This Court implores Defendants [President Biden, et al.] to examine the results of their unflagging support of the military siege against the Palestinians in Gaza."

The ICJ ordered, in pertinent part, that "Israel must, in accordance with its obligations under the Genocide Convention, in relation to Palestinians in Gaza, take all measures within its power to prevent the commission of all acts within the scope of Article II of this Convention, in particular: (a) killing members of the group; (b) causing serious bodily or mental harm to members of the group; (c) deliberately inflicting on the group conditions of life calculated to bring about its physical destruction in whole or in part; and (d) imposing measures intended to prevent births within the group." The ICJ further ordered "that Israel must take immediate and effective measures to enable the provision of urgently needed basic services and humanitarian assistance to address the adverse conditions of life faced by Palestinians in the Gaza Strip."

Israel and its patron, the United States, responded quickly to this order, but not in compliance thereof. Rather, they acted quickly to do the exact opposite of what was being ordered, and to therefore show their profound contempt for the ICJ and the rule of international law.

Thus, while the ICJ ordered Israel to prevent the killing of Palestinians in Gaza, the AP explained that "Since the ruling, Israel has continued its military offensive . . . and hundreds more Palestinians have been killed."[18] Indeed, within just forty-eight hours of the ICJ decision,

"Euro-Med Monitor reported that the Israeli army had killed over 373 Palestinians—including 345 civilians—and injured over 643 more."[19] In flagrantly refusing to abide by the ICJ decision, Israel officials denounced the ICJ's decision, issued by fifteen of the ICJ's seventeen judges, as anti-Semitic.[20] The fifteen judges who signed on to the decision were approved by the UN General Assembly and are from the United States, Lebanon, Slovakia, France, Somalia, China, India, Japan, Germany, Australia, Mexico, Romania, and South Africa, respectively. It defies belief that all these judges were motivated by anti-Semitic hatred. However, the absurdities did not end with this claim, with some Israeli officials complaining that the ICJ "remained silent during the Holocaust."[21] Of course, the ICJ was not even created until after the Holocaust and World War II were ended. While still other Israeli officials complained that the ICJ decision "cheapens the very essence of the term 'genocide,'"[22] it is Israeli officials who do so, and who also cheapen the idea of anti-Semitism itself, by making such patently ridiculous charges.

For its part, the United States, along with several other Western allies and at the urging of Israel, aggressively flaunted the ICJ's admonition "to take immediate and effective measures to enable the provision of urgently needed basic services and humanitarian assistance to address the adverse conditions of life faced by Palestinians in the Gaza Strip." To wit, within hours of the ICJ ruling, the United States, Germany, Canada, Netherlands (*ironically, where the ICJ is based*), United Kingdom, Italy, Australia, and Finland suspended all of the aid they were providing to UNRWA.[23] This amounted to the severance of around 57 percent of all of UNRWA's funding.[24]

This represents a severe blow to the Palestinian population of Gaza, and elsewhere as well, at the very time of their extreme desperation. As Al Jazeera explained in no uncertain terms, UNRWA is "considered a lifeline for two million people in the besieged enclave" of the Gaza Strip,[25] and these nine Western countries decided to cut that lifeline when it was most needed.

For all of the West's chest-thumping about human rights and international law, and its use of alleged human rights and international law violations to justify military interventions, this has always been mere theater.

Indeed, the United States time and again has shown utter contempt for the international law system. The most glaring example is its response to the most important ICJ case before the current one involving Israeli genocide, and that is the case of *Nicaragua v. United States* (1986). In that case, the ICJ ruled that the United States was violating international customary law by supporting the Contra forces against Nicaragua, mining Nicaragua's harbors and blowing up Nicaragua's oil installations.

The ICJ ordered the United States to cease support for the Contras and to compensate Nicaragua for the damage done by the US's terror campaign against the country. In response, the US Congress did vote to end Contra aid. However, the Reagan administration, not deterred either by domestic or international law, continued to secretly arm the Contras through illegal arms sales to Iran and by proceeds from CIA-facilitated cocaine trafficking on the streets of US inner cities.[26] This became known as the Iran-Contra scandal. In addition, the United States has, to this day, refused to compensate Nicaragua as ordered by the ICJ. This all puts into perspective Nicaragua's decision to bring its own ICJ case against Western countries for their role in aiding and abetting Israel's genocide in Gaza. There appears to be some poetic justice here.

The justification for the terrible act of cutting off Gaza's humanitarian lifeline was Israel's unverified claim, made over 100 days after the fact, that a handful of UNRWA staff people participated in the October 7 attacks against Israel. Originally, Israel claimed that it was twelve staff members who were so involved, but that number quickly was reduced to six staff who allegedly infiltrated Israel on October 7, and only four who allegedly were involved in kidnapping Israelis that day.[27]

The publication *Mondoweiss* described the absurdity, and obvious "cruelty," of this decision:

> On January 26, Israeli allegations against a dozen UNRWA employees surfaced. The agency immediately fired nine of them and said that two others were dead, hoping their swift and pre-emptive action would stave off rash US actions. Nonetheless, the United States and a host of other countries immediately suspended funding for UNRWA, over the actions of 12 of over 30,000 employees, 13,000 of whom are in Gaza.

It's worth pausing over that last fact for a moment. Twelve out of 13,000 Gaza employees have caused all of this, and it's based on evidence that has not been made public. You'd never know that from much of the media coverage, which is, once again, treating Israeli allegations as proven facts. Nor could you tell by the US response. Secretary of State Antony Blinken stated, "We haven't had the ability to investigate [the allegations] ourselves. But they are highly, highly credible."[28]

As *Mondoweiss* also explains, Israel's claims about UNRWA staff is undermined by the fact that the "UNRWA submits lists of all of its employees in the West Bank and Gaza to Israel. Somehow, Israel had no problem with these twelve, despite their supposedly extensive knowledge of the membership of Hamas and other Palestinian groups."

Moreover, as *Mondoweiss* also emphasizes, despite any alleged bad apples, Israel itself has acknowledged the valuable work that UNRWA does, and that, in fact, while Israel starves out the people of Gaza, it can and does point to UNRWA and its work to try to claim that the civilians of Gaza are at least receiving some support and protection. That is, the existence of UNRWA has provided a fig leaf for Israel's genocidal campaign.

Still, Israel wants to severely weaken and undermine UNRWA, and has always wanted to, in order to further its goal of eliminating the Palestinian people. This fact was underscored in an announcement by Jewish Voices for Peace (JVP) headlined, "Defunding UNRWA is another heinous act of Genocide," which condemned the cuts to UNRWA and demanded that the funding be immediately restored. As JVP explained, "The Israeli government has sought to undermine UNRWA for decades, recently accusing it of 'perpetuating the refugee problem'—in other words, keeping Palestinians alive."[29] And, lest there be any doubt about this, the *Times of Israel* reported on December 29, 2023—that is, even before the allegations about the UNRWA staff were made—that Israel plans to push UNRWA entirely out of Gaza after the war.[30]

JVP pointed out the glaring hypocrisy of the Biden administration immediately cutting off funding for UNRWA over unverified claims about a handful of staff (as JVP notes, accounting for only "0.0004 percent of their total workforce") while at the same time refusing "to even place conditions on the billions of dollars in weapons and aid to the Israeli state and military—despite mountains of evidence in international court that Israel is committing genocide." Indeed, as noted above, the Biden administration has worked to lift any conditions, including human rights conditions, on military assistance to Israel even as it has been pummeling Gaza. As JVP pointed out, "at least 153 UNRWA workers have been killed in Gaza by the Israeli military in the last few months—a war crime, one to which the US government has yet to respond."

On February 5, 2024, *Channel 4* of Britain, after a detailed review of the mere six-page dossier Israel provided as the basis for its claims, concluded that it contained "no evidence to support its explosive new claim that UNRWA staff were involved in the terror attacks on Israel."[31] Despite this lack of evidence, UNRWA has been brought to the edge of disaster, stating that if funding is not restored by the end of February 2024, it will have to discontinue its operations altogether.[32]

As if to highlight its utter contempt for the ICJ and international law, Israel even destroyed a UNRWA convoy loaded with food for people in Gaza on February 4. As of the time of this writing, UNRWA had claimed that this was the third time that Israel had attacked such a humanitarian aid convoy.[33] In addition, UNRWA announced that only four of its twelve health facilities in Gaza were operational as the result of Israeli attacks.[34]

As the *Arab News* explained, "Philippe Lazzarini, the agency's commissioner general, said that although the agency notifies Israel of all aid convoys and coordinates with authorities on their movements, they continue to come under fire. . . . 'We cannot deliver humanitarian aid under fire,' the agency said."[35] The whole point is to prevent humanitarian aid from being delivered.

Indeed, the Associated Press reported on February 9, 2024, that Israel was intentionally blocking a UNRWA shipment of food bound from Turkey for the people of Gaza. As the AP explained, "That stoppage means 1,049 shipping containers of rice, flour, chickpeas, sugar, and cooking oil—enough to feed 1.1 million people for one month—are stuck, even as an estimated 25 percent of families in Gaza face catastrophic hunger."[36] Scores of Israeli citizens have been happy to help out this mission by blocking aid trucks attempting to get into Gaza.[37]

In addition, Israel has punished some countries that have refused to go along with the decision to cut off aid to UNRWA, for example by bombing Belgium's Embassy in Gaza shortly after Belgium announced that it would be continuing funding to the agency.[38]

But UNRWA is not the only relief agency that Israel targeted after the ICJ decision. Thus, on February 9, 2024, news services reported that Israel was targeting the headquarters of the Palestinian Red Crescent in Gaza. Ironically, the Red Crescent (the Arab version of the Red Cross) is not just tasked with providing humanitarian and medical relief; it is also tasked with monitoring compliance with international humanitarian law in conflict zones. The *Middle East Monitor* quoted a Red Crescent spokesperson as stating, "The Israeli army deliberately targeted the society's headquarters and vehicles to put them out of service. . . . The Israeli army is still besieging the society's Al-Amal Hospital, west of Khan Younis, from all sides, depriving Palestinians sheltering there of food, water, medical supplies, basic needs, and oxygen. The hospital houses more than 200 patients, medical, and administrative staff."[39]

Another incident took place after the ICJ decision, which became emblematic for Palestinians about Israel's nefarious intentions in Gaza, and this involved the killing of a six-year-old girl named Hind Rajab along with two Palestinian Red Crescent Society (PRCS) paramedics. As Al Jazeera reported, Hind was riding in a family car when it was "peppered with bullets" by IDF forces.[40] Her uncle, aunt, and their three children were in the car at the time and were killed immediately. Hind survived and called emergency services for help: "'I'm so scared, please come. Please call someone to come and take me,' she was heard crying desperately in the call that PRCS said lasted three hours in an effort to calm the frightened child." A PRCS ambulance, manned with two paramedics, was dispatched to save her. Despite the fact that the PRCS coordinated with the IDF to make this rescue, the IDF shot up the ambulance and the two paramedics inside. In addition, they shot Hind Rajab while she cowered in the car along with the bodies of her relatives. It took twelve days for the PRCS to figure out what had happened to its ambulance, paramedics, and to Hind.

This incident is being pointed to as evidence that Israel has absolutely no regard for the lives of Palestinians, including little children, and it indeed appears to be so. This is nothing new. As Pulitzer Prize–winning journalist Chris Hedges said when reporting from Gaza in 2003, "Children have been shot in other conflicts I have covered. But never have I watched as soldiers enticed children like mice into a trap and murdered them for sport."

The depths of hatred that the Israeli government and most Israelis have for the Palestinian people cannot be overstated. If more evidence need be given, *Haaretz* provided it on February 4, 2024 in a shocking story about the IDF's running a Telegram channel, known a "72 Virgins—Uncensored," which runs what some have referenced as "snuff films" of Palestinians being murdered.[41] As *Haaretz* explained, this gruesome channel was created for the purpose of influencing Israeli opinion, apparently because Israelis generally respond so well to the graphic killing of Palestinians.

Haaretz described the site as follows:

The channel's administrators posted graphic content, such as images of the dead bodies of Hamas terrorists, captioned "Shatter the terrorists' fantasy," on a daily basis. . . . They uploaded thousands of videos and still images of the killing of terrorists and destruction in the Strip, and encouraged the channel's followers to share the content so that "everyone can see we're screwing them."

The operators used coarse language in a bid to obscure the IDF's involvement in the channel. An October post read: "Burning their mother . . . You won't believe the video we got! You can hear their bones crunch. We'll post it right away, get ready." Photos of Palestinian men captured by the IDF in the Strip and the bodies of terrorists were captioned: "Exterminating the roaches . . . exterminating the Hamas rats . . . Share this beauty." A video of a soldier allegedly dipping machine gun bullets in pork fat is captioned: "What a man!!!!! Greases bullets with lard. You won't get your virgins." Another caption was: "Garbage juice!!!! Another dead terrorist!! You have to watch it with the sound, you'll die laughing."

It must be emphasized that the Palestinians *Haaretz* refers to as "terrorists" in this story without comment or qualification are often just civilians, and in any case, are people being killed without warrant or trial. But even for *Haaretz*, a well-respected Israeli paper that is about as objective as any paper in Israel, this is of no matter. I would say that this is the case because, for most Israelis, Palestinians are guilty until proven innocent. However, Palestinians are rarely given an opportunity to prove their innocence and so they simply remain guilty forever.

As *Haaretz* also reported, "The channel administrators didn't stop at images from Gaza. On October 11, hundreds of Israelis, including members of the Beitar Jerusalem soccer team's violently racist fan club La Familia rioted at Sheba Medical Center, Tel Hashomer, near Tel Aviv, following a rumor that Hamas terrorists who had invaded Israel were being treated there. People roamed the hospital, cursing out and spitting on medical professionals. Within an hour, a video of the riot was posted to the 72 Virgins channel with the title, 'My brothers, the heroessss, La Familia fans, love you!!!!!!! What heroes, they came to screw the Arabs.'"

For its part, the *New York Times* reported on February 6, 2024, about the proliferation of Tik Tok videos posted by Israeli soldiers, some of which are being viewed by tens of thousands of people. The title of the article says it all: "What Israeli Soldiers' Videos Reveal: Cheering Destruction and Mocking Gazans."[42] As the *Times* explains, many of these videos "capture soldiers vandalizing local shops and school classrooms, making derogatory comments about Palestinians, bulldozing what appear to be civilian areas and calling for the building of Israeli settlements in Gaza, an inflammatory idea that is promoted by some far-right Israeli politicians." Still, many other videos show members of Israel's Combat Engineering Corps, which is responsible for the controlled demolitions in Gaza, celebrating as they bring down civilian structures such as residential buildings.

In short, Israel has proven that it has no regard for international law or for the lives and welfare of the Palestinians whose lands it occupies. This is why this occupation must end, for Israel will not stop oppressing and killing the Palestinians until every Palestinian in historic Palestine is either ejected or dead. And be sure that the Palestinians will never stop resisting this as is their right to do. This is why Israel can no longer exist as a state that, by its very definition, is exclusive, non-pluralistic and chauvinistic; a state reserved for only one people—people the state defines as Jewish. I say as the state defines who is Jewish because that has actually changed over time as the Israeli government has deemed it necessary. Thus, as Uri Davis explained to me, Jewishness in Israel is defined by a law of 1950, as amended in 1970. This first defined a Jew as having a Jewish mother and having never converted to another religion. As of 1970, this was changed to having one Jewish parent or grandparent even if one had converted. This change was made to guarantee Jewish majority in Israel—a big preoccupation of the government.

At one point, there was a large consensus over two states—one Jewish and one Arab, and this was agreed to in 1993 between Israel and the PLO in the Oslo Accords. However, it is Israel which, beginning before the ink on this agreement was even dry, has made this impossible, and it has done so intentionally. The only remaining option is a multiethnic, multireligious, and pluralistic state where each person, regardless of race or religion, has equal rights and one vote.

One of the most famous and respected Palestinian intellectuals, the late Edward Said, who taught at Columbia University, expressed the need for such a one-state solution back in 1999 in a *New York Times* opinion piece. In this piece, Said explains how such a state is the only solution remaining for both Jews and Palestinians living in historic Palestine. But first, he explains why the two-state solution, then contemplated in the Oslo Accords, was not then a viable solution and really never was.

As Said explained:

The conflict appears intractable because it is a contest over the same land by two peoples who always believed they had valid title to it and who hoped that the other side would in time give up or go away. One side won the war, the other lost, but the contest is as alive as ever. We Palestinians ask why a Jew born in Warsaw or New York has the right to settle here (according to Israel's Law of Return), whereas we, the people who lived here for centuries, cannot. After 1967, the conflict between us was exacerbated. Years of military occupation have created in the weaker party anger, humiliation, and hostility.[43]

Said further relates that "In the West Bank, Jerusalem and Gaza, the situation is deeply unstable and exploitative. Protected by the army, Israeli settlers (almost 350,000 of them) live as extraterritorial, privileged people with rights that resident Palestinians do not have. (For example, West Bank Palestinians cannot go to Jerusalem and in 70 percent of the territory are still subject to Israeli military law, with their land available for confiscation.) Israel controls Palestinian water resources and security, as well as exits and entrances. Even the new Gaza airport is under Israeli security control. You don't need to be an expert to see that this is a prescription for extending, not limiting, conflict. Here the truth must be faced, not avoided or denied."

Things have only gotten much worse for the Palestinians since these words were written a quarter of a century ago. Back in 1999, Said mentions "the new Gaza airport." Israel did not allow that airport (the Yasser Arafat International Airport)—the one airport in Gaza—to stand for very long, bombing the radar station and control tower in December 2001 and then going so far as to bulldoze the runway in January 2002. And, as already discussed above, Israel, in its latest round of mass bombardments of Gaza since October 7, 2023, has left nearly no other infrastructure standing. Gaza is left in rubble. The possibility of any viable Palestinian state being built from the rubble and ash has been made impossible for a long time to come. That was the intention of Netanyahu who has been repeating his unwavering position that there will be no Palestinian statehood.

As for the West Bank, the illegal settlements referred to by Said have only mushroomed. While Said talked of 350,000 Israeli settlers—then living in both Gaza and the West Bank—there are now 500,000 such settlers in the West Bank alone and another 250,000 in East Jerusalem. In the article, "Israeli Settlers Are Causing Mayhem in the West Bank," the *Economist* explained, "Some 500,000 Israelis live in settlements (excluding East Jerusalem) in the West Bank regarded as illegal by the UN and foreign governments. They are often cited as an obstacle in peace talks and plainly undermine the territorial integrity of a future Palestinian state. The building of settlements has steadily increased since the Israeli-Palestinian peace accords signed in Oslo in 1993."[44]

As explained above, the "mayhem" created by these settlers, with the full backing of the IDF, has only increased since October 7, with the *Economist* explaining, "Last year [2022] was already the deadliest for Palestinians in the West Bank for twenty years. Settler groups have become bolder, and the army has intensified its raids on Palestinian towns and cities. But since October 7th things have dramatically worsened. At the current rate, the four weeks following the Hamas attack will have been more deadly for Palestinians in the West Bank than the whole of last year."

In short, if conditions for a two-state solution were inhospitable back in 1999 when Said was writing, they are only much more so now. And again, this has been as per the intention of the Israeli state. Of all the difficult and challenging options available, it seems that the one-state solution, which really should have been the solution to begin with, is the only one which makes any sense now.

As Said, who was magnanimous in the future state he was conceiving, concluded:

> The beginning is to develop something entirely missing from both Israeli and Palestinian realities today: the idea and practice of citizenship, not of ethnic or racial community, as the main vehicle for coexistence. In a modern state, all its members are citizens by virtue of their presence and the sharing of rights and responsibilities. Citizenship therefore entitles an Israeli Jew and a Palestinian Arab to the same privileges and resources. A constitution and a bill of rights thus become necessary for getting beyond Square 1 of the conflict because each group would have the same right to self-determination; that is, the right to practice communal life in its own (Jewish or Palestinian) way, perhaps in federated cantons, with a joint capital in Jerusalem, equal access to land and inalienable secular and juridical rights. Neither side should be held hostage to religious extremists.

As Said correctly noted, "The alternatives are unpleasantly simple: either the war continues (along with the onerous cost of the current peace process) or a way out, based on peace and equality (as in South Africa after apartheid) is actively sought, despite the many obstacles."

Said explains that "the millennia-long history of Palestine provides at least two precedents for thinking in such secular and modest terms. First, Palestine is and has always been a land of many histories; it is a radical simplification to think of it as principally or exclusively Jewish or Arab. While the Jewish presence is longstanding, it is by no means the main one. Other tenants have included Canaanites, Moabites, Jebusites and Philistines in ancient times, and Romans, Ottomans, Byzantines, and Crusaders in the modern ages. Palestine is multicultural, multiethnic, multireligious. There is as little historical justification for homogeneity as there is for notions of national or ethnic and religious purity today."

In addition to historic Palestine, and South Africa as well, which Said mentions, another historic precedent is the United States of America. The US is a pluralistic society of many races, ethnicities, religions, and beliefs. That is not to say that the United States is perfectly so, and it is not. And the United States, like Israel, was built on settler-colonialism and ethnic cleansing and genocide against the indigenous population. The US also has a history of something that Israel does not—the enslavement of Africans imported from Africa.

Despite this terrible history, and other historical stains such as Jim Crow segregation and the internment of Japanese Americans during World War II, the United States, with an evolving Constitution, which—through a bloody civil war over slavery, amendments, and progressive Court interpretations, and with the push of protest movements and demonstrations and struggle—protects the equal rights of all peoples without regard to race, religion, national origin, or gender. And, in 2008, this country elected an African American named Barack Hussein Obama as president, and he remains the most popular president so far this century. If such a state could be built in the United States—a country that often has appeared to be infertile ground for true equality and pluralism—it can be built in Israel/Palestine.

HOMILY OF LUTHERAN MINISTER

Christ in the Rubble
A Liturgy of Lament
Rev. Dr. Munther Isaac
Evangelical Lutheran Christmas Church Bethlehem
Saturday, December 23rd, 2023

We are angry!

We are broken!

This should have been a time of joy; instead, we are mourning. We are fearful.

20,000 killed. Thousands under the rubble still. Close to 9,000 children killed in the most brutal ways. Day after day after day. 1.9 million displaced! Hundreds of thousands of homes were destroyed. Gaza as we know it no longer exists. This is an annihilation. A genocide.

The world is watching; Churches are watching. Gazans are sending live images of their own execution. Maybe the world cares? But it goes on . . .

We are asking, could this be our fate in Bethlehem? In Ramallah? In Jenin? Is this our destiny too?

We are tormented by the silence of the world. Leaders of the so-called "free" lined up one after the other to give the green light for this genocide against a captive population. They gave the cover. Not only did they make sure to pay the bill in advance, they veiled the truth and context, providing political cover. And, yet another layer has been added: the theological cover with the Western Church stepping into the spotlight.

The South African Church taught us the concept of "The state theology," defined as "the theological justification of the status quo with its racism, capitalism and totalitarianism." It does so by misusing theological concepts and biblical texts for its own political purposes.

Here in Palestine, the Bible is weaponized against. Our very own sacred text. In our terminology in Palestine, we speak of the Empire. Here we confront the theology of the Empire. A disguise for superiority, supremacy, "chosenness," and entitlement. It is sometimes given a nice cover using words like mission and evangelism, fulfillment of prophecy, and spreading freedom and liberty. The theology of the Empire becomes a powerful tool to mask oppression under the cloak of divine sanction. It divides people into "us" and "them." It dehumanizes and demonizes. It speaks of land without people even when they know the land has people—and not just any people. It calls for emptying Gaza, just like it called the ethnic cleansing in 1948 "a divine miracle." It calls for us Palestinians to go to Egypt, maybe Jordan, or why not just the sea?

"Lord, do you want us to command fire to come down from heaven and consume them?" they said of us. This is the theology of Empire.

This war has confirmed to us that the world does not see us as equal. Maybe it is the color of our skin. Maybe it is because we are on the wrong side of the political equation. Even our kinship in Christ did not shield us. As they said, if it takes killing 100 Palestinians to get a single "Hamas militant" then so be it! We are not humans in their eyes. (But in God's eyes . . . no one can tell us we are not!)

The hypocrisy and racism of the Western world is transparent and appalling! They always take the words of Palestinians with suspicion and qualification. No, we are not treated equally. Yet, the other side, despite a clear track record of misinformation, is almost always deemed infallible!

To our European friends. I never ever want to hear you lecture us on Human rights or international law again. We are not white—it does not apply to us according to your own logic.

In this war, the many Christians in the Western world made sure the Empire has the theology needed. It is self-defense, we were told! (And I ask How?)

In the shadow of the Empire, they turned the colonizer into the victim, and the colonized into the aggressor. Have we forgotten that the state was built on the ruins of the towns and villages of those very same Gazans?

We are outraged by the complicity of the church. Let it be clear: Silence is complicity, and empty calls for peace without a ceasefire and end to occupation, and the shallow words of empathy without direct action—are all under the banner of complicity. So here is my message: Gaza today has become the moral compass of the world. Gaza was hell on earth before October 7th.

If you are not appalled by what is happening; if you are not shaken to your core—there is something wrong with your humanity. If we, as Christians, are not outraged by this genocide, by the weaponizing of the Bible to justify it, there is something wrong with our Christian witness, and compromising the credibility of the Gospel!

If you fail to call this a genocide. It is on you. It is a sin and a darkness you willingly embrace.

Some have not even called for a ceasefire.

I feel sorry for you. We will be ok. Despite the immense blow we have endured, we will recover. We will rise and stand up again from the midst of destruction, as we have always done as Palestinians, although this is by far the biggest blow we have received in a long time.

But again, for those who are complicit, I feel sorry for you. Will you ever recover from this?

Your charity, your words of shock AFTER the genocide, won't make a difference. Words of regret will not suffice for you. We will not accept your apology after the genocide. What has been done, has been done. I want you to look at the mirror . . . and ask: where was I?

To our friends who are here with us: You have left your families and churches to be with us. You embody the term accompaniment—a costly solidarity. "We were in prison and you visited us." What a stark difference from the silence and complicity of others. Your presence here is the meaning of solidarity. Your visit has already left an impression that will never be taken from us. Through you, God has spoken to us that "we are not forsaken." As Father Rami of the Catholic Church said this morning, you have come to Bethlehem, and like the Magi, you brought gifts with, but gifts that are more precious than gold, frankincense, and myrrh. You brought the gift of love and solidarity.

We needed this. For this season, maybe more than anything, we were troubled by the silence of God. In these last two months, the Psalms of lament have become a precious companion. We cried out: My God, My God, we have you forsaken Gaza? Why do you hide your face from Gaza?

In our pain, anguish, and lament, we have searched for God, and found him under the rubble in Gaza. Jesus became the victim of the very same violence of the Empire. He was tortured. Crucified. He bled out as others watched. He was killed and cried out in pain—My God, where are you?

In Gaza today, God is under the rubble.

And in this Christmas season, as we search for Jesus, he is to be found not on the side of Rome, but our side of the wall. In a cave, with a simple family. Vulnerable. Barely, and miraculously surviving a massacre. Among a refugee family. This is where Jesus is found.

If Jesus were to be born today, he would be born under the rubble in Gaza. When we glorify pride and richness, Jesus is under the rubble . . .

When we rely on power, might, and weapons, Jesus is under the rubble . . .

When we justify, rationalize, and theologize the bombing of children, Jesus is under the rubble . . .

Jesus is under the rubble. This is his manger. He is at home with the marginalized, the suffering, the oppressed, and displaced. This is his manger.

I have been looking, contemplating on this iconic image -- God with us, precisely in this way. THIS is the incarnation. Messy. Bloody. Poverty.

This child is our hope and inspiration. We look and see him in every child killed and pulled from under the rubble. While the world continues to reject the children of Gaza, Jesus says: "just as you did it to one of the least of these brothers and sisters of mine, you did it to me." "You did it to ME." Jesus not only calls them his own, he is them!

We look at the holy family and see them in every family displaced and wandering, now homeless in despair. While the world discusses the fate of the people of Gaza as if they are unwanted boxes in a garage, God in the Christmas narrative shares in their fate; He walks with them and calls them his own.

This manger is about resilience. The resilience of Jesus is in his meekness; weakness, and vulnerability. The majesty of the incarnation lies in its solidarity with the marginalized. Resilience because this very same child, rose up from the midst of pain, destruction, darkness and death to challenge Empires; to speak truth to power and deliver an everlasting victory over death and darkness.

This is Christmas today in Palestine and this is the Christmas message. It is not about Santa, trees, gifts, lights . . . etc. My goodness how we twisted the meaning of Christmas. How we have commercialized Christmas. I was in the USA last month, the first Monday after Thanksgiving, and I was amazed by the amount of Christmas decorations and lights, all the commercial goods. I couldn't help but think: They send us bombs, while celebrating Christmas in their land. They sing about the prince of peace in their land, while playing the drum of war in our land.

Christmas in Bethlehem, the birthplace of Jesus, is this manger. This is our message to the world today. It is a gospel message, a true and authentic Christmas message, about the God who did not stay silent, but said his word, and his Word is Jesus. Born among the occupied and marginalized. He is in solidarity with us in our pain and brokenness.

This manger is our message to the world today—and it is simply this: this genocide must stop NOW. Let us repeat to the world: STOP this Genocide NOW.

This is our call. This is our plea. This is our prayer. Hear oh God. Amen.

(Transcript from RedLetterChristians.org)

APPENDIX B

STATEMENT OF ARMENIAN PATRIARCHATE

ԴԻՒԱՆԱՏՈՒՆ
ՊԱՏՐԻԱՐՔՈՒԹԵԱՆ ՀԱՅՈՑ
ԵՐՈՒՍԱՂԵՄԻ

CHANCELLERY
ARMENIAN PATRIARCHATE OF
JERUSALEM

Թուական:
Date: .... 28 December, 2023 ....

URGENT COMMUNIQUE

A MASSIVE AND COORDINATED PHYSICAL ATTACK WAS LAUNCHED ON BISHOPS, PRIESTS, DEACONS, SEMINARIANS, AND OTHER ARMENIAN COMMUNITY MEMBERS IN JERUSALEM WITHIN ONE HOUR OF THIS ANNOUNCEMENT. SEVERAL PRIESTS, STUDENTS OF THE ARMENIAN THEOLOGICAL ACADEMY, AND INDIGENOUS ARMENIANS ARE SERIOUSLY INJURED.

Over 30 armed provocateurs in ski-masks with lethal and less-than-lethal weaponry including powerful nerve-agents that have incapacitated dozens of our clergy broke into the grounds of the Cow's Garden and began their vicious assault. We stress again, several priests, deacons and students of the Armenian Theological Academy along with indigenous Armenians are seriously injured. **ARMENIAN CLERICS IN JERUSALEM ARE FIGHTING FOR THEIR LIVES AGAINST IMPUNE PROVACATEURS.**

This is the criminal response we have received for the submission of a lawsuit to the District Court of Jerusalem for the Cow's Garden, which was officially received by the Court less than 24 hours ago. This is how the Australian-Israeli businessman Danny Rothman (Rubenstein) and George Warwar (Hadad) react to legal procedures.

The Armenian Patriarchate's existential threat is now a physical reality. Bishops, Priests, Deacons, Seminarians, and indigenous Armenians are fighting for their very lives on the ground. We are calling on authorities around the world and the International Media to help us save the Armenian Quarter from a violent demise that is being locally supported by unnamed entities.

We call upon the Israeli Government and Police to start an investigation against Danny Rothman (Rubenstein) and George Warwar (Hadad) for organizing their continuous criminal attacks on the Armenian Patriarchate and Community, attacks which seem to have no end in sight.

Israel is a State of law and order and such criminal behavior cannot be tolerated and go unpunished.

DIVAN OF THE ARMENIAN PATRIARCHATE

P.O.Box: 14235 Jerusalem Zip Code 9191141 / TEL: (972) 2-6282331, E Email: armpattivan@yahoo.com

RESIGNATION LETTER
OF CRAIG MOKHIBER

United Nations   Nations Unies

HEADQUARTERS | SIEGE | NEW YORK, NY 10017
TEL.: + ███████████ | ███████████

28 October 2023

Dear High Commissioner,

This will be my last official communication to you as Director of the New York Office of the High Commissioner for Human Rights.

I write at a moment of great anguish for the world, including for many of our colleagues. Once again, we are seeing a genocide unfolding before our eyes, and the Organization that we serve appears powerless to stop it. As someone who has investigated human rights in Palestine since the 1980s, lived in Gaza as a UN human rights advisor in the 1990s, and carried out several human rights missions to the country before and since, this is deeply personal to me.

I also worked in these halls through the genocides against the Tutsis, Bosnian Muslims, the Yazidi, and the Rohingya. In each case, when the dust settled on the horrors that had been perpetrated against defenseless civilian populations, it became painfully clear that we had failed in our duty to meet the imperatives of prevention of mass atrocites, of protection of the vulnerable, and of accountability for perpetrators. And so it has been with successive waves of murder and persecution against the Palestinians throughout the entire life of the UN.

High Commissioner, we are failing again.

As a human rights lawyer with more than three decades of experience in the field, I know well that the concept of genocide has often been subject to political abuse. But the current wholesale slaughter of the Palestinian people, rooted in an ethno-nationalist settler colonial ideology, in continuation of decades of their systematic persecution and purging, based entirely upon their status as Arabs, and coupled with explicit statements of intent by leaders in the Israeli government and military, leaves no room for doubt or debate. In Gaza, civilian homes, schools, churches, mosques, and medical institutions are wantonly attacked as thousands of civilians are massacred. In the West Bank, including occupied Jerusalem, homes are seized and reassigned based entirely on race, and violent settler pogroms are accompanied by Israeli military units. Across the land, Apartheid rules.

This is a text-book case of genocide. The European, ethno-nationalist, settler colonial project in Palestine has entered its final phase, toward the expedited destruction of the last remnants of indigenous Palestinian life in Palestine. What's more, the governments of the United States, the United Kingdom, and much of Europe, are wholly complicit in the horrific assault. Not only are these governments refusing to meet their treaty obligations "to ensure respect" for the Geneva Conventions, but they are in fact actively arming the assault, providing economic and intelligence support, and giving political and diplomatic cover for Israel's atrocities.

—Volker Turk, High Commissioner for Human Rights
Palais Wilson, Geneva

In concert with this, western corporate media, increasingly captured and state-adjacent, are in open breach of Article 20 of the ICCPR, continuously dehumanizing Palestinians to facilitate the genocide, and broadcasting propaganda for war and advocacy of national, racial, or religious hatred that constitutes incitement to discrimination, hostility, and violence. US-based social media companies are suppressing the voices of human rights defenders while amplifying pro-Israel propaganda. Israel lobby online-trolls and GONGOS are harassing and smearing human rights defenders, and western universities and employers are collaborating with them to punish those who dare to speak out against the atrocities. In the wake of this genocide, there must be an accounting for these actors as well, just as there was for radio *Milles Collines* in Rwanda.

In such circumstances, the demands on our organization for principled and effective action are greater than ever. But we have not met the challenge. The protective enforcement power Security Council has again been blocked by US intransigence, the SG is under assault for the mildest of protestations, and our human rights mechanisms are under sustained slanderous attack by an organized, online impunity network.

Decades of distraction by the illusory and largely disingenuous promises of Oslo have diverted the Organization from its core duty to defend international law, international human rights, and the Charter itself. The mantra of the "two-state solution" has become an open joke in the corridors of the UN, both for its utter impossibility in fact, and for its total failure to account for the inalienable human rights of the Palestinian people. The so-called "Quartet" has become nothing more than a fig leaf for inaction and for subservience to a brutal status quo. The (US-scripted) deference to "agreements between the parties themselves" (in place of international law) was always a transparent slight-of-hand, designed to reinforce the power of Israel over the rights of the occupied and dispossessed Palestinians.

High Commissioner, I came to this Organization first in the 1980s, because I found in it a principled, norm- based institution that was squarely on the side of human rights, including in cases where the powerful US, UK, and Europe were not on our side. While my own government, its subsidiary institutions, and much of the US media were still supporting or justifying South African apartheid, Israeli oppression, and Central American death squads, the UN was standing up for the oppressed peoples of those lands. We had international law on our side. We had human rights on our side. We had principle on our side. Our authority was rooted in our integrity. But no more.

In recent decades, key parts of the UN have surrendered to the power of the US, and to fear of the Israel Lobby, to abandon these principles, and to retreat from international law itself. We have lost a lot in this abandonment, not least our own global credibility. But the Palestinian people have sustained the biggest losses as a result of our failures. It is a stunning historic irony that the Universal Declaration of Human Rights was adopted in the same year that the Nakba was perpetrated against the Palestinian people. As we commemorate the 75th Anniversary of the UDHR, we would do well to abandon the old cliché that the UDHR was born out of the atrocities that proceeded it, and to admit that it was born *alongside* one of the most atrocious genocides of the 20th Century, that of the destruction of Palestine. In some sense, the framers were promising human rights to everyone, *except* the Palestinian people. And let us remember as well, that the UN itself carries the original sin of helping to facilitate the dispossession of the Palestinian people by ratifying the European settler colonial project that seized Palestinian land and turned it over to the colonists. We have much for which to atone.

But the path to atonement is clear. We have much to learn from the principled stance taken in cities around the world in recent days, as masses of people stand up against the genocide, even at risk of beatings and arrest. Palestinians and their allies, human rights defenders of every stripe, Christian and Muslim organizations, and progressive Jewish voices saying "not in our name", are all leading the way. All we have to do is to follow them.

Yesterday, just a few blocks from here, New York's Grand Central Station was completely taken over by thousands of Jewish human rights defenders standing in solidarity with the Palestinian people and demanding an end to Israeli tyranny (many risking arrest, in the process). In doing so, they stripped away in an instant the Israeli *hasbara* propaganda point (and old antisemitic trope) that Israel somehow represents the Jewish people. It does not. And, as such, Israel is solely responsible for its crimes. On this point, it bears repeating, in spite of Israel lobby smears to the contrary, that criticism of Israel's human rights violations is not antisemitic, any more than criticism of Saudi violations is Islamophobic, criticism of Myanmar violations is anti-Buddhist, or criticism of Indian violations is anti-Hindu. When they seek to silence us with smears, we must raise our voice, not lower it. I trust you will agree, High Commissioner, that this is what speaking truth to power is all about.

But I also find hope in those parts of the UN that have refused to compromise the Organization's human rights principles in spite of enormous pressures to do so. Our independent special rapporteurs, commissions of enquiry, and treaty body experts, alongside most of our staff, have continued to stand up for the human rights of the Palestinian people, even as other parts of the UN (even at the highest levels) have shamefully bowed their heads to power. As the custodians of the human rights norms and standards, OHCHR has a particular duty to defend those standards. Our job, I believe, is to make our voice heard, from the Secretary- General to the newest UN recruit, and horizontally across the wider UN system, insisting that the human rights of the Palestinian people are not up for debate, negotiation, or compromise *anywhere* under the blue flag.

What, then, would a UN-norm-based position look like? For what would we work if we were true to our rhetorical admonitions about human rights and equality for all, accountability for perpetrators, redress for victims, protection of the vulnerable, and empowerment for rights-holders, all under the rule of law? The answer, I believe, is simple—if we have the clarity to see beyond the propagandistic smokescreens that distort the vision of justice to which we are sworn, the courage to abandon fear and deference to powerful states, and the will to truly take up the banner of human rights and peace. To be sure, this is a long-term project and a steep climb. But we must begin now or surrender to unspeakable horror. I see ten essential points:

1. ***Legitimate action***: First, we in the UN must abandon the failed (and largely disingenuous) Oslo paradigm, its illusory two-state solution, its impotent and complicit Quartet, and its subjugation of international law to the dictates of presumed political expediency. Our positions must be unapologetically based on international human rights and international law.

2. ***Clarity of Vision***: We must stop the pretense that this is simply a conflict over land or religion between two warring parties and admit the reality of the situation in which a disproportionately

powerful state is colonizing, persecuting, and dispossessing an indigenous population on the basis of their ethnicity.

3. ***One State based on human rights***: We must support the establishment of a single, democratic, secular state in all of historic Palestine, with equal rights for Christians, Muslims, and Jews, and, therefore, the dismantling of the deeply racist, settler-colonial project and an end to apartheid across the land.

4. ***Fighting Apartheid***: We must redirect all UN efforts and resources to the struggle against apartheid, just as we did for South Africa in the 1970s, 80s, and early 90s.

5. ***Return and Compensation***: We must reaffirm and insist on the right to return and full compensation for all Palestinians and their families currently living in the occupied territories, in Lebanon, Jordan, Syria, and in the diaspora across the globe.

6. ***Truth and Justice***: We must call for a transitional justice process, making full use of decades of accumulated UN investigations, enquiries, and reports, to document the truth, and to ensure accountability for all perpetrators, redress for all victims, and remedies for documented injustices.

7. ***Protection***: We must press for the deployment of a well-resourced and strongly mandated UN protection force with a sustained mandate to protect civilians from the river to the sea.

8. ***Disarmament***: We must advocate for the removal and destruction of Israel's massive stockpiles of nuclear, chemical, and biological weapons, lest the conflict lead to the total destruction of the region and, possibly, beyond.

9. ***Mediation***: We must recognize that the US and other western powers are in fact not credible mediators, but rather actual parties to the conflict who are complicit with Israel in the violation of Palestinian rights, and we must engage them as such.

10. ***Solidarity***: We must open our doors (and the doors of the SG) wide to the legions of Palestinian, Israeli, Jewish, Muslim, and Christian human rights defenders who are standing in solidarity with the people of Palestine and their human rights and stop the unconstrained flow of Israel lobbyists to the offices of UN leaders,

where they advocate for continued war, persecution, apartheid, and impunity, and smear our human rights defenders for their principled defense of Palestinian rights.

This will take years to achieve, and western powers will fight us every step of the way, so we must be steadfast. In the immediate term, we must work for an immediate ceasefire and an end to the longstanding siege on Gaza, stand up against the ethnic cleansing of Gaza, Jerusalem, and the West Bank (and elsewhere), document the genocidal assault in Gaza, help to bring massive humanitarian aid and reconstruction to the Palestinians, take care of our traumatized colleagues and their families, and fight like hell for a principled approach in the UN's political offices.

The UN's failure in Palestine thus far is not a reason for us to withdraw. Rather it should give us the courage to abandon the failed paradigm of the past, and fully embrace a more principled course. Let us, as OHCHR, boldly and proudly join the anti-apartheid movement that is growing all around the world, adding our logo to the banner of equality and human rights for the Palestinian people. The world is watching. We will all be accountable for where we stood at this crucial moment in history. Let us stand on the side of justice.

I thank you, High Commissioner, Volker, for hearing this final appeal from my desk. I will leave the Office in a few days for the last time, after more than three decades of service. But please do not hesitate to reach out if I can be of assistance in the future.

Sincerely

Craig Mokhiber

Craig Mokhiber

NOTES

Preface

1 Chotiner, Isaac. "Does the Biden Administration Want a Long-Lasting Ceasefire in Gaza?" *The New Yorker*, February 28, 2024. https://www .newyorker.com/news/q-and-a/does-the-biden-administration-want-a-long -lasting-ceasefire-in-gaza.

2 Nader, Ralph. "Stop the Worsening Undercount of Palestinian Casualties in Gaza." Ralph Nader, March 5, 2024. https://nader.org/2024/03/05 /stop-the-worsening-undercount-of-palestinian-casualties-in-gaza/.

3 Abulhawa, Susan. "History Will Record That Israel Committed a Holocaust." *The Electronic Intifada*, March 6, 2024. https://electronicintifada.net /content/history-will-record-israel-committed-holocaust/45006.

4 Reuters Staff. "UNRWA Report Says Israel Coerced Some Agency Employees to Falsely . . ." Reuters, March 8, 2024. https://www.reuters.com/world /middle-east/unrwa-report-says-israel-coerced-some-agency-employees -falsely-admit-hamas-links-2024-03-08/.

5 Israel/OPT: UN Experts Appalled by Reported Human Rights Violations . . ." UN High Commission for Human Rights, February 19, 2024. https://www .ohchr.org/en/press-releases/2024/02/israelopt-un-experts-appalled -reported-human-rights-violations-against.

6 Grim, Ryan, and Jeremy Scahill. "The Story behind the New York Times October 7 Exposé." *The Intercept*, March 2, 2024. https://theintercept .com/2024/02/28/new-york-times-anat-schwartz-october-7/.

7 Hudson, John. "U.S. Floods Arms into Israel despite Mounting Alarm over War's . . ." *Washington Post*, March 6, 2024. https://www.washingtonpost .com/national-security/2024/03/06/us-weapons-israel-gaza/.

8 Maté, Aaron. "The Biden Doctrine in Gaza: Bomb, Starve, Deceive," March 8, 2024. https://www.aaronmate.net/p/the-biden-doctrine-in-gaza-bomb-starve.

9 Brown, Paul. "What Video and Eyewitness Accounts Tell Us about Gazans Killed around Aid Convoy." BBC News, March 1, 2024. https://www.bbc .com/news/world-middle-east-68445973.

10   France 24 Staff. "Sleepless Nights for Mothers of Palestinians Jailed in Occupied West Bank." France 24, March 8, 2024. https://www.france24 .com/en/live-news/20240308-sleepless-nights-for-mothers-of-palestinians -jailed-in-occupied-west-bank.

11   Klippenstein, Ken. "Leaked U.S. Cable: Israeli Invasion of Rafah Would Have 'Catastrophic Humanitarian Consequences.'" The Intercept, March 6,2024. https://theintercept.com/2024/03/05/israel-rafah-humanitarian-aid -us-cable/.

Introduction

1   Arnaud Bertrand, Twitter, Feb. 14, 2024 https://x.com/rnaudbertrand/statu s/1757971532218044827?s=46

2   Berg, Matt and Alexander Ward. "US won't punish Israel for Rafah op that doesn't protect civilians," Politico. Feb. 13, 2024. https://www.politico .com/newsletters/national-security-daily/2024/02/13/us-wont-punish-israel -for-rafah-op-that-doesnt-protect-civilians-00141013.

3   Urquhart, Conal "The Goldstone Report: A History." The Guardian, April 14, 2011. https://www.theguardian.com/world/2011/apr/14/goldstone-report -history.

4   "HUMAN RIGHTS IN PALESTINE AND OTHER OCCUPIED ARAB TERRITORIES," Report of the United Nations Fact-Finding Mission on the Gaza Conflict, UN Human Rights Council (September 25, 2009). https://documents.un.org/doc/undoc/gen/g09/158/66/pdf/g0915866.pdf.

5   "Gaza in 2020: A Livable Place?" A Report by the United Nations Country Team in the Palestine Occupied Territory (August 2012). https://www .unrwa.org/userfiles/file/publications/gaza/Gaza%20in%202020.pdf.

6   Schwegel, Justin. "The Greenhouse Propaganda-How Gazan History Is Being Rewritten to Dehumanize Palestinians." Mondoweiss, August 10, 2014. https://mondoweiss.net/2014/08/propaganda-dehumanize-palestinians/.

7   "Amnesty International Report 2016/17—Palestine (State Of)." Refworld, February 22, 2017. https://www.refworld.org/docid/58b033c5a.html.

8   Balousha, Hazem, and Miriam Berger. "The U.N. once predicted Gaza would be 'uninhabitable' by 2020." Washington Post. January 5, 2020. https://www.washingtonpost.com/world/2020/01/01/un-predicted-gaza -would-be-uninhabitable-by-heres-what-that-actually-means/.

9   Shani, Ayelett. "Gaza Kids Live in Hell: A Psychologist Tells of Rampant Sexual Abuse, Drugs and Despair." Haaretz.com, November 10, 2017. https: //www.haaretz.com/middle-east-news/palestinians/2017-11-11/ty-article -magazine/gaza-kids-live-in-hell-a-psychologist-tells-of-sex-abuse-drugs -and-despair/0000017f-e6f1-df2c-a1ff-fef16fd30000.

10   Abram, Epstein. "Naftali Bennett's Visit to Tree of Life Synagogue," Times of Israel. October 30, 2018. https://www.timesofisrael.com/israels-chief -rabbi-wont-call-pittsburghs-tree-of-life-a-synagogue/.

11 Kovalik, Daniel. "The Need to Address the Palestinian Plight," Jurist. December 13, 2021. https://www.jurist.org/commentary/2021/12/daniel-kovalik-palestinian-tragedy/.

12 "The Gazan Doctor Whose Phone Call on Live TV Shook Israelis to the Core 15 Years Ago." CNN, January 15, 2024. https://www.cnn.com/2024/01/15/opinions/palestinian-doctor-trauma-children-abuelaish/index.html.

13 Segal, Aidan. "The Absurdity of a Human Rights Professor's Anti-Semitism." Jewish News Syndicate. February 3, 2022. https://www.jns.org/the-absurdity-of-a-human-rights-professors-anti-semitism/.

14 O'Connor, Tom. "U.S. Fights Turkey-Backed Syrian Rebels CIA Once Funded." *Newsweek*, August 29, 2017. https://www.newsweek.com/us-military-battles-syria-rebels-supported-cia-backed-turkey-656617.

15 Tsurkov, Elizabeth. "Inside Israel's Secret Program to Back Syrian Rebels." *Foreign Policy*, September 6, 2018. https://foreignpolicy.com/2018/09/06/in-secret-program-israel-armed-and-funded-rebel-groups-in-southern-syria/.

16 Gallagher, Tom. "Christians in Syria Struggle amid Violent Clashes." *National Catholic Reporter*, March 12, 2012. https://www.ncronline.org/news/world/christians-syria-struggle-amid-violent-clashes.

17 Al Jazeera Staff. "Sabra and Shatila Massacre: What Happened in Lebanon in 1982?" Al Jazeera, September 16, 2022. https://www.aljazeera.com/news/2022/9/16/sabra-and-shatila-massacre-40-years-on-explainer.

18 Rashid Khaladi, *The Hundred Years' War on Palestine, A History of Settler Colonialism and Resistance, 1917–2017* (New York, Henry Holt & Company), 2020 at p .128.

Chapter One

1 Pappe, Ilan, *The Ethnic Cleansing of Palestine*. (Oxford: Oneworld Publications) 2006, p. xiv.

2 *Democracy Now!* "'Utterly Illegal': U.N. Special Rapporteur Slams Netanyahu's 'Voluntary Migration' Plan for Gazans." *Democracy Now!*, December 29, 2023. https://www.democracynow.org/2023/12/29/utterly_illegal_un_special_rapporteur_slams.

3 Pappe, Ilan. *The Ethnic Cleansing of Palestine* (Oxford: Oneworld Publications), 2006.

4 Knell, Yolande. "Balfour Declaration: The Divisive Legacy of 67 Words." BBC News, November 2, 2017. https://www.bbc.com/news/world-middle-east-41765892.

5 "Jewish & Non-Jewish Population of Israel/Palestine (1517-Present)." Jewish Virtual Library. Accessed February 13, 2024. https://www.jewishvirtuallibrary.org/jewish-and-non-jewish-population-of-israel-palestine-1517-present.

6   "The Mandate Years: Colonialism and the Creation of Israel." *The Guardian*, May 31, 2001. https://www.theguardian.com/books/2001/may/31/london reviewofbooks.

7   Pappe, Ilan, p. 13.

8   Gaal, Ferenc. "German military exports to Israel up nearly 10-fold as Berlin Fast Tracks Permits," Reuters. https://www.reuters.com/world/europe /german-military-exports-israel-up-nearly-10-fold-berlin-fast-tracks-permits -2023-11-08/.

9   Al Tahhan, Zena. "More than a Century on: The Balfour Declaration Explained." Al Jazeera, November 2, 2018. https://www.aljazeera.com /features/2018/11/2/more-than-a-century-on-the-balfour-declaration -explained.

10   Ibid.

11   Glass, Charles, "The Mandate Years," ibid.

12   Pappe, Ilan, at p. 12.

13   "The Truth about Why Many Evangelical Christians Support Israel." MSNBC, October 22, 2023. https://www.msnbc.com/opinion/msnbc-opinion/truth -many-evangelical-christians-support-israel-rcna121481.

14   Wong, Edward. "The Rapture and the Real World: Mike Pompeo Blends Beliefs and Policy." *New York Times*, March 30, 2019. https://www.nytimes .com/2019/03/30/us/politics/pompeo-christian-policy.html.

15   Lecker, Maya. "Mike Pence Shouldn't Have Signed His Name on an Israeli Bomb." Haaretz.com, January 7, 2024. https://www.haaretz.com /israel-news/haaretz-today/2024-01-07/ty-article/.highlight/mike-pence -shouldnt-have-signed-his-name-on-an-israeli-bomb/0000018c-e4a6 -d765-ab9d-f4ffc84e0000.

16   Al Jazeera Staff. "Israeli Settlers Storm Al-Aqsa Mosque Complex on Fifth Day of Sukkot." Al Jazeera, October 4, 2023. https://www.aljazeera.com /news/2023/10/4/israeli-settlers-storm-al-aqsa-mosque-complex-on-fifth -day-of-sukkot.

17   Ibid.

18   Al Jazeera Staff. "What's behind the Ramadan Raids at Jerusalem's Al-Aqsa Mosque?" Al Jazeera, April 5, 2023. https://www.aljazeera.com /news/2023/4/5/al-aqsa-mosque-compound-and-recurrent-ramadan-tensions.

19   Al Jazeera Staff. "What's behind the Ramadan Raids at Jerusalem's Al-Aqsa Mosque?" Al Jazeera, April 5, 2023. https://www.aljazeera.com /news/2023/4/5/al-aqsa-mosque-compound-and-recurrent-ramadan -tensions.

20   Al Tahan, Zena, ibid.

21   Pappe, Ilan at p. 13.

22   Pappe, Ilan at pp. 7–8.

23   Glass, Charles, ibid.

24 Ibid.

25 Pappe, Ilan, p. 50.

26 Pappe, Ilan, at pp. 29–30.

27 Ibid., p. 34.

28 Institute for Middle East Understanding. "Quick Facts about the Palestinian Nakba," April 5, 2023. https://imeu.org/article/quick-facts-the-palestinian -nakba.

29 Green, David B. "This Day in Jewish History: Irgun Blows up British HQ at Jerusalem's King David Hotel." Haaretz.com, July 22, 2021. https://www .haaretz.com/israel-news/2021-07-22/ty-article/this-day-in-jewish-history -irgun-blows-up-british-hq-at-jerusalems-king-david-hotel/0000017f-f5f9 -ddde-abff-fdfd85990000.

30 https://www.haaretz.com/israel-news/2017-07-16/ty-article-magazine /testimonies-from-the-censored-massacre-at-deir-yassin/0000017f-e364 -d38f-a57f-e77689930000.

31 Al Jazeera Staff. "The Deir Yassin Massacre: Why It Still Matters 75 Years Later." Al Jazeera, April 26, 2023. https://www.aljazeera.com/news/2023/4/9 /the-deir-yassin-massacre-why-it-still-matters-75-years-later.

32 Albert Einstein Letter to the *New York Times*. December 4, 1948, Internet Archive https://archive.org/details/AlbertEinsteinLetterToTheNew YorkTimes.December41948/page/n1/mode/1up.

33 "Bombing Halts as Reagan Sends a Warning." *New York Times*, August 15, 1982. https://www.nytimes.com/1982/08/15/weekinreview/bombing -halts-as-reagan-sends-a-warning.html.

34 Burgis, Ben. "Exclusive: In the '80s, Joe Biden Speculated to Israel's PM about Wiping out Canadians." *Jacobin*. October 22, 2023. https://jacobin .com/2023/10/joe-biden-menachem-begin-israel-lebanon-war-civilian -casualties-canada-gaza.

35 McKernan, Bethan. "UK Study of 1948 Israeli Massacre of Palestinian Village Reveals Mass Grave Sites." *The Guardian*, May 25, 2023. https: //www.theguardian.com/world/2023/may/25/study-1948-israeli-massacre -tantura-palestinian-village-mass-graves-car-park.

36 Shavit, Ari. "An Interview with Benny Morris." CounterPunch.org, January 16, 2004. https://www.counterpunch.org/2004/01/16/an-interview -with-benny-morris/.

37 Zogby, James J. "On the 'the River to the Sea' Controversy." Twitter, November 11, 2023. https://twitter.com/jjz1600/status/17234799000304 27459?lang=en.

38 Middle East Monitor. "The Politics behind the Flight of Christians from the Holy Land." Middle East Monitor, December 25, 2015. https://www .middleeastmonitor.com/20151225-the-politics-behind-the-flight-of-christians -from-the-holy-land/.

39   UN General Assembly Resolution 194, UNRWA.org https://www.unrwa
      .org/content/resolution-194.

40   "Palestinian Refugees and the Right of Return in International Law."
      OHRH. May 14, 2018. https://ohrh.law.ox.ac.uk/palestinian-refugees-and
      -the-right-of-return-in-international-law/.

41   Soussi, Alasdair. "The Mixed Legacy of Golda Meir, Israel's First Woman PM."
      Al Jazeera, March 18, 2019. https://www.aljazeera.com/features/2019/3/18
      /the-mixed-legacy-of-golda-meir-israels-first-female-pm.

42   Kellman, Laurie. "'No Such Thing' as Palestinian People, Top Israeli
      Minister Says." PBS, March 20, 2023. https://www.pbs.org/newshour
      /world/no-such-thing-as-palestinian-people-top-israeli-minister-says.

43   "1948 No Catastrophe Says Israel, as Term Nakba Banned from Arab
      Children's Textbooks." *The Guardian*, July 22, 2009. https://www.the
      guardian.com/world/2009/jul/22/israel-remove-nakba-from-textbooks.

44   Israel passes laws forbidding remembrance of 1948 takeover of Palestine."
      International Middle East Media Center. March 24, 2011. https://imemc
      .org/article/60927/.

45   Ibid.

46   Beinart, Peter. "A Jewish Case for Palestinian Return," *The Guardian*. May 18,
      2021. https://amp.theguardian.com/news/2021/may/18/a-jewish-case-for
      -palestinian-refugee-return.

Chapter Two

1   Feeney, Brian. "'Genocide Joe' Biden Has Got the Gaza Crisis Wrong in
      Every Way." *The Irish News*. December 29, 2023. https://www.irishnews
      .com/opinion/genocide-joe-biden-has-got-the-gaza-crisis-wrong-in-every
      -way-brian-feeney-PVL4BQU4YZFZ7FLC67S2APUYDU/.

2   Haaretz Staff. "Holocaust Survivors Condemn Israel for 'Gaza Massacre,'
      Call for Boycott." Haaretz.com, August 23, 2014. https://www.haaretz
      .com/2014-08-23/ty-article/holocaust-survivors-condemn-israel-for-gaza
      -massacre/0000017f-e738-dea7-adff-f7fb2fbe0000.

3   Rashid Khalidi, *The Hundred Years' War on Palestine* (New York: Henry Holt
      & Company), 2020 at p. 94.

4   Ibid.

5   Sterling, Rick. "From Dallas to Gaza: How JFK's Assassination Was Good
      for Zionist Israel." Antiwar.com, December 13, 2023. https://original.anti
      war.com/rick_sterling/2023/12/14/from-dallas-to-gaza-how-jfks
      -assassination-was-good-for-zionist-israel/.

6   See, Khalidi, Rashid, *The Hundred Years' War on Palestine* at pp. 96–137.

7   Ibid. at 106.

8   Ibid.

9   Ibid. at p. 107.

10 Pensack, Miriam. "Fifty Years Later, NSA Keeps Details of Israel's USS Liberty Attack Secret." *The Intercept*, September 20, 2019. https://theintercept.com/2017/06/06/fifty-years-later-nsa-keeps-details-of-israels-uss-liberty-attack-secret/.

11 Ibid.

12 Ibid.

13 Abier. "A 3-4 Year Old Palestinian Child Is ' Young Lady'" Twitter, January 10, 2024. https://twitter.com/abierkhatib/status/1744988715930280327.

14 *The Onion*. "'New York Times' Invents Entirely New Numerical System to Avoid Reporting Gazan Death Toll." *The Onion*, November 6, 2023. https://www.theonion.com/new-york-times-invents-entirely-new-numerical-system-1850996369.

15 Adam Johnson, and Othman Ali. "Coverage of Gaza War in the New York Times and Other Major Newspapers Heavily Favored Israel, Analysis Shows." *The Intercept*, January 10, 2024. https://theintercept.com/2024/01/09/newspapers-israel-palestine-bias-new-york-times/.

16 McGreal, Chris. "CNN Staff Say Network's pro-Israel Slant Amounts to 'Journalistic Malpractice.'" *The Guardian*, February 4, 2024. https://www.theguardian.com/media/2024/feb/04/cnn-staff-pro-israel-bias.

17 Houghtaling, Ellie Quinlan, and Tori Otten. "You Won't Believe How Much AIPAC Is Spending to Target the Squad in 2024." *The New Republic*, February 14, 2024. https://newrepublic.com/post/176959/aipac-spending-target-squad-2024-election.

18 Khalidi, Rashid at pp. 136–37.

19 Ibid.

20 See, Jimmy Carter, *Palestinian Peace Not Apartheid* (New York: Simon & Schuster) (2006).

21 Roy, Sara. "The Long War on Gaza." *The New York Review of Books*, January 9, 2024. https://www.nybooks.com/online/2023/12/19/the-long-war-on-gaza/.

22 Barakat, Ibtisam. "A Palestinian Whose Childhood Was Destroyed by War Pleads for Peace." *The Nation*, January 2, 2024. https://www.thenation.com/article/world/palestine-gaza-children-peace/.

23 Brunnstrom, David. "Trump cuts more than $200 million in U.S. aid to Palestinians." August 24, 2018. https://www.reuters.com/article/idUSKCN1L923C.

Chapter Three

1 Ageel, Ghada. "Gaza's Orphans: Pain without Borders." Al Jazeera, December 28, 2023. https://www.aljazeera.com/opinions/2023/12/26/gazas-orphans-pain-without-borders.

2   Ahmed, Sulaiman. "Hamas Al-Aqsa Flood Operation." Twitter, January 21, 2024. https://twitter.com/ShaykhSulaiman/status/1749065290137128971.

3   Ibid.

4   Ibid.

5   Ibid.

6   Ibid.

7   France 24 Staff. "Israel Social Security Data Reveals True Picture of Oct 7 Deaths." France 24, December 15, 2023. https://www.france24.com/en /live-news/20231215-israel-social-security-data-reveals-true-picture-of-oct -7-deaths.

8   Euro-Med Monitor. "In 4th Month of Israeli Genocide, 4 Percent of Gaza's Population Dead, Missing, or Injured." ReliefWeb, January 5, 2024. https: //reliefweb.int/report/occupied-palestinian-territory/4th-month-israeli-genocide -4-percent-gazas-population-dead-missing-or-injured-70-percent-strips -infrastructure-destroyed-enar.

9   Ibid.

10   Atalay, Dildar Baykan. "Another Israeli witness confirms Israeli tanks killed own citizens," Anadolu Ajansi November 12, 2023. https://www.aa.com.tr /en/middle-east/another-israeli-witness-confirms-israeli-tanks-killed-own -citizens-on-oct-7/3079514.

11   Frankel, Julia. "New York Times Report Says Israel Knew about Hamas Attack over a Year in Advance." AP News, December 1, 2023. https: //apnews.com/article/new-york-times-hamas-attack-israel-gaza-6088cad 78f5e4153d671fe9b5b819308.

12   Al Jazeera Staff. "Who Are the Palestinian Prisoners Israel Released on Friday?" Al Jazeera, November 24, 2023. https://www.aljazeera.com/news/2023/11/24 /who-were-the-palestinian-prisoners-israel-released-on-friday.

13   "Children in Israeli Military Detention—UNICEF Report—Question of Palestine." United Nations. June 3, 2013. https://www.un.org/unispal /document/auto-insert-208566/.

14   Ibid.

15   Ibid.

16   "Israel: 240 Palestinian Children 'sexually Abused' in Jerusalem Detention Centres, Group Claims." Middle East Children's Alliance, February 8, 2024. https://www.mecaforpeace.org/israel-240-palestinian-children-sexually -abused-in-jerusalem-detention-centres-group-claims/.

17   Al Jazeera Staff. "Palestinian Children Abused in Israeli Detention: NGO." Al Jazeera, July 10, 2023. https://www.aljazeera.com/news/2023/7/10 /palestinian-children-abused-in-israeli-detention-ngo.

18   Ibid.

19   Madar, Revital. "Beyond Male Israeli Soldiers, Palestinian Women, Rape, and War." Berghahn Journals, June 1, 2023. https://www.berghahnjournals .com/view/journals/conflict-and-society/9/1/arcs090105.xml.

20   Al Jazeera Staff. "Who Are the Palestinian Prisoners Israel Released on Friday?" Al Jazeera, November 24, 2023. https://www.aljazeera.com/news/2023/11/24 /who-were-the-palestinian-prisoners-israel-released-on-friday.

21   Id.

22   Id.

23   Borger, Julian. "Israeli government report admits systematic torture of Palestinians," *The Guardian*. February 11, 2000. https://www.theguardian.com /world/2000/feb/11/israel

24   Staff, The New Arab. "Surge in Abuse, Torture against Palestinians in Israel Jails." The New Arab. January 3, 2024. https://www.newarab.com/news /surge-abuse-torture-against-palestinians-israel-jails.

25   Ibid.

26   Ibid.

27   Ibid.

28   Editorial, Haaretz. "Israel Must Stop Abusing and Humiliating Palestinian Prisoners: Editorial." Haaretz.com, January 3, 2024. https://www.haaretz .com/opinion/editorial/2024-01-03/ty-article-opinion/israel-must-stop -the-beating-and-humiliation-of-palestinian-prisoners/0000018c-cbf7-dc35 -adee-cbf7961c0000.

29   Ibid.

30   Al Jazeera Staff. "Israeli Captive Endured 'hell' in Attack, but Treated 'Well' in Gaza." Al Jazeera, October 24, 2023. https://www.aljazeera.com /news/2023/10/24/israeli-captive-endured-hell-in-attack-but-treated-well -in-gaza.

31   Goldenberg, Tia. "Freed Israeli Hostage Describes Deteriorating Conditions While Being Held by Hamas." AP News, November 28, 2023. https: //apnews.com/article/hostage-gaza-freed-israel-captive-408f65fc c1b8f016f3735cd5022163eb.

32   Ibid.

33   Ibid.

34   "US Intel: No Evidence of Viagra as Weapon in Libya." NBCNews.com, April 29, 2011. https://www.nbcnews.com/id/wbna42824884.

35   Rozovsky, Liza, and Josh Breiner. "Israeli Police Ask Victims and Witnesses to Testify about Hamas Sexual Violence." Haaretz.com, January 4, 2024. https://www.haaretz.com/israel-news/2024-01-04/ty-article/.premium /israeli-police-ask-victims-and-witnesses-to-testify-about-hamas-sexual -violence/0000018c-d580-d751-ad8d-ffa4acf40000.

36   Halah Jaber, Twitter, February 10, 2024. https://twitter.com/halajaber/statu s/1756294089593508277?s=46.

37   Blumenthal, Max, and Mate, Aaron. "NY Times October 7 Hoax Exposed." *The Grayzone*, December 31, 2023. https://www.youtube.com /watch?v=BXdCd8VPo4g.

       and Abunimah, Ali. "Watch: Debunking Israel's 'Mass Rape' Propaganda." The Electronic Intifada, February 3, 2024. https://electronicintifada.net /blogs/ali-abunimah/watch-debunking-israels-mass-rape-propaganda.

38   Blumenthal, Max and Maté. Aaron. "Screams without Proof: Questions for NYT about Shoddy 'Hamas Mass Rape' Report." *The Grayzone*, January 10, 2024. https://thegrayzone.com/2024/01/10/questions -nyt-hamas-rape-report/.

39   Porter, Gareth. "How Israel Leverages Genocide with Hamas 'Massacres.'" Consortium News, Volume 29, Number 38, January 7, 2024. https: //consortiumnews.com/2024/01/06/how-israel-leverages-genocide -with-hamas-massacres/.

40   Al Jazeera Staff. "White House Walks Back Biden's Claim He Saw Children Beheaded by Hamas." Al Jazeera, October 30, 2023. https://www.aljazeera. com/news/2023/10/12/white-house-walks-back-bidens-claim-he-saw -children-beheaded-by-hamas.

41   Scahill, Jeremy. "Joe Biden Keeps Repeating His False Claim That He Saw Pictures of Beheaded Babies." *The Intercept*, December 14, 2023. https: //theintercept.com/2023/12/14/israel-biden-beheaded-babies-false/.

42   "Israelis Could Be Charged with War Crimes." Salt Cube Analytics, January 4, 2024. https://www.youtube.com/watch?v=SHwyquMunWM&t=10s.

43   "Why the Oct. 7 Attack Wasn't Israel's 9/11." Rand Corporation, Nov. 2023. https://www.rand.org/pubs/commentary/2023/11/why-the-oct-7-attack -wasnt-israels-9-11.html.

44   Certo, Peter. "Mowing the Lawn in Gaza—FPIF." Foreign Policy In Focus, March 3, 2021. https://fpif.org/mowing-lawn-gaza/.

45   Horowitz, Michael. "42 Survivors of the Nova Rave Massacre Sue Defense Establishment for Negligence." *Times of Israel*, January 1, 2024. https: //www.timesofisrael.com/42-survivors-of-the-nova-rave-massacre-sue -defense-establishment-for-negligence/.

46   Blumenthal, Max. "Full YNet Investigation on Oct 7." Twitter, January 16, 2024. https://twitter.com/maxblumenthal.

47   Winstanley, Asa. "Israeli HQ Ordered Troops to Shoot Israeli Captives on 7 October." *The Electronic Intifada*, January 22, 2024. https: //electronicintifada.net/blogs/asa-winstanley/israeli-hq-ordered-troops -shoot-israeli-captives-7-october.

48   Laub, Karin, Najib Jobain, and Jack Jeffery. "Israeli Military Says It Mistakenly Killed 3 Israeli Hostages in Gaza." PBS, December 15, 2023. https://www.pbs.org/newshour/world/israeli-military-says-it-mistakenly -killed-3-israeli-hostages-in-gaza.

49   Fink, Rachel. "'Unlawful, Unethical, Horrifying': IDF Ethics Expert on Controversial Hannibal Directive." Haaretz.com, January 17, 2024. https://www.haaretz.com/israel-news/2024-01-17/ty-article/.premium /unlawful-unethical-horrifying-idf-ethics-expert-on-controversial-hannibal -directive/0000018d-186c-dd75-addd-faedd2b80000.

Chapter Four

1   Teibel, Amy. "An Israeli ministry, in a 'concept paper,' proposes transferring Gaza civilians to Egypt's Sinai," AP (October 30, 2023).

2   Rempfer, Kyle. "In 1948, Israeli Forces Drove 750,000 Palestinians out in the Nakba. Many Fear a Repeat." *Washington Post*, November 3, 2023. https: //www.washingtonpost.com/history/2023/11/03/israel-nakba-history-1948/.

3   "Gaza: Forced and Protracted Displacement of Palestinians Would Constitute a Serious Breach of International Law and an Atrocity Crime." Norwegian Refugee Council, December 26, 2023. https://www.nrc.no/news /2023/december/gaza-displacement/..

4   Ruebner, Josh. "Israel Is Threatening a Second Nakba—But It's Already Happening." *The Hill*, November 17, 2023. https://thehill.com/opinion /international/4313276-israel-is-threatening-a-second-nakba-but-its-already -happening/.

5   "Israeli Intelligence Ministry Policy Paper on Gaza's Civilian Population, October 2023." Unofficial translation by *+972 Magazine*, Scribd. October 2023. https://www.scribd.com/document/681086738/Israeli-Intelligence -Ministry-Policy-Paper-on-Gaza-s-Civilian-Population-October-2023.

6   Ibid.

7   "Gaza Is 'Running out of Time' UN Experts Warn." Office of the High Commissioner for Human Rights, November 2023. https://www.ohchr.org /en/press-releases/2023/11/gaza-running-out-time-un-experts-warn -demanding-ceasefire-prevent-genocide-0.

8   "70 Killed after Convoys of Evacuees in Gaza Hit by Israeli Airstrikes." NBCNews.com, October 14, 2023. https://www.nbcnews.com/news/world /live-blog/israel-hamas-war-live-updates-rcna120252.

9   https://www.aljazeera.com/news/liveblog/2023/11/3/israel-hamas-war -live-israeli-forces-gather-outside-gaza-city.

10   Al Jazeera Staff. "Palestinians Fleeing to Khan Younis Still Face Israeli Air Attacks." Al Jazeera, October 14, 2023. https://www.aljazeera.com/gallery/2023/10/14 /palestinians-who-fled-to-khan-younis-still-under-israeli-airstrikes.

11   Power, Samantha. "Humanitarian Pause in Gaza: Press Release." U.S. Agency for International Development, November 27, 2023. https://www.usaid.gov /news-information/press-releases/nov-24-2023-humanitarian-pause-gaza.

12   "In a Matter of Hours, Israel Carries out the Bloodiest Massacre in Its History." Euro-Med Monitor, November 7, 2023. https://euromedmonitor

.org/en/article/5922/In-a-matter-of-hours,-Israel-carries-out-the-bloodiest
-massacre-in-its-history.

13   Ibid.

14   Euro-Med Monitor. "In 4th Month of Israeli Genocide, 4 Percent of Gaza's
      Population Dead, Missing, or Injured." ReliefWeb, January 5, 2024. https:
      //reliefweb.int/report/occupied-palestinian-territory/4th-month-israeli
      -genocide-4-percent-gazas-population-dead-missing-or-injured-70-percent
      -strips-infrastructure-destroyed-enar.

15   Ibid.

16   Leatherby, Lauren. "Gaza Civilians, under Israeli Barrage, Are Being Killed
      at Historic Pace." *New York Times*, November 25, 2023. https://www
      .nytimes.com/2023/11/25/world/middleeast/israel-gaza-death-toll.html.

17   Malsin, Jared, and Nancy A Youssef. "U.S. Sends Israel 2,000-Pound
      Bunker Buster Bombs" *Wall Street Journal*, December 1, 2023. https:
      //www.wsj.com/world/middle-east/u-s-sends-israel-2-000-pound-bunker
      -buster-bombs-for-gaza-war-82898638.

18   Stein, Robin, Haley Willis, Ishaan Jhaveri, Danielle Miller, Aaron Byrd,
      and Natalie Reneau. "A Times Investigation Tracked Israel's Use of One of
      Its Most Destructive Bombs in South Gaza." *New York Times*, December
      22, 2023. https://www.nytimes.com/2023/12/21/world/middleeast/israel
      -gaza-bomb-investigation.html.

19   Malsin, Jared, and Nancy A Youssef. "U.S. Sends Israel 2,000-Pound
      Bunker Buster . . ." *Wall Street Journal*, December 1, 2023. https://www
      .wsj.com/world/middle-east/u-s-sends-israel-2-000-pound-bunker-buster
      -bombs-for-gaza-war-82898638.

20   Kullab, Samya, and Najib Jobain. "Their Families Wiped out, Grieving
      Palestinians in Gaza Ask Why." AP News, November 18, 2023. https://apnews
      .com/article/palestinians-israel-airstrikes-gaza-hamas-war-689624bc
      9069c10b5fa154a762f6da6f.

21   Graham-Harrison, Emma. "Israeli Airstrike Kills Gaza Aid Worker and
      70 of His Extended Family, Un Says." *The Guardian*, December 24, 2023.
      https://www.theguardian.com/world/2023/dec/23/israeli-airstrike-kills
      -gaza-aid-worker-and-70-of-his-extended-family-un-says.

22   Ibid.

23   Harb, Ali, and Brian Osgood. "'So What?': Israeli PM Netanyahu Reiterates
      Rejection of Palestinian State." Al Jazeera, January 19, 2024. https:
      //www.aljazeera.com/news/liveblog/2024/1/18/israels-war-on-gaza-live
      -medicine-arrives-for-captives-palestinians.

24   Ahmed, Kaamil. "Lack of Clean Drinking Water for 95% of People in Gaza
      Threatens Health Crisis." *The Guardian*, November 4, 2023. https://www
      .theguardian.com/global-development/2023/nov/04/lack-of-clean-drinking
      -water-for-95-of-people-in-gaza-threatens-health-crisis.

25 Gayle, Damien, and Nina Lakhani. "Flooding Hamas Tunnels with Seawater Risks 'Ruining Basic Life in Gaza', Says Expert." *The Guardian*, December 23, 2023. https://www.theguardian.com/world/2023/dec/23 /israel-flooding-hamas-tunnels-seawater-risks-ruining-basic-life-gaza-expert.

26 Euro-Med Monitor. "Israel Is Waging an Extensive War of Starvation against Gaza's Civilian Population [En/Ar]—Occupied Palestinian Territory." ReliefWeb, November 5, 2023. https://reliefweb.int/report/occupied -palestinian-territory/israel-waging-extensive-war-starvation-against-gazas -civilian-population-enar.

27 Alijla, Abdalhadi. "'Black Moment in Human History.'" Twitter, November 7, 2023. https://twitter.com/alijla2021/status/1721819986170171420?s=4 6&t=uhXUfUMFVhRd-WfTfl-Mvw.

28 Oshin, Olafimihan. "Cindy McCain Says Gaza 'on the Brink of Famine.'" Yahoo! News, November 26, 2023. https://www.yahoo.com/news/cindy -mccain-says-gaza-brink-232438715.html.

29 Al Jazeera Staff. "Disease Could Kill More Palestinians in Gaza than Bombs, Says Who." Al Jazeera, November 28, 2023. https://www.aljazeera.com /news/2023/11/28/disease-could-kill-more-in-gaza-than-bombs-who-says -amid-israeli-siege.

30 Rahhou, Jihane. "UN Chief: 4 out of 5 Hungriest People Globally Are in Gaza." Morocco World News, December 23, 2023. https://www.morocco worldnews.com/2023/12/359739/un-chief-4-out-of-5-hungriest-people -globally-are-in-gaza.

31 Chotiner, Isaac. "Gaza Is Starving." *The New Yorker*, January 3, 2024. https://www.newyorker.com/news/q-and-a/gaza-is-starving.

32 Burke, Jason. "Aid Officials Believe There Are 'Pockets of Famine' in Gaza." *The Guardian*, January 16, 2024. https://www.theguardian.com/world/2024 /jan/16/no-food-no-water-no-heating-famine-exists-in-gaza-say-officials.

33 Sridhar, Devi. "It's Not Just Bullets and Bombs. I Have Never Seen Health Organisations as Worried as They Are about Disease in Gaza." *The Guardian*, December 29, 2023. https://www.theguardian.com/commentisfree/2023 /dec/29/health-organisations-disease-gaza-population-outbreaks-conflict.

34 The New Arab Staff. "Israeli General Praises Spread of Disease in Gaza." The New Arab, November 21, 2023. https://www.newarab.com/news/israeli -general-praises-spread-disease-gaza.

35 Al-Mughrabi, Nidal. "Gaza Death Toll Tops 10,000; UN Calls It a Children's Graveyard . . ." Reuters, November 6, 2023. https://www .reuters.com/world/middle-east/pressure-israel-over-civilians-steps-up -ceasefire-calls-rebuffed-2023-11-06/.

36 Charlton, Angela, and Jeffrey Schaeffer. "France Has Banned Pro-Palestinian Protests and Vowed to Protect Jews from Resurgent Antisemitism." AP News,

October 12, 2023. https://apnews.com/article/france-israel-palestinians
-war-protests-banned-5626bafec480b32226dcb97d0c92a553.

37 Sinmaz, Emine. "Gaza's Largest Hospital Being Bombarded, WHO
Says." *The Guardian*, November 10, 2023. https://www.theguardian.com
/world/2023/nov/10/netanyahu-says-israel-is-not-seeking-to-occupy-gaza.

38 Save the Children. "Gaza: 3,195 Children Killed in Three Weeks Surpasses
Annual Number of Children Killed in Conflict Zones since 2019–Occupied
Palestinian Territory." ReliefWeb, October 29, 2023. https://reliefweb.int
/report/occupied-palestinian-territory/gaza-3195-children-killed-three
-weeks-surpasses-annual-number-children-killed-conflict-zones-2019.

39 Euro-Med Human Rights Monitor. "Over 10,000 Infants and Children
Killed in Israel's Gaza Genocide, Hundreds of Whom Are Trapped beneath
Debris." Euro-Med Human Rights Monitor, November 9, 2023. https:
//euromedmonitor.org/en/article/6020/.

40 "Facing Life in the Gaza Strip with a New Disability." UNICEF State of
Palestine, December 21, 2023. https://www.unicef.org/sop/stories/facing-life
-gaza-strip-new-disability.

41 Hearst, Katherine. "Over 1,000 Children in Gaza Have Limbs Amputated,
UNICEF Says." Middle East Eye, December 29, 2023. https://www.middle
easteye.net/news/war-gaza-israel-palestine-over-1000-children-have-limbs
-amputated-unicef.

42 Nichols, Michelle. A child killed on average every 10 minutes in Gaza, says who
chief . . ., November 10, 2023. https://www.reuters.com/world/middle-east
/child-killed-average-every-10-minutes-gaza-says-who-chief-2023-11-10/.

43 Asmar, Marwan. "Israel's War on Gaza Hospitals Continues Unabated."
Jordan Times, November 11, 2023. https://jordantimes.com/opinion/marwan
-asmar/israels-war-gaza-hospitals-continues-unabated.

44 Stepansky, Joseph. "'We Have a Duty': US Doctor Says Ceasefire an 'ethical
Imperative' in Gaza." Al Jazeera, December 20, 2023. https://www.aljazeera
.com/news/2023/12/19/we-have-a-duty-us-based-doctor-says-ceasefire-an
-ethical-imperative-in-gaza.

45 Scahill, Jeremy. "Al-Shifa Hospital, Hamas's Tunnels, and Israeli Propaganda."
The Intercept, December 4, 2023. https://theintercept.com/2023/11/21
/al-shifa-hospital-hamas-israel/.

46 Goodwin, Allegra, Jomana Karadsheh, Abeer Salman, Florence Davey-
Attlee, and Mihir Melwani. "Al-Nasr Hospital: Infants Found Dead and
Decomposing in Evacuated Gaza ICU. Here's What We Know." CNN,
December 8, 2023. https://www.cnn.com/2023/12/08/middleeast/babies
-al-nasr-gaza-hospital-what-we-know-intl/index.html.

47 "The Kuwaiti Incubator Hoax." *Washington Post*, February 25, 1994.
https://www.washingtonpost.com/archive/opinions/1994/02/26/the
-kuwaiti-incubator-hoax/35b1e882-f796-4acb-a106-9280a7dda521/.

48 Ismail, Aymann. "We Can All See the Horrors of War Now." *Slate Magazine*, October 13, 2023. https://slate.com/news-and-politics/2023/10/decapitated -babies-claim-intent-dehumanization.html.

49 Maté, Aaron. "Biden Endorses Israel's War to Eliminate Gaza." Substack, November 25, 2023. https://open.substack.com/pub/mate/p/biden-endorses -israels-war-to-eliminate?r=7fv5q&utm_medium=ios&utm_campaign =post.

50 Jones, Kathy. "Journalist Casualties in the Israel-Gaza War." Committee to Protect Journalists, February 15, 2024. https://cpj.org/2024/01/journalist -casualties-in-the-israel-gaza-conflict/.

51 Al Jazeera Staff. "Gaza Media Office Says 100 Journalists Killed since Israeli Attacks Began." Al Jazeera, December 23, 2023. https://www.aljazeera .com/news/2023/12/23/gaza-media-office-says-100-journalists-killed -since-israeli-attacks-began.

52 Frankel, Julia. "Israel's Military Campaign in Gaza Seen as among the Most Destructive in Recent History, Experts Say." AP News, January 11, 2024. https://apnews.com/article/israel-gaza-bombs-destruction-death-toll -scope-419488c511f83c85baea22458472a796.

53 Hill, Evan, Imogen Piper, Meg Kelly, and Jarrett Ley. "Destruction in Gaza Outpaces Other Recent Conflicts, Evidence Shows . . ." *Washington Post*, December 23, 2023. https://www.washingtonpost.com/investigations/inter active/2023/israel-war-destruction-gaza-record-pace/.

54 "Israel: White Phosphorus Used in Gaza, Lebanon." Human Rights Watch, October 13, 2023. https://www.hrw.org/news/2023/10/12/israel-white -phosphorus-used-gaza-lebanon.

55 Middle East Monitor Staff. "Report: Nearly 25,000 Children in Gaza Now Orphans." Middle East Monitor, December 11, 2023. https://www .middleeastmonitor.com/20231211-report-nearly-25000-children-in-gaza -now-orphans/.

56 Rouqa, Doaa. "Orphans of Gaza War Left with No Close Relatives to Care for Them." Reuters, December 12, 2023. https://www.reuters.com /world/middle-east/orphans-gaza-war-left-with-no-close-relatives-care -them-2023-12-12/.

57 Euro-Med Human Rights Monitor. "Fate of Baby and Other Palestinian Children Is Unknown after Israeli Army Forcibly Transfers Them out of Gaza Strip." Euro-Med Human Rights Monitor, January 2, 2024. https: //euromedmonitor.org/en/article/6074/Fate-of-baby-and-other-Palestinian -children-is-unknown-after-Israeli-army-forcibly-transfers-them-out -of-Gaza-Strip.

58 Parker, Claire, and Emily Raulala. "South Africa's Genocide Case against Israel." *Washington Post*. January 26, 2024. https://www.washingtonpost .com/world/2024/01/10/south-africa-israel-icj-genocide-case/.

59   Defense of Children International—Palestine v. Joseph R. Biden (Complaint). N.D. of California (2023). https://ccrjustice.org/sites/default/files/attach/2023/11/Complaint_DCI-Pal-v-Biden_w.pdf.

60   Conley, Julia. "Israeli MP Says It Clearly for World to Hear: 'Erase All of Gaza from the Face of the Earth.'" Common Dreams, November 4, 2023. https://www.commondreams.org/news/israel-gaza-genocide.

61   Dag, Burak. "Israeli Journalist Says Army Should Have Killed 100,000 Palestinians in Gaza." Anadolu Ajansı, December 21, 2023. https://www.aa.com.tr/en/middle-east/israeli-journalist-says-army-should-have-killed-100-000-palestinians-in-gaza/3089253.

62   Lowkey, Twitter, November 2, 2023. https://twitter.com/Lowkey0nline/status/1720018165571231998?lang=en.

63   Tharoor, Ishaan. "Welcome to the New, 'New' Middle East." Washington Post, October 16, 2023. https://www.washingtonpost.com/world/2023/10/16/new-new-middle-east-israel-region-saudi-relations-fututre/.

64   Euro-Med Human Rights. "Int'l Committee Must Investigate Israel's Holding of Dead Bodies in Gaza." Euro-Med Human Rights Monitor, November 26, 2023. https://euromedmonitor.org/en/article/5982/Int%E2%80%99l-committee-must-investigate-Israel%E2%80%99s-holding-of-dead-bodies-in-Gaza%E2%80%8B.

65   Block, Elizabeth. "'Operation al-Aqsa Flood' Day 82: Israel Accused of Harvesting Organs from Dead Gazans." Mondoweiss, December 28, 2023. https://mondoweiss.net/2023/12/operation-al-aqsa-flood-day-82-israel-accused-of-harvesting-organs-from-dead-gazans/.

66   "'A Textbook Case of Genocide': Israeli Holocaust Scholar on Israel's Gaza Assault." Democracy Now!, October 31, 2023. https://www.democracynow.org/2023/10/16/raz_segal_textbook_case_of_genocide; and Pilkington, Ed. "Top UN Official in New York Steps Down Citing 'genocide' of Palestinian Civilians." The Guardian, October 31, 2023. https://www.theguardian.com/world/2023/oct/31/un-official-resigns-israel-hamas-war-palestine-new-york.

67   Segal, Raz. "Opinion: Here's What the Mass Violence in Gaza Looks like to a Scholar of Genocide." Los Angeles Times, November 19, 2023. https://www.latimes.com/opinion/story/2023-11-19/israel-hostages-gaza-bombing-civilians-genocide-holocaust-studies.

68   Ibid.

69   Wilkins, Brett. "UN Experts Warn of 'Grave Risk of Genocide' in Gaza." Common Dreams, November 3, 2023. https://www.commondreams.org/news/gaza-genocide-warning.

70   Katz, Bruce. "The Blockade of Gaza: It's All about the Natural Gas." The Canada Files, July 12, 2000. https://www.thecanadafiles.com/.

71   Samuels, Ben, and Amir Tibon. "U.S. to Push Israel to Allow Gaza Offshore Gas Reserves to Revitalize Palestinian Economy." Haaretz.com, November 20, 2023. https://www.haaretz.com/israel-news/2023-11-20/ty-article/.premium /u-s-to-push-israel-to-allow-gaza-offshore-gas-reserves-to-revitalize -palestinian-economy/0000018b-ed90-ddc3-afdb-fdd1ff250000 ?lts=1701105314619.

72   Klippenstein, Ken. "Joe Biden Moves to Lift Nearly Every Restriction on Israel's Access to U.S. Weapons Stockpile." *The Intercept*, December 1, 2023. https: //theintercept.com/2023/11/25/biden-israel-weapons-stockpile-arms-gaza/.

73   Sugihartono, Sekarsari. "The Ben Gurion Project and Its Relation to Israel's Occupation in Gaza." *Modern Diplomacy*, December 3, 2023. https: //moderndiplomacy.eu/2023/11/24/the-ben-gurion-project-and-its -relation-to-israels-occupation-in-gaza/.

Chapter Five

1   Alsaafin, Linah. "The Colour-Coded Israeli ID System for Palestinians." Al Jazeera, November 18, 2017. https://www.aljazeera.com/news/2017/11/18 /the-colour-coded-israeli-id-system-for-palestinians/.

2   Nesher, Talila. "Israel Admits Ethiopian Women Were given Birth Control Shots." Haaretz.com, January 27, 2013. https://www.haaretz.com/israel -news/2013-01-27/ty-article/.premium/ethiopians-fooled-into-birth -control/0000017f-f512-d044-adff-f7fb92c30000.

3   https://www.aljazeera.com/opinions/2014/4/13/uganda-doing-israels -dirty-work.

4   Yerushalmi, Shalom. "Israel in Talks with Congo and Other Countries on Gaza 'voluntary Migration' Plan." *Times of Israel*, January 3, 2024. https://www.timesofisrael.com/israel-in-talks-with-congo-and-other -countries-on-gaza-voluntary-migration-plan/.

5   Tampa, Vava. "It's Time to Ask Why the US and UK Fund Rwanda While Atrocities Mount up in DRC." *The Guardian*, February 14, 2024. https: //www.theguardian.com/global-development/2024/feb/14/why-us-and -uk-fund-rwanda-while-atrocities-mount-up-in-drc-vava-tampa.

6   Barrows-Friedman, Nora. "Day 77 Roundtable: Gaza's Christians; Craig Mokhiber on Genocide." *The Electronic Intifada*, February 3, 2024. https: //electronicintifada.net/blogs/nora-barrows-friedman/day-77-roundtable -gazas-christians-craig-mokhiber-genocide.

7   Middle East Monitor Staff. "Israel Settlers Attack Farmers, Pollute Drinking Water in Jericho." Middle East Monitor, July 10, 2023. https://www .middleeastmonitor.com/20230710-israel-settlers-attack-farmers-pollute -drinking-water-in-jericho/.

8   "The Pogroms Are Working - the Transfer Is Already Happening." The Israeli Information Center for Human Rights in the Occupied Territories. Accessed

February 15, 2024. https://www.btselem.org/publications/202309_the
_pogroms_are_working_the_transfer_is_already_happening.

9   Feeney, Brian. "'Genocide Joe' Biden Has Got the Gaza Crisis Wrong in
Every Way." *The Irish News*, December 29, 2023. https://www.irishnews
.com/opinion/genocide-joe-biden-has-got-the-gaza-crisis-wrong-in-every
-way-brian-feeney-PVL4BQU4YZFZ7FLC67S2APUYDU/.

10 Guiora, Amos N. "US Must Respond to Israel's Toleration of West Bank
Settlers' Pogroms, Terrorism." *The Hill*, July 14, 2023. https://thehill
.com/opinion/international/4095672-us-must-respond-to-israels-toleration
-of-west-bank-settlers-pogroms-terrorism/.

11 Mezzofiore, Gianluca, Celine Alkhaldi, Abeer Salman, and Nima Elbagir.
"Israel's Military Called the Settler Attack on This Palestinian Town a
'pogrom.' Videos Show Soldiers Did Little to Stop It." CNN, June 15, 2023.
https://www.cnn.com/2023/06/15/middleeast/huwara-west-bank-settler
-attack-cmd-intl/index.html.

12 Salman, Abeer, Hadas Gold, and Richard Allen Greene. "Inside the
Palestinian Town That Far-Right Israeli Minister Wants 'Erased.'" CNN,
March 3, 2023. https://edition.cnn.com/2023/03/03/middleeast/inside
-palestinian-town-minister-wants-erased-mime-intl/index.html.

13 Al Jazeera Staff. "Israel Hits Bethlehem in Christmas Raids on Occupied
West Bank." Al Jazeera, December 25, 2023. https://www.aljazeera.com
/news/2023/12/25/israel-intensifies-occupied-west-bank-raids-on-christmas
-day.

14 Salam, Ali. "Israeli Forces Invade Jericho and Nablus." IMEMC News,
December 23, 2023. https://imemc.org/article/israeli-forces-invade-jericho
-and-nablus/.

15 "Deir Ghassana: Riwaq—Centre for Architectural Conservation." Riwaq.
Accessed February 15, 2024. https://www.riwaq.org/content/deir-ghassana
.16 "Bani Zeid." Palestine tales of hospitality, March 16, 2021. https://www
.palestinetalesofhospitality.com/bani-zeid/?lang=en.

17 Williamson, Lucy. "Released Palestinians Allege Abuse in Israeli Jails." BBC
News, December 1, 2023. https://www.bbc.com/news/world-middle-east
-67581915.

18 Engel, Sune, Omar Abdel-BaquiFollow, and Fatima AbdulKarim. "Israel
Intensifies Raids against Palestinians in West Bank." *Wall Street Journal*,
January 19, 2024. https://www.wsj.com/world/middle-east/israel-intensifies
-raids-against-palestinians-in-west-bank-424cb246.

19 "Israeli Settlers Assault Farmers in Kafr Al-Dik." Palestinian News &
Information Agency—WAFA, July 1, 2023. https://english.wafa.ps/.

20 Elias, Hana. "For Palestinians in the West Bank, This Olive Harvest Is Literally
Life-Threatening." *The Nation*, November 15, 2023. https://www.thenation
.com/article/society/settler-attacks-threaten-palestinian-olive-harvest/.

21   @hiphopo3, Twitter, October 7, 2023. https://twitter.com/hiphopo3/status
     /1710734867934142685?s=46.

Chapter Six

1   Cook, Jonathan. *Israel and the Clash of Civilizations: Iraq, Iran and the Plan
     to Remake the Middle East* (London: Pluto Press, 2007), p. 92.
2   "Kafr Qasim Massacre, 29 October 1956." Institute for Palestine Studies,
     November 14, 2023. https://www.palestine-studies.org/en/node/1651786.
3   Shilon, Avi. "Why Israel Supported South Africa's Apartheid Regime."
     Haaretz.com, December 11, 2013. https://www.haaretz.com/opinion/2013
     -12-11/ty-article/.premium/why-israel-supported-apartheid-regime/00000
     17f-e3ae-df7c-a5ff-e3fe965a0000.
4   Ahren, Raphael. "Nelson Mandela Was Close to Jews, Resolutely Loyal to
     Palestinians . . ." *Times of Israel*, December 6, 2013. https://www.timesofisrael
     .com/nelson-mandela-was-close-to-jews-resolutely-loyal-to-palestinians/.
5   Shakir, Omar. "A Threshold Crossed." Human Rights Watch, March
     28, 2023. https://www.hrw.org/report/2021/04/27/threshold-crossed/israeli
     -authorities-and-crimes-apartheid-and-persecution.
6   Tharoor, Ishaan. "Why Christmas Is Canceled in Bethlehem." *Washington
     Post*, November 29, 2023. https://www.washingtonpost.com/world/2023/11
     /29/palestinian-christians-christmas-ceasefire-cancel/.
7   Mallinder, Lorraine. "Under Israeli Attack: Who Are the Christians of Gaza?"
     Al Jazeera, November 2, 2023. https://www.aljazeera.com/news/2023/11/1
     /under-israeli-attack-who-are-the-christians-of-gaza.
8   "Jewish Palestine at the Time of Jesus." Encyclopædia Britannica. Accessed
     February 15, 2024. https://www.britannica.com/biography/Jesus/Jewish
     -Palestine-at-the-time-of-Jesus.
9   https://cmep.salsalabs.org/pr-dec0123.
10   Moench, Mallory. "Reverend Delivers 'christ in the Rubble' Sermon." *Time*,
     December 24, 2023. https://time.com/6550851/bethlehem-christmas-sermon
     -nativity-rubble/.
11   Middle East Monitor Staff. "Remembering Israel's Siege of the Church of
     the Nativity in Bethlehem." Middle East Monitor, April 8, 2022. https:
     //www.middleeastmonitor.com/20220408-remembering-israels-siege-of
     -the-church-of-the-nativity-in-bethlehem/.
12   Ibid.
13   Ibid.
14   Harel, Amos. "250 under Siege in Church of Nativity." Haaretz.com, April
     3, 2002. https://www.haaretz.com/2002-04-04/ty-article/250-under-siege
     -in-church-of-nativity/0000017f-f80a-d460-afff-fb6e35970000.
15   Al Jazeera Staff. "Israel Hits Bethlehem in Christmas Raids on Occupied
     West Bank." Al Jazeera, December 25, 2023. https://www.aljazeera.com
     /news/2023/12/25/israel-intensifies-occupied-west-bank-raids-on-christmas
     -day.

16 Cook, Jonathan. "Bit by Bit Israel Aims to Squeeze out the Palestinian Christians." Jonathan Cook reporting on Israel and Palestine and the Middle East, January 6, 2020. https://www.jonathan-cook.net/2020-01-07/israel-gaza-palestinian-christians/.

17 Najib, Mohammed. "Israeli Police Storm Christians Heading to Jerusalem Church." Arab News, April 15, 2023. https://www.arabnews.com/node/2287326/middle-east.

18 Ibid.

19 Ibid.

20 Ibid.

21 Husseini, Ibrahim. "Mob Attacks Jerusalem Armenian Quarter amid 'Land Grab.'" The New Arab, December 28, 2023. https://www.newarab.com/news/mob-attacks-jerusalem-armenian-quarter-amid-land-grab.

22 Ibid.

23 Ibid.

24 Ibid.

25 Debre, Isabel. "Israeli Arms Quietly Helped Azerbaijan Retake Nagorno-Karabakh, to the Dismay of Region's Armenians." AP News, October 5, 2023. https://apnews.com/article/armenia-azerbaijan-nagorno-karabakh-weapons-israel-6814437bcd744acc1c4df0409a74406c.

26 Censored Man, "Merry Christmas to All!" Twitter, December 24, 2023 https://twitter.com/censoredmen/status/1739063578466951596?s=46.

27 Nassim Nicholas Taleb, Twitter, December 28, 2023. https://twitter.com/nntaleb/status/1740455323180335280?s=46.

28 Atshan, Sa'ed. "Opinion: Palestinian Christians Are Losing Loved Ones in Israel's Bombing in Gaza. Where's the Outcry from Western Christian Communities?" Los Angeles Times, November 2, 2023. https://www.latimes.com/opinion/story/2023-11-02/israel-palestine-gaza-christians-church-bombing-baptisms-st-porphyrius.

29 Tharoor, Ishaan. "Why Christmas Is Canceled in Bethlehem." Washington Post, November 29, 2023. https://www.washingtonpost.com/world/2023/11/29/palestinian-christians-christmas-ceasefire-cancel/.

30 Veltman, Chloe. "More than 100 Gaza Heritage Sites Have Been Damaged or Destroyed by Israeli Attacks." NPR, December 3, 2023. https://www.npr.org/2023/12/03/1216200754/gaza-heritage-sites-destroyed-israel.

31 Karadsheh, Jomana, and Heather Chen. "Gaza: Pope Speaks out after IDF Sniper Kills Two Women inside Church, per Catholic Authorities." CNN, December 18, 2023. https://www.cnn.com/2023/12/16/middleeast/idf-sniper-gaza-church-deaths-intl-hnk/index.html.

32 Al Jazeera Staff. "Israel Army Kills 2 Christian Women in 'Cold Blood' at Gaza Church Compound." Al Jazeera, December 18, 2023. https://www.aljazeera.com/news/2023/12/17/israeli-forces-kill-two-christian-women-in-cold-blood-inside-gaza-church.

33 Banco, Erin. "Congressional Staff Tried to Protect Gazan Churches by Sending Locations to Israel." *Politico*, December 21, 2023. https://www.politico.com/news/2023/12/21/congress-gazan-churches-location-israel-00132915.

34 Kilani, Hazar. "Israel Attacks 600-Year-Old Monastery in South Lebanon a Day before Christmas Eve." Doha News | Qatar, December 24, 2023. https://dohanews.co/israel-attacks-600-year-old-monastery-in-south-lebanon-a-day-before-christmas-eve/.

35 Haaretz Staff. "Empty Book on Palestinian History Becomes Instant Best-Seller on Amazon." Haaretz.com, June 22, 2017. https://www.haaretz.com/middle-east-news/palestinians/2017-06-22/ty-article/empty-book-on-palestinian-history-is-amazon-best-seller/0000017f-ea3a-d4a6-af7f-fefef6820000.

36 Maçães, Bruno. "Israel Erased the Civil Registry in Gaza." Twitter, January 21, 2024. https://twitter.com/macaesbruno/status/1749072533054206114?s=46.

37 Chomsky, Noam. "The Responsibility of Intellectuals, Redux." *Boston Review*, September 7, 2023. https://www.bostonreview.net/articles/noam-chomsky-responsibility-of-intellectuals-redux/.

38 "On Religion and Politics, Noam Chomsky Interviewed by Amina Chaudary." *Islamica Magazine*, Issue 19, April 1, 2007. https://chomsky.info/200704__/.

39 Palencia-Frener, Sergio. "Memory and Forgetting in Guatemala: Catholic Church Sets the War Record Straight." openDemocracy, June 6, 2021. https://www.opendemocracy.net/en/democraciaabierta/memory-and-forgetting-in-guatemala-catholic-church-sets-war-record-straight/.

40 Middle East Monitor. "Israel's Role in the Guatemalan Genocide." Middle East Monitor, October 5, 2015. https://www.middleeastmonitor.com/20151005-israels-role-in-the-guatemalan-genocide/.

41 Sofuoglu, Murat. "Israel's Role in War Crimes Committed during the Guatemalan Civil War." TRT World—Breaking News, Live Coverage, Opinions and Videos, February 18, 2021. https://www.trtworld.com/magazine/israel-s-role-in-war-crimes-committed-during-the-guatemalan-civil-war-44285.

42 Sofuoglu, Murat. "Israel's Role in War Crimes Committed during the Guatemalan Civil War." TRT World—Breaking News, Live Coverage, Opinions and Videos, February 18, 2021. https://www.trtworld.com/magazine/israel-s-role-in-war-crimes-committed-during-the-guatemalan-civil-war-44285.

43 Ibid.

44 "Colombian Priest Killed in Continuing Trend of Violence." Catholic News Agency, February 5, 2013. https://www.catholicnewsagency.com/news/26513/colombian-priest-killed-in-continuing-trend-of-violence.

45 Cohen, Dan. "New Investigation Reveals Role of Israeli Operatives in Colombia's 'Political Genocide.'" MR Online, June 5, 2021. https://mro nline.org/2021/06/05/new-investigation-reveals-role-of-israeli-operatives -in-colombias-political-genocide/.

46 Al Jazeera Staff. "Israel's Latin American Trail of Terror." Al Jazeera, June 5, 2003. https://www.aljazeera.com/news/2003/6/5/israels-latin-american-trail -of-terror.

47 Ibid.

48 Schalk, Owen. "Israel's Support for the Far-Right in Latin America Goes Back Decades." *Canadian Dimension*, August 29, 2022. https://canadiandimension .com/articles/view/israels-support-for-the-far-right-in-latin-america-goes -back-decades.

49 Ibid.

50 Salisbury-Corech, Michael. "Israelis Demand State Open up Past Ties to Argentine Junta." *+972 Magazine*, March 24, 2016. https://www.972mag .com/israelis-demand-state-opens-up-past-ties-to-argentine-junta/.

51 Spraragen, Avraham B. "Argentina-Israel Relations: Nazi Trials and Terrorist Tribulations." Jerusalem Center for Public Affairs, July 20, 2017. https: //jcpa.org/article/argentina-israel-relations-nazi-trials-terrorist-tribulations/.

52 The New Arab Staff. "Israeli Police Attack Anti-Zionist Jews amid Gaza War." The New Arab, November 2, 2023. https://www.newarab.com/news /israeli-police-attack-anti-zionist-jews-amid-gaza-war.

53 Chomsky, Noam," Responsibility of Intellectuals, Redux," ibid.

54 Schalk, Owen, ibid.

Conclusion

1 Jaanan, Zeeshan. Twitter, January 17, 2024. https://twitter.com/Zeeshan Jaanam/status/1747037258002133053.

2 Al Jazeera Staff. "What's in Hamas's 135-Day Proposal for a Gaza Truce?" Al Jazeera, February 8, 2024. https://www.aljazeera.com/amp/news/2024/2/7 /whats-in-hamass-135-day-proposal-for-a-gaza-truce.

3 Ibid.

4 Ibid.

5 RT International. "The Footage Reportedly Shows the Moment Israel Blew up the University of Palestine in Gaza City Using 315 Mines." Twitter, January 18, 2024. https://www.rt.com/.

6 Abraham, Leanne, Bora Erden, Nader Ibrahim, Elena Shao, and Haley Willis. "Israel's Controlled Demolitions Are Razing Neighborhoods in Gaza." *New York Times*, February 1, 2024. https://www.nytimes.com /interactive/2024/02/01/world/middleeast/Israel-gaza-war-demolish.html.

7 Hearst, Katherine. "Killing of Gaza's Academics Amounts to 'Educide,' Say Campaigners." Middle East Eye, January 31, 2024. https://www.middle

easteye.net/news/war-gaza-israel-killing-academics-educide-campaigners
-say.

8   Irfan, Anne. "Why Palestinians Are Known as the World's 'Best Educated
     Refugees.'" Columbia University Press Blog, August 3, 2023. https://cupblog
     .org/2023/08/23/why-palestinians-are-known-as-the-worlds-best-educated
     -refugeesanne-irfan/.

9   "Brismes Demands Government Action on Gaza." BRICUP. Accessed
     March 8, 2024. https://bricup.org.uk/article/brismes-british-government
     -must-pressure-israel-to-stop-destruction-of-education-system-in-gaza/.

10   Crean, Rosabel. "100 Palestinian Children Killed in West Bank since 7
     October." The New Arab, February 16, 2024. https://www.newarab.com
     /news/100-palestinian-children-killed-west-bank-7-october.

11   Ibid.

12   "Over 7,000 Palestinians Detained by Israel in West Bank since October
     7." Palestinian News & Information Agency—WAFA, February 13, 2024.
     https://english.wafa.ps/Pages/Details/141642.

13   Al Jazeera Staff. "Israeli Forces Kill Three Palestinians in West Bank
     Hospital Raid." Al Jazeera, January 31, 2024. https://www.aljazeera.com
     /news/2024/1/30/israel-troops-kill-three-palestinians-in-west-bank-hospital
     -ministry.

14   T.R. "Israeli Colonists Attack Arab Bedouin Community West of Jericho,
     Steal Sheep." Palestinian News & Information Agency—WAFA, November
     28, 2023. https://english.wafa.ps/.

15   International Court of Justice Decision, January 26, 2024. https://www
     .icj-cij.org/sites/default/files/case-related/192/192-20240126-ord-01-00
     -en.pdf.

16   "Stories of Loss and Grief: At Least 17,000 Children Are Estimated to
     Be Unaccompanied or Separated from Their Parents in the Gaza Strip."
     UNICEF, February 2, 2024. https://www.unicef.org/press-releases/stories
     -loss-and-grief-least-17000-children-are-estimated-be-unaccompanied-or.

17   Defense of Children International—Palestine v. Joseph R. Biden, N.D.
     California, Order Granting Motion to Dismiss, January 31, 2024. https:
     //ccrjustice.org/sites/default/files/attach/2024/01/91_1-31-24_Order
     -granting-MTD_w.pdf.

18   Imray, Gerald, and Sebabatso Mosamo. "South Africa Says Israel Is Already
     Ignoring Un Court Ruling Ordering It to Prevent Deaths in Gaza." AP
     News, January 31, 2024. https://apnews.com/article/israel-gaza-genocide
     -south-africa-palestinians-d4724119dfd23d118350175c39fb4534.

19   Euro-Med Human RightsMonitor. "Two Days after ICJ Ruling, Euro-Med
     Monitor Says Israel Has Maintained Its Rate of Killing in Gaza." ReliefWeb,
     January 29, 2024. https://reliefweb.int/report/occupied-palestinian-territory
     /two-days-after-icj-ruling-euro-med-monitor-says-israel-has-maintained
     -its-rate-killing-gaza-enar.

20 McKernan, Bethan. "Israeli Officials Accuse International Court of Justice of Antisemitic Bias." *The Guardian*, January 26, 2024. https://www.theguardian.com/world/2024/jan/26/israeli-officials-accuse-international-court-of-justice-of-antisemitic-bias.

21 "Ben Gvir Slams ICJ as Antisemitic, Says Israel Should Ignore Ruling . . ." *Times of Israel*, January 26, 2024. https://www.timesofisrael.com/liveblog_entry/ben-gvir-slams-icj-as-antisemitic-says-israel-should-ignore-ruling-on-provisional-measures/.

22 Jerusalem Post Staff. "ICJ's Anti-Israel Ruling a 'Dark Day for Justice'—Jewish Organizations." *The Jerusalem Post*, January 26, 2024. https://www.jpost.com/israel-hamas-war/article-783880.

23 Al Jazeera Staff. "Which Countries Have Cut Funding to UNRWA, and Why?" Al Jazeera, January 31, 2024. https://www.aljazeera.com/news/2024/1/28/which-countries-have-cut-funding-to-unrwa-and-why.

24 Ibid.

25 Ibid.

26 "The Contras, Cocaine, and Covert Operations." National Security Archives, George Washington University. Accessed February 16, 2024. https://nsarchive2.gwu.edu/NSAEBB/NSAEBB2/index.html.

27 Bunkall, Alistair. "Israeli Intelligence Report Claims Four UNRWA Staff in Gaza Involved in Hamas Kidnappings." Sky News, January 30, 2024. https://news.sky.com/story/israeli-intelligence-report-claims-four-unrwa-staff-in-gaza-involved-in-hamas-kidnappings-13059967.

28 Plitnick, Mitchell. "U.S. Admits It Hasn't Verified Israel's UNRWA Claims, Media Ignores It." *Mondoweiss*, February 6, 2024. https://mondoweiss.net/2024/02/u-s-admits-it-hasnt-verified-israels-unrwa-claims-media-ignores-it/.

29 "Defunding UNRWA is Genocide," Jewish Voices for Peace, January 31, 2024. https://www.jewishvoiceforpeace.org/2024/01/31/defunding-unrwa-is-genocide/.

30 TOI Staff. "Israel Hoping to Push UNRWA out of Gaza Post-War." *Times of Israel*, December 29, 2023. https://www.timesofisrael.com/israel-hoping-to-push-unrwa-out-of-gaza-post-war-report/.

31 Mizzi, Oliver. "'No Evidence' for Israeli UNRWA Claims in Six-Page Dossier." The New Arab, February 6, 2024. https://www.newarab.com/news/no-evidence-israeli-unrwa-claims-six-page-dossier.

32 "UNRWA Could Shut down by End of February If Funding Does Not Resume." Reuters, February 1, 2024. https://www.reuters.com/world/middle-east/unrwa-could-shut-down-by-end-february-if-funding-does-not-resume-2024-02-01/.

33 UNRWA, "This was the third time a humanitarian convoy led by has been hit," Twitter, February 6, 2024 https://x.com/UNRWA/status/175490886

8172185774?s=20https://x.com/UNRWA/status/175490886817218577
4?s=20.

34   UNRWA, Twitter, February 6, 2024. https://twitter.com/unrwa/status/17
      54863818839069139?s=46https://twitter.com/unrwa/status/1754863818
      839069139?s=46.

35   Arab News Staff. "Un Aid Convoy Hit by Israeli Gunfire in Northern Gaza."
      Arab News, February 6, 2024. https://www.arabnews.com/node/2454561
      /middle-east.

36   Frankel, Julia. "Israel Is Holding up Food for 1.1 Million Palestinians
      in Gaza, the Main UN Aid Agency There Says." AP News, February 9,
      2024. https://apnews.com/article/israel-palestinians-gaza-unwra-bank-aid
      -4ed5e0652dd81b875055679a01a19371.

37   KAMPEAS, RON. "Protesters Blocking Delivery of Aid to Gaza Plan March
      to Jerusalem." Times of Israel, February 3, 2024. https://www.timesofisrael
      .com/protesters-blocking-delivery-of-aid-to-gaza-plan-march-to-jerusalem/.

38   "Belgium Summons Israeli Ambassador after Its Building in Gaza Is
      Bombed." Reuters, February 2, 2024. https://www.reuters.com/world
      /middle-east/belgium-summons-israeli-ambassador-after-its-building-gaza
      -is-bombed-2024-02-02/.

39   Middle East Monitor Staff. "Israel Targets Red Crescent Headquarters in
      Gaza." Middle East Monitor, February 9, 2024. https://www.middleeast
      monitor.com/20240209-israel-targets-red-crescent-headquarters-in-gaza/.

40   Al Jazeera Staff. "Body of 6-Year-Old Killed in 'Deliberate' Israeli Fire
      Found after 12 Days." Al Jazeera, February 10, 2024. https://www.aljazeera
      .com/news/2024/2/10/body-of-6-year-old-killed-in-deliberate-israeli
      -fire-found-after-12-days.

41   Kubovich, Yaniv. "Israeli Army Admits Running Unauthorized Graphic Gaza
      Influence Op." Haaretz.com, February 4, 2024. https://www.haaretz.com
      /israel-news/security-aviation/2024-02-04/ty-article/.premium/israeli
      -army-its-admits-staff-was-behind-graphic-gaza-telegram-channel
      /0000018d-70b4-dd6e-a98d-f4b6a9c00000.

42   Toler, Aric, Sarah Kerr, Adam Sella, Arijeta Lajka, and Chevaz Clarke.
      "What Israeli Soldiers' Videos Reveal: Cheering Destruction and Mocking
      Gazans." New York Times, February 6, 2024. https://www.nytimes.com
      /2024/02/06/world/middleeast/israel-idf-soldiers-war-social-media-video
      .html.

43   Said, Edward. "The One-State Solution." New York Times, January 10, 1999.
      https://www.nytimes.com/1999/01/10/magazine/the-one-state-solution
      .html.

44   "Israeli Settlers Are Causing Mayhem in the West Bank." The Economist,
      November 6, 2023. https://www.economist.com/middle-east-and-africa/2023
      /11/06/settlers-are-causing-mayhem-in-the-west-bank.

INDEX

216